Under The Banana Moon

Under The Banana Moon

living, loving, loss and Aspergers

by Kimberly Gerry Tucker

ISBN-13:978-1505728866

ISBN-10:150572886X

Create Space, Charleston, SC

FOR MY ASPIE FRIENDS

CONTENTS

Foreword

To say I cried when I read Kimberly's book is an understatement. I cried buckets. But this is not a miserable book, far from it. It's a gritty, gutsy, moving, sometimes even funny book about the worst and best of life. It's a book about childhood and innocence, and about entrapment, selling-out and smiling whilst you do the unbelievable,
simply because your back is to the wall and you damned well have to.

Kimberly's husband, Howie, develops ALS (Lou Gehrig's disease), one of the most challenging of all diseases and one which stripped him of almost every function, with the exception of his intellect and sexuality.

Kimberly, a remarkable woman with Asperger's struggling with life-long selective mutism lives in an invisible cage of her own, struggling with being known, being dependent on others, showing her feelings openly. Yet in their incredible journey together it is Howie's obvious imprisonment that overshadows Kimberly's own at every turn.

In spite of very real anxiety disorders, anxiety disorders her own invisible cage compels her to hide from others, she is expected to 'pull herself together' and function where many non-autistic adults would crumble.

The crazy thing is, she does.

There are many on the autistic spectrum who do not feel excruciating social phobia to the degree they are compulsively compelled to hide, lose their natural voice, their connection to their own expressions and actions, but as the author of *Exposure Anxiety; The Invisible Cage of Involuntary Self Protection Responses*, I know of these things too well and I know where Kimberly has been. Most people with severe Exposure Anxiety as part of their autism don't speak and Kimberly surely struggled and still does, with verbal communication.

We are not all desperate for attention, easily to accept praise, cope with feeling overwhelming gratitude or connection, or want to be known. Some of us are lucky if we manage that with a single friend or partner and Kimberly achieved that, only to lose that partner.

What's so much more remarkable is that whilst Kimberly has an obvious natural rapport with others on the autistic spectrum, she was also able to dare to be known by her non-autistic husband who often couldn't see her. For all his faults (and he is unashamedly portrayed here in all his gritty glory) Howie stands out in this book as a real rough diamond.

What she's written here is a monument to him, but also an act of enormous daring and self honesty. Howie was no monster but he was not politically correct either. He was a 'rough-and-ready' type of bloke from the same raw, tell it like it is, reality Kimberly grew up in. She saw him beyond his often insensitive, even flippant reactions and still saw him beyond what his disease reduced him to. She saw him even when she's stopped seeing herself. And it is this that leaves me so awestruck about Kimberly Tucker. I identify with her in so many ways.

I am proud of her. Let her hide from the world if she is

safest in such a 'cat corner', but her individuality and humanity will still jump out
as long as she allows us that window through her ARTism, through her writing.

Dare to read this book. She dared to write it. You won't forget it.

Donna Williams, author of the
international bestseller, *Nobody Nowhere.*

Author's Note

"**W**abi-sabi" is Asian. In a nutshell, it is a feeling of embracing the perfection of imperfection. It can be felt quietly as the humble beauty of the weed in the sidewalk growing. It's the subtle statement of bubbly seeds in hand-blown bottles and the lovely placement of discarded glass shards into haphazard pattern in a mosaic. It can be a way of life.

When I saw the movie, The King's Speech, I identified with it in a big way. The King's stammering was like the third person in the room. I related to his anger, frustration, humiliation and sadness. Not because I stammer, but because there are horrible times my words are gone unsaid, never expressed. It *feels* like my tongue swells to monstrous proportions. It seems like my throat is an elevator in freefall and the bottom drops out. It's like that cartoon about the fire-breathing dragon and it opens its mouth and then nothing comes out but a wisp of smoke.

The title of my book is derived from the camaraderie I share with a special little boy- Jaden. One evening, we stood outside in line at a farm, under a starlit sky, waiting our turn to order farm-fresh ice cream. He was mesmerized by the night sky, and he finally grasped the meaning of the Twinkle, Twinkle song. He discovered that stars really do twinkle.

"What do you think of this beautiful sky?" I asked him.

"I think sometimes the moon is a ball and sometimes it's a banana moon," he answered, and with that I felt that as long as I had banana moons above me, I would have the innocence of the young in my heart.

And hope come what may.

In many ways this book is a regurgitation; an attempt to paint a sensitive and bittersweet life onto the quietness of paper.

It's painting the chameleon by hand every day. It's just another autiebiography in the big scheme of things. It's wabi-sabi in the details.   -K.G.T.

PART ONE
Chapter One: The Tooth Debacle, 2005

I was concerned about the tooth, of all things. After he was pronounced dead, I consoled the nurse. "You did everything you could for him," I said, patting her back. Her eyes were round and moist. I was numb. She kept apologizing, but I knew that lungs operating at less than five percent capacity for so long do not reinflate.

And I was ready to escape the small gallery of mourners and leave for home. Two weeks of living in a hospital by someone's bedside without leaving the building had me starving for fresh air. I would cry at home, in private cuddled with my little girl. The bedside cot I'd been provided for my two week stay concealed my fanny pack that I'd stashed in its tangle of crisp white sheets. Or so I thought. I rooted for it. The search went on for an hour. I rummaged through every trash can in the unit. It never turned up. My mourning was mixed with anger. I lost fifty dollars and all my important cards and photos, but I would also mourn the keepsakes from my pack that were stolen at some point as he lay dying. I would miss the bolt I carried everywhere.

Amid all this, the gold tooth glinted in my mind, like the intrusion of an internet pop-up ad.

I was always skilled in doing as I was told, but this time he was telling me like a madcap auctioneer from inside my head, "Will ya' fulfill my wishes? Do I hear a yes? Do I hear a yes from the woman in the big canary-yellow shirt? Pull the tooth before it's too late."

The funeral director was predictably somber and out of breath for some reason. He wore creased pants that didn't reach his shoes. I could see whenever he crossed his legs, the silky dark socks that stretched up very high. He took me by surprise every time he spoke, his words pressing air like the low keys on an organ. I raised an eyebrow and was startled when he said surreal things about a person who he now spoke of as "the body." My mood state was flat and that was normal for me. I was labeled dysthymic after all; but overall I liked to fancy myself quite composed. Starr sat beside me and Sue sat across from me where she kept falling apart.

It was her son after all.

The funeral guy told us he took an actual fingerprint from "the body's thumb," and I jumped in my seat but no one else did. They nodded. The funeral director told us we could make jewelry with the body's thumbprint that we could order from him. (Like kindergarten all over again when I put my hand in the plaster. Only not.)

He asked if we had any questions and whether anyone minded that he removed his coat. We didn't. My mother-in-law's face exploded. I passed the tissue box. "Excuse me." She apologized. I was the one who was going to have to apologize to *her,* after the words that were about to come out of my mouth but it had to be said. I had to silence the auctioneer's voice.

I had been staring at the tan carpet the whole time but now I looked in Starr's direction for the strength the action might lend me.

"Well," I started, swallowing down any hint of a smile. "There's this funny thing. Starr, remember how he always said that he wanted me to have his gold tooth?" I cleared my throat. I clasped my hands. Somewhere classical music played.

"I do remember that, yeah," she said. She nodded. She was a frequent visitor at the end of his life, treating us to her good cheer and sunshine aura.

Sue sat up straight and plunked the tissue box down on its side table. "I didn't know my son had a gold tooth," she said, searching my face and Starr's. Then she searched the commercial grade carpet with her wet eyes. I wondered if she saw the lint and hair caught there, as I did. "The gold tooth must've been in the back of his mouth."

"It was," I said. "A souvenir of when our finances were a little better." Hooray for me- I made a giant sentence! I was always pretty good at talking one-on-one with people but there were three people in the room so I was doing A-OK! The voice in my head urged me on- "Spit it out, already. Good thing you aren't paying him for his time."

I spit it out. "Anyway he wanted me to have it. Is there any chance you could pull-"

Sue swiped for her tissue box. At first I thought she was swiping for *me* and I almost ducked. Actually I did duck a little. The funeral guy swiveled his chair toward me, nearly spilling the paperwork off his well-dressed lap.

"I do not feel comfortable with pulling a tooth from the body, no. I can't do that," he said, running quickly chosen words together.

Starr spoke up with her usual conviction. "I think if it's something he really wanted her to have and if it means something to the family then there has to be someone who'll get the tooth for them for a keepsake before he's cremated."

Well you could just pat that silence on the back. You could offer it some paperwork to fill out and watch silence pick up the pen. That's how palpable it was. But I felt calm. The voice in my head was just-gone. Sue was a shade lighter than milk.

I was sitting there, hands still clasped and wondering if the funeral guy was going to reply to Starr when he finally did. "I- I'm just not comfortable with that. Sounds like he just wanted something to represent his memory, something for the family to cherish of him, and I strongly recommend our fingerprint jewelry. That's an alternative." He handed me the brochure.

"But," I said, experimenting with new ways to cross my legs, uncross them and swing my feet around, "What happens after cremation? Will his gold tooth be left in the ashes? He worried about that. That someone might steal it. Hey…will it be in the ashes that you give me so I can see it and fish it out later for myself to keep?"

Sue leaned forward like she had a stomach ache. The funeral guy explained that the heat from the cremation process was so great that it would obliterate the tooth completely.

"I'll get it," Starr said point blank. She shrugged and leaned back in her chair.

And then my mother-in-law's words *had* to come out. Her dam was only so strong. The words gushed. "What do you mean, you'll get it?" It was admirable. I saw that behind her wet eyes she was trying to have on her smiling public face. But she was a mess. I was sorry for the frightened look across her features. I could not imagine losing a child.

Starr had a plan. With the voice of a conspirator she said, "After the wake I'll go in and get it out."

"And just how you do you propose to get the tooth out of my son's head?" Sue asked, eyes wider than ever.

"I got some tools in the trunk," Starr said. I knew she would do it. She once got my dropped dollar bill back from a mean kid at the movies when I was seven. She would face down a bull if she had to and I had no doubt it would back off whimpering.

Within a few days the "body" was on display in a closed casket and I was back inside the funeral parlor. The cremation was going to be held sometime after the wake. The funeral parlor building held uneasy memories for me. When I was twelve, two older girls who smoked and wore a swipe of shiny blue shadow across their upper eyelids chased me past the deli, all the way down the hill, and into the funeral parlor's parking lot. I dared not go further so I turned and faced them, out of breath and scared.

"So," one of them said, laughing at my tears and lighting a cigarette, "whaddya say we put you in there?" She pointed at the white building with the dark shutters.

His body was in the casket because they couldn't arrange a cremation right away. After most everyone had left the building, I found myself standing alone in the room in front of the closed casket with a handful of mourners. I wondered if he was wearing the hospital coat or was naked inside the casket.
Flowers were lined up on the floor and more hung from the

walls. Some had cursive words in gold script across the fronts of the flower sprays: *Loving Brother, Father, Beloved Son, Son-In- Law*. At a diagonal, to the left behind the casket was a heart shaped wreath of white and red flowers hanging from the stark white wall.

Across the front was the word: Husband. This was the one Sue had ordered for me. With my financial affairs still not in order ever since my fanny pack had been stolen, she had paid for this wreath for me.

After the funeral she announced I needed to decide which flowers to take home. But there were no voices today and I couldn't answer. She said we could donate them to a nursing home or to the hospital. Howie's sister loaded the *Brother* arrangement into her car. Everyone, save for us, was already en route to her house for the 'after-funeral' get-together. Since Howie was to be cremated later, there would be no gathering at a cemetery because there would be no burial and no headstone.

Maybe I'd pluck one rose to press in a book next to my four-leafed clovers but no, I shook my head. Maybe I didn't want any at all. After over twenty years of having a man make every decision for you it was damned hard to decide if you wanted something or didn't! And then it happened so fast, landing on the smiling portrait of him and me. The *Husband* flowers had a life of their own and fell over face-forward onto the casket. That's not supposed to happen. The red and white heart surged forward on its own.

It landed onto the casket right in front of me. If that sort of thing happened a lot in the old black shuttered funeral home, no wonder the funeral guy always looked like a snail in a weasel hole. I stood there, frozen to the spot, reading *Husband* for a moment.

We were all alabaster statues fixated on the picture that the flowers had crashed into-and working out in all our minds the impossible route in our heads the flowers had taken.

I broke the silence. "I'll take those home!" I announced to everyone. At least I finally answered Sue's question. I suspected someone was still trying to make decisions for me.

In the parking lot, I loaded my *Husband* wreath into someone's car. Starr came up to me, her limp barely noticeable. She would never let M.S. get an upper hand. She hooked a thumb over her shoulder conspiratorially, back toward the intimidating funeral home.

I waited for her to speak. She was going to tell a creepy joke or something. I expected she might hum the twilight zone theme close to my ear.

Her eyebrows were up. *Uh-oh*. A partner-in-crime look.

She said, "Should I go back in there and get that tooth? No one needs to know."

I smiled, at a loss for my true want. I knew *his* want. He wanted me to have his gold tooth. That want was recorded on his talking machine at home.

The sky was cloudless. It matched my ugly blue shirt with the fake blue rose attached, chosen because it was his favorite color. I knew I would later throw it away as it'd be tainted with the honor of being the *funeral shirt*. I smiled at Starr's devotion, avoiding her eyes. "No, I think we'll let it go." I said, surprising myself. Empowering my self.

"Are you sure? I'll do it if it's important," she said, "I remember him saying it. Got the tools in the trunk. Not a big deal. When everyone's gone." She made a hand gesture in the air, a movement like operating pliers.

Howie would've approved. You better believe it. *Excuse me, funeral guy. We'd like alone time with the body. Please grant us privacy here.* Oh yes, if he were still here long enough to concoct the plan himself he would've approved right down to making me be the one who clamped the monkey wrench down on his gleaming three hundred dollar dental atrocity of a molar. Or whatever it cost. I wasn't allowed to touch the checkbook.

Really, I wasn't allowed to even touch it. When Starr asked if I was sure, you better believe I considered it. I looked to the heavens that June day and imagined every detail of the caper right down to the "Mission Impossible" theme music as we lifted the lid of the casket. As we ran out into the parking lot, the gleaming dental prize held high in the air and then the "Laverne and Shirley" song would have to play. *Schlemiel, schlimazel!* Yep. In that instant I wanted the caper more than the tooth.

"I'm sure," I said, smiling.

"Okay kiddo," she said. She pivoted on her good leg and paused to look at me over her shoulder as she headed toward her car.

It was as if she hoped I'd change my mind. Maybe she wanted a caper too.
I shrugged.
She turned and kept walking.

Chapter Two: The First Gray House

My earliest memory: Aunt Nat running around the side of the grey house popping up in front of the window and tapping the glass. I'm giggling so hard I can't catch my breath and then where is she? Pop! There she is! I'm giggling again. I'm laughing so hard tears are flowing and I nearly tip over. There's a separation I don't quite get- a pane of glass that makes it safe between Aunt Nat and me. She ducks down outside: disappears and reappears. But she can't touch me. She can't even hear me laugh.

I have that memory frozen in Polaroid, in shades of grey. My parents took lots of pictures in the grey house back when pictures were black and white, appropriately enough. In grey, you could see Mommy's cold coffee. You could see dilapidated garages. In shades of grey, you saw the world that was black and white TV.
You saw home.
The grey house of my childhood, all two stories of it, stood sentinel on a patchy hill by the highway with its windows for eyes. My crooked curtain beyond the bottom porch was a winking lid. The house on the hill had caterpillars that liked to crawl up over the house where the bare board peeked through peeling paint. In the grey of the grey house, you could see sky colors, and looking deeper, you could see the eye colors of my parents, and of Starr.
Most of the cousins' eyes were dark; rich, like fine wood or Vermont dirt, creamy as hot chocolate pudding. Not my eyes. My eyes were hazel. Like the nuts.
My room was ordered clutter, piled as curiously as Picasso's art. I never saw the bottoms of the walls where they joined the floor but I assumed they were there. In a feat that seemed to me akin to scaling

Everest, I bruised my girl knees climbing the precariously positioned
things that walled the valley path to my bed. Who knew
when we would need a salvaged bicycle tire, a coat two sizes too big
or a little gold corkscrew in the shape of a wicked faced boy with the
flip-up corkscrew being his wee-wee?
My mother chose the pattern for my curtains and bed canopy.
Evermore, blue and white checks meant "mother."
When I dared to dig into the piles, I usually started at the bottom and
hoped against thing-slides and object-lanches. I found mysterious
outdated gadgets for which I assigned my own uses in the yard. I
often smashed thermometers to play with the mercury.
Eggbeaters with a jump-rope attached became gas pumps for my
bike. With things in my company, I never felt bored or lonely.
When I looked out my window from inside my room, I saw
Ilana's weathered porch with its lovely expanse of peeling grey
boards jutting out from under my window outside in an interesting
linear perspective. Ilana was the woman who rented the apartment
upstairs from ours. Later in my life, upon seeing Van Gogh's painting
of his room, I would think of the boards of the porch that seemed to
distortedly run away from my view. The image of them would
remain, as many images do, air-brushed inside my head like a poster.
Ilana greeted these boards daily. Jumping spiders siesta-ed
around the porch rails and by the bicycle and old plant pots.

One bright day I sat on her porch step thinking about the place
between nothing and everything, watching air particles square dance.
She came round the corner and greeted me in the eyes. We both
looked away. She hoisted up the steps, getting some spiders to
hopping.
As she passed me, I got an eye-level view of her oversized ankles
and legs decorated with purple lines. I couldn't *not* look at them.
Ilana shuffled up past me turtle-like as ever, and across the fine
boards, her colorful dress swaying. A puff of white-blonde hair
framed her face as she smiled my way with cherry red lips.
Her apartment laid spread out on our ceilings like a dark secret. If I
could see her things, familiarize myself with the things she
surrounded herself with, only then could I, only then would I, know
her.
One Halloween, I figured *here's my chance!* As I stood on the
topmost part of her unlit claustrophobia-inducing hall stairs, I

knocked on her door. It was incredibly dark. But I *sparkled*. I was wearing *the* princess mask with glitter for eye shadow above the eye slits. The door opened a crack, revealing her red painted mouth. Plump fingers crawled through the crack with Chiclets gum. The yellow packet fell neatly into the hollow of the plastic pumpkin. I strained to see into the room behind her. *Was that a stove?!* It was crow-black, clunky and so quirky with its funny curving pipe, it reminded me of a type I'd seen illustrated in a storybook. Ilana lived in a cartoon kitchen! Smiling at her doughy hand, she closed her door till it clicked. I heard a clasp latch. My mask dropped a bit on one side. Already the princess was cracked at the single staple that held the elastic band to the yellow plastic hair. But insanely, she smiled. Beneath it, I exhaled hot breath from my no-expression face.

My grey house had a soul and a heart, and also an innards, which was where I lived, where I slept and dreamed and ate and defecated. My house had quiet mystery too. It had skin which ———— swirled with more than simple grey if you bothered to look. I never did see hidden colors inside of blue for instance. Blue's just blue. But grey; grey was so much.
It was never dull in the grey house. The highway noise lulled me to sleep like no nursery rhyme could. In the daylight hours I'd seen a tractor trailer take down a Lassie dog, and assorted other wildlife and pets alike were smashed into road kill. I'd seen and heard vehicles struck by other vehicles. That Lassie dog jumped up like it was making to catch a high flying Frisbee; its front limbs all flayed out but it caught the headlights of that tractor trailer instead.

"Don't let Kimmy outside! This one she don't have to see. Blood all over the windshield. I don't think this guy's makin' it," my father said one day.

Then he was walking down the hill toward the scene.
We were privy to such excitement so often that there were times we could barely get through a Laugh-In or Hee-Haw episode on TV. My mother pulled me away from the screened door and told me to go and do something. I knew better than to ask her just what I should do because she just might tell me to twiddle my thumbs again and I didn't like doing that. So I froze, thinking.

Thinking was "doing something."
My father, I knew, would be a comfort to whomever had crashed. He knew the tow-truck driver next door by first name and his talent was such that he could take a car apart and put it back together. My father, that is. He was 'Mr. Reliable.'

"That Joe," said the owner of the gas station. "He can Mickey Mouse any car into running."

Daddy said that someday he'd own a place called Joe's Garage.

He jogged into the house. "There's a redhead down there- oh she's a mess, Carol," he told my mother. "I gotta' make some calls for her. The other guy- I think he's a goner."

The people victims were carried away by ambulances. The animals were flattened until they disappeared entirely, flattened so completely that their remnants could lift and blow across the lanes. I stopped expecting little animal ambulances and animal stretchers to appear on the highway a long time ago.
The black undertakers usually arrived, to make off with entrails and such and rightfully so, in the scheme of things. But they disturbed me just the same. It was something about their voices. The crows cackled. Everything was so damn funny to them. It wasn't until I met an actual undertaker many years later that I wondered if he too cackled. In private, maybe.

One night I saw something stupid on the big floor model television. "That would never happen. The news isn't true. It's dumb," I told Mommy, who was crocheting.
"What's so dumb?" she asked me.

"All that for one person? All those fire trucks? All those people? It's only one little kid trapped in a house but a TV person comes and they go to all that trouble to rescue one kid with that big ladder! That's a crowd of people to help one person! It could never happen, Mommy!" I told her. I figured cops and the like weighed the importance of rescues.

"It happened. It happens all the time. People help other people; whether it's one person or *ten people* who're trapped," She said with a matter-of-fact air, never putting down her yarn.

I looked at her,
cocking my head to the side.
I had no choice but to believe her.
She wouldn't lie.

Chapter Three: Uncle Rooster

I was about five. We were visiting Grandma in Vermont.
Relatives were gathered in the country kitchen all around the great
Formica table; gabbing, laughing, swearing, eating, and smoking.
Cousins darted after each other, more boisterous than I dared to be.
I sat on Daddy's lap, blurring and staring into nothing; stuck in good
between the table's edge and his stomach. Voices were rising and
falling; undecipherable gibberish. I was staring.

I didn't know it was Uncle Rodney's voice asking me a question until I heard my father explaining me in an un-Daddy-like voice.

"Here," Daddy said. He tossed Rodney the cigarette pack. It skimmed across the table neat as a whisper- *swoosh!*

Then Daddy said, "Kimmy won't pass these to ya." She doesn't touch 'em. Never has. She goes way out of her way to avoid 'em. Heh, heh."

Uncle Rodney looked at me as if for the first time ever.
Shaking, I dared see his face. A long man who tended to dart about quickly, he had a gravelly voice that tumbled out of a pasted-on Cheshire cat grin. My father's word for him was "cocky." I thought of "rooster" when I heard that word and so my father's word seemed to fit Rodney.

"That so? Doesn't touch 'em?" said Uncle Rodney.

He shoved the pack across the table toward me as if we were playing some game together. I jerked my hand away in time. From the missile. The pack skidded across the table right to where my hand had been moments before!

"I asked Kimmy to pass 'em," Uncle Rodney said, grinning.

Yikesyikesyikesyikes. I couldn't breathe.

"Let it go, Rod. Heh, heh," My father laughed. "She won't. She never has. I don't know why she's like that."

Good. It's all explained. Get on with playing, all you cousins.

I tilted my head to see into my father's face and saw the stubble there. He was smiling cockeyed lopsided at me. What was worse, Daddy was averting his gaze from everyone. An outgoing man, he always looked people in the face. When we were out in public together and he held my hand, I wore his essence like a familiar mitten. The aunts and uncles were looking at me now too, not just Daddy. Even the cousins had ceased their darting about to glare at me. The humming voices stopped.
I tried to make my get-away but I was wedged in too tight. My throat felt constricted. It happened so fast! Uncle Rodney leapt up, the sound of his metal-legged chair screaming the way I should have. He rubbed the crinkle of that pack all over my arms and face. Bits of tobacco, the antithesis of the flower stamens I loved to dissect, were sprinkling out and tainting me. I whipped my face from side to side to avoid contact with the cigarette pack. He towered over me, grinding it into my cheeks. And my hair. My *ears*. Soon my face was wet with waterfall tears. The sound of the pack crinkling in my ears was more than I could stand. I dared not swat at it for fear of touching it.
"Gonna git you! Bad ciggie gonna git you!" Uncle Rodney taunted.

I willed the cousins and aunts to swarm him like a mad sci-fi thriller plot and reveal hidden stingers from their backsides. No one heeded my thought vibes.
Then nothing.
Grandma's rooster clock made a startlingly loud click. Click. Click.

Uncle Rodney sat down and leaned back against his chair, lighting a bent cigarette from the wadded pack he'd terrorized me with. He smoked like a cartoon villain. Silence reined in the kitchen except that I could hear his amusement. He was laughing. It was high-pitched like a shriek.

He asked my father something then, quite seriously, "How long she been like that, Joe? If that ain't the damnedest thing."

Always the wonder in the voice when the people tried to figure me out. I did not hear my father's answer if there was one. I managed to wriggle onto my feet at last. I could hear no more and see no one. I spun in a slow circle with my soiled arms held straight out and I cried with no sound.

I was
      a deaf,
            mute and
                  blind kid.

Chapter Four: Blond Mommy

For the most part my beautiful mother was tolerant of my behaviorisms. I couldn't step on the torn places on the living room floor where the grey swirls in the linoleum were turned black. That was the bad territory. I'd probably get a disease and have to squeeze my fingers a hundred times then run outside till my breath came in hitches to erase the black from my feet and that wasn't even a surefire cure.
I couldn't sit in the chairs at Starr's house. The embossed swirlies in her chairs were called "vinyl" and were intolerable. They made my blood stop flowing. They didn't have that effect on anyone except me. I was the only one the chairs disliked. Styrofoam coolers were a top secret operation. I wasn't sure who was behind that; but it had to do with the spies who invented the sounds in dog whistles. I didn't know who was behind that plot against me.

I was in the process of reading the book *Harriet the Spy* and I was keeping an eye on everybody.

"I won't wear this shirt," I told my mother one day.

"It'll go with your eyes. It's your color! Try it on, stubborn kid," she said, handing the "paisley" shirt to me. She held it up. It had long sleeves and a wild pattern. I'd checked it out already but rendered it unwearable.

"Didn't you read the label, Mommy?" I said.

She read the name on the tag aloud, "Marlboro Clothing Company. Aren't you taking this smoking thing of yours a little far? This is a clothing company, for cryin' out loud!"

It was more than just boycotting cigarettes. Intellectually I did know that the clothing company was coincidentally named the same as the cigarette company. Or was it? I couldn't wear loud shoes either. Couldn't step on bumpy things. Couldn't speak when expected, my vocabulary was large but words got stuck. I didn't think of my self as shy. Not having words was far different than being shy.
I knew what I liked. Diarrhea medicine from the refrigerator had a superb chalk taste. *I knew that because I enjoyed actual chalk.* I scooped spoonfuls of white creamy shortening straight out of the can and in fact I tasted anything in the house labeled 'non-toxic'.
Not something I'd recommend.
For a long time I loved newspaper. The smell. The feel. Taste. Silky texture as the paper melted on my tongue. I swirled the wet goo around till it was mush. Then chewed. Not quite the same taste as paste, but similar. I gave up eating newspaper when I thought there was bleach in the paper making my teeth sensitive to hot and cold. I licked rocks to see them change color. I could not touch anything associated with bad smells. Not cigarettes, matches or lighters, ashtrays, or cigarette packages or cellophane wrappers from cigarette packages, and not labels on shirts that mentioned the cigarettes' names.

My mother knew all this and still persisted that day about the shirt. "At least wear it long enough for me take your picture with you holding Duchess' puppies. You can sit by the pool in the grass," She said.

Duchess the hound was the new dog; a heart on a
string. Now she had puppies. I took the shirt from her as if it were maggot-infested. I sat cross-legged in the damp grass alongside the pool, trying to keep three black and white puppies from bumbling off my lap.
The suffocation intensified with every movement my body made. I could not send an expression to my face. *Click!* Went the camera. My arms were stiff rods for the photo. She seemed content enough to take my picture without benefit of a pleasant facial expression to enhance the photo. *Click!* It went again.
My fingers went under my nose to detect whether the smell of the shirt was coming off on my skin. The tag against the back of my neck was a reminder taunting me: The Marlboro Company has designed this shirt for you and all its workers chain smoked while sewing the teeny buttons on. Their nicotine stained fingers were all over this thing!
I spilled the puppies into the grass and made for the house, careful not to run because when I was agitated I didn't turn out my left foot correctly and I tripped over it. I didn't register any pain, just a tearing that I could hear as well as feel; as my wart was clipped clean off on the screened door's bad nail; the seed wart that used to rub against pencils when I wrote things. Soon I would be rid of the shirt too!
In the bathroom I fumbled with too-tiny buttons, unable to remove the shirt fast enough. Crying silently I feared I was soiled forever. Red rivulets in a watercolor painting couldn't have been prettier than that which trickled over my hand and down my wrist as I turned it. The color was pure; mesmerizing. I studied the spot in the linoleum that I could not let the bottoms of my feet touch. The ashtray was on a table next to the toilet. A lot of mapping went on in this small room to avoid bad things.

When I left the bathroom, bleeding all over myself; I said to her, "I hope you're satisfied. I'm never wearing that shirt again."

But the pear tree was a delight to my senses. With its golden

✗ fruits, like the partridge song, it was a silhouette against the sky near
the picnic table. I heard it growing. I saw it hyper-visually, in
symbols.

If I were a driver on the two-lane highway at the bottom of the
scraggy hill, surely I'd wreck the car! I'd be craning my neck to see
such a wonder as these golden pears:

food presented- no, *sprung* really from mere wood.

Oh the pear tree with its golden fruit heavy and mottled, affixed
on its intricate branches. It was like so many Christmas ornaments, it
seemed. Christmas under the sun. Pears in piles, pungent, soft upon
the ground, nested in leaf litter. The tree was noisy. It buzzed with
bees that endlessly twirled through and around it; busy, busy, all this
silhouetted against the sky. My favorite sky, grey.

Starr would feast on the fruits one after another while
contemplating the dissymmetry of her posterior against my
splintered picnic table. I never bit into a pear's flesh. Never did I plan
to. I ate glue, sand and shortening, but I much preferred
ketchup sandwiches and nothing but ketchup sandwiches at home.
If there was even a smear on the plate below my sandwich of red
glorious ketchup, I licked my plate till it shone with my spit.
Variety was not my strong suit. I wanted toast cut into three strips
with butter going all the way to the edges. And nothing but toast cut
into threes.

My parents were concerned about my limited diet but the good
doctor told my mother not to worry, I was only seven and I would
somehow get the nutrients I needed; even if I was known to lick the
occasional rock and chew driveway grit between my teeth, savoring
the glass-like crunchies.

My parents hoped I would one day try a vegetable, or juice, or
meat. They followed the doctor's advice. No one mentioned to the
doctor my staring spells, my mutism, my lack of interest in friends,
(that were not rocks, bugs, trees, or otherwise invisible) my need to
control my cousins when I did play with them, my sleepwalking,
need for structure and routine, or the fact that I was in grade school
and my mother still put me on the table and dressed me because I
couldn't do buttons. That's not to say that the doctor would've picked
up on it back then anyway. But today when a kid has a cluster of
behaviorisms a trained professional should look at the overall
picture. Not just one aspect. Oh well. I wasn't hurting anybody.

I got good grades but I was drawing the attention of the teachers who worried that I never spoke spontaneously except when called upon; and then monosyllabically. I never interacted with the other kids. And I stared a lot in class.
I spoke to Starr, but not if others were present. Not at school.
Some relatives had never heard my voice.
Starr tolerated me. She lived in close proximity. Sometimes I thought if there were other girls to choose from by the highway, she would prefer playing with them and forget me altogether. But mostly I gave her more credit than that and felt she really liked me.
Starr's mother thought us to be "too close" and requested to the school that Starr and I never ever have any classes together. She sensed something off about comical me who didn't speak among groups, and she couldn't wait for her daughter to form other friendships. There were things that happened which bonded us; like the untimely death of her little sister and a man who lived nearby and

lured us...
into his house-
with the promise
of sourball candy.
He called me Timmy.
I guess he couldn't pronounce the K sound.

I asked Mommy and Daddy why I didn't have a little brother like Starr, and was told they were "trying." Whatever the process, I figured it was pretty delicate, pretty difficult to make people. *Then why did the Aunt and Uncle have four kids?* My mother chided me as I lay on the living room's swirly linoleum at night, coloring with carefully chosen crayon colors in my coloring book. There were no popular TV character or movie coloring books then. The pages had practical scenes: kids on bicycles, Daddies with hammers. Mommies baking cookies or rocking babies.

Mommy said sternly, "Why?! Why do you make all the Mommies with black hair? Why?" She kneeled on the floor long enough to put a yellow crayon into my fist and to toss the black crayon I'd been using. It went rolling away. "There, there. A blond Mommy," she said. "Do a blond one."

She started the picture with her own lemon crayon. I assumed she thought the Mommies should have hair like she did. I closed the book across her hand. I was dark-haired and everyone should be. I knew how disappointed she was by my long horse tail black hair and my height. The doctor had said I would be taller than the both of them.

I knew her disappointment because once I hid in secret behind my father's mother's curtain which separated the kitchen from the sewing room where toys were kept when I heard my mother crying. We were in Massachusetts; I was holding a one-armed doll with roll-back eyes in one hand and a small tractor with no wheels in the other when I overheard her say:

"Why couldn't she at least *look like me?*" And later in the conversation:

 "She never hugs back."

She was bawling.

Chapter Five: Sidekick

Every morning I knew that my Daddy disappeared into a factory where he was a foreman and he dyed patterns onto cloth. Sometimes he brought home "flawed" material. He said that his factory would only have chucked the flawed stuff in the trash compactor. Oh we were a family of trash rescuers. I knew that much. I may not have been too savvy about people rescues.
But there were no *things* that went to their demises in our house. Not if we could help it!
In the mid-evening we sometimes picked Daddy up from work when only one car was running and they had to share one vehicle. I liked to look down in the crap-brown canal in front of the factory where eels lined up in flowing dark ribbons near the banks when Mommy and me would park in front of the factory. Daddy would come bounding out with his arms full. He would store bundles of cloth in the trunk for later.

My father had his arms full with bolts of fabrics with the so-called 'misprints' on them. Grayed-down colors where the dye had not saturated the cloth, zigzags that were not lightning sharp- but foggy instead, double struck anchors laid one upon another. Teacups, cornucopias and vegetables were overlapping where they weren't intended to overlap. I could cut out all the pictures and make them have parties with each other! Who was the judge of flaws and mistakes? My father made pattern and color when he left for work! How many fathers could do that?

I followed Daddy under Ilana's hall staircase, where the indoor entrance to the cellar was. The bundles would be piled down there with the rest of the flawed pieces. I followed him; I wanted to see what we had in storage. My father's footfalls on the wooden steps were heavy but sure. I saw a blur flash from the depths. The staircase creaked as we descended. I froze halfway down.

"What's that?" I asked him, knowing full well what 'it' was that had leapt from one lopsided clothes barrel to another.

"Just a rat, Booby," he said. "They're more afraid o' you than you are o' them." Daddy laughed.

"I change my mind Daddy!" I said. I zipped back up to the dark linoleumed hall from which I'd come, listening to my father's hooting laughter follow him into the cellar.

I accompanied him bowling too, doing my puzzles till it was his turn to throw the ball, then I set down my maze book and watched. I sat in the curved plastic orange seats while Daddy bowled with his league friends: Long Earl, Paul, and the others. Those seats were almost as good as the Laundromat seats with their bump in the middle made just-so, to fit my hiney, how did they know?

Those sleek and spectacular seats, all alike but the Laundromat ones somehow different from the bowling ones. How I liked collections of things that were alike but different too.

Every Friday night I got to see Daddy's name up in lights over the place where the shoes were kept in cubby holes. He held the record score. His picture had been in the newspaper several times, shaking hands and receiving trophies.

The accomplishment was his, but he made like it was mine

when, ball in hand, just before his turn to bowl, he faced me and asked, "Should I win you a trophy?"

I liked the 'alleys'. The owners, an orange haired woman who drew on her eyebrows and a short reserved man with black pasted on hair and glasses, let a dog and a cat roam free inside the building, and the animals knew to stay off the lanes. I liked following the pets over to the couch and TV area to pet them.
The kitty liked to rub her scent over the long line of bowling balls. The dog often roamed into the owners' back room. They let me follow her in there and sit with her while my father bowled. Among a desk, a dog bed, bowling posters that punned the words "spare" and "strike," framed black and white photos and cartoon bowlers, I was never at a loss for something to look at or to read.
I sat in the windowless, cluttered room next to the dog bed, tolerating the stack of cigar boxes, and I read the puns over and over again, giggling silent laughs with a hand held over my mouth:
"Think you can spare a strike?"

Daddy taught me to bait hooks, to cast a line. I learned the importance of catching and releasing. We walked upstream in a quest for better fishing spots, and the bank would turn to shrubs, vines, or pricker bushes. It became necessary to cross the streams to the other side. Daddy tested the rocks in the stream with a steel toe, prodding for loosened ones that might upend me. If enough rocks did not exist to precipitate my safe crossing, he rearranged rocks into quaint lines of stepping stones. He warned me of the mossy or slick ones that nearly upended him.

Sometimes he 'fell in' up to his shin or knee and hooting with laughter, he announced, "Better me than you, Poopsie!"

Always he guided me with a big callused hand held lightly over mine; sausage fingers over smooth little white ones. Usually the stepping rocks, however smartly placed, were a bit too far apart for my legs and he would tell me, "Just hold on. I'm not gonna' let you fall in..." I trusted him and let his hand swallow mine.
When we had to cross logs, suspended where they crashed over streams during storms, sometimes several feet in air over the rushing

water, it was the same. He held my hand. We walked sideways over the fallen trees, slowly, and I wasn't too afraid.

"I got your hand. Pretend you're walking on level ground. Don't slow up. Just walk steady now. Almost there. Don't look down", he'd say. So the trick to this was in the pretending.

Chapter Six: Grandma

I had an older cousin who liked to shampoo her long red hair in Grandma's brook. I had no concept as to why she'd do that. Nevertheless I admired her free spirit and her long flowing sunset hair that tried to follow the water downstream. I was happy enough with faucets. Grandma had a perfectly good bathtub in the house. Grandma was a fragile woman with a playful air about her. It seemed she could read everyone's lips but mine. The beloved but prim Aunt Hannah who lived with Grandma, liked to say I didn't "e-nun-ci-ate" clearly. Sometimes I thought she just enjoyed the opportunity to use the word "enunciate" in a sentence. But no matter, Grandma and I had our own way to communicate. I wrote her long sprawling notes in my grade school scrawl and she read every word silently to herself. Then she answered me aloud, a cigarette balanced in her trembling hand.

"Were any new kittens born since last time I was here? How old are they? Which cat is the mother this time?" This and more I jotted on paper.

She began the ritual of pulling a cigarette from the pack, coughing, lighting it, clearing her throat. Then she winked
and began answering me aloud. With my elbows on the table and my hands supporting my chin, I watched her talk. I watched her lips, her fingers, I savored her presence. When it appeared she'd answered every question, and she checked the notes to see that she did, I wrote some more notes to her. We carried on for hours.
With Grandma it was always a delightful task for me to choose which utensil to write with, from the washed soup can on the table. Another group of things that were alike but somehow different.

There were stubby pencils in the can that wrote rich and darkly like smooth liquid grey velvet and some pencils were yellow with long silvery points. I tested pen after pen on paper. Some did not give out ink at all. These I put aside.
Other pens appeared brand new and made red or green marks. Sometimes if I was giddy I alternated pens; making colorful notes.

I wrote on the paper plate I'd used for my toast strips: "Grandma, I have to throw these pens away. They don't write anymore." I held the dry pens in my fist for her to see.

She read the words on the plate, winked, nodded. I threw them away. "Don't throw the paper plate away! Just brush the crumbs off. You can use the plate again," she told me in her crackly Grandma voice.

I kept Grandma busy while my mother chatted with her sister, Hannah. My mother drank coffee, smoked, helped Hannah solve her beloved crossword puzzles from the newspaper, and read her dog-eared paperback romance novels. Often simultaneously! We always visited Grandma in the kitchen.
Hannah lived in the big white house with Grandma. Hannah had a grown son Louie who had darting eyes and fuzzy hair and who only sometimes slept in one of the many rooms of the house. There were always lots of cats milling about outside and sunning themselves on the roof levels. The house had enough charm to be a Matisse painting. It was as if the shingles themselves were brushstrokes. I had the set of World Book encyclopedias at home so I knew about such things. The faces of relatives were Matisse's subjects; sometimes 'jumbled' but interesting.

I had an all-white cat at home that was born in Grandma's shed. Before we took her home to Connecticut, Hannah had had her checked by a vet who said the cat was deaf. My deaf cat Puff did not like to touch the floor. We even kept her food dish on the counter. Puff liked to sleep on top of the refrigerator. The higher up she could get, the better. She had creative ways of hopping from cabinet to television to table to stool to counter to refrigerator. People thought this to be odd but I could relate to her altering her behavior to make her environment more tolerable. Her disability challenged her; she

34

developed agility to compensate. When she was up high, she had some control. No surprises. She could see everything coming. She *never* touched the floor.

I *never* touched smoking things. Or the vinyl chairs in Starr's kitchen, or cotton or sauces, seafood or torn spots on linoleum.

I'd heard say that when the cat population at Grandma's got too numerous, Cousin Louie drowned some in a pillowcase in the brook over the hill.

I was designing a puzzle one day when Aunt Hannah left for the race-track where she sold hot dogs. I was startled in my kitchen chair when Louie jumped up, shaking the table. He was inches from Grandma's face, yelling, his mouth so wide open I could see his pale gums and holes where teeth should've been. I continued to write words for my puzzle. Mommy was acting normal too.

Louie was raving about Grandma finding his expensive pot and pipe in his pocket and throwing it out. When his hand clenched into a fist I tensed. His spittle flew. He paced for a bit then got into her face again.

She held her cigarette as best she could with her hand tremor and the acrid haze of her smoke made me hold my breath. She would not look at him.

When the gun flashed I put down my
pencil.

My pencil rolled and I let it go. Grandma swatted at the handgun touching her forehead with a shaky but determined hand. Louie put it up against her head again. His eyes were big and wild. His finger caressed the trigger. Grandma swatted again; but the gun returned. She swatted. It was as if she were shoeing a pesky horsefly buzzing around her head and not the nose of a gun. Her forehead never looked more fragile to me and frail with its blue veins and receding hairline of grey hair so thin that her entire head of hair could be rolled up with a total of only ten of Mommy's soft pink curlers! Mommy closed her book; surprisingly calm and quiet as we watched Grandma rise and head for the black wall phone with the big dial. He followed her, gun waving through the air.

She meant to *use* the phone, I thought, something I had never seen her do, and a ripple of an unnamed feeling surged through me. She was going to dial the phone. She had the receiver in her hand. He raved some illiterate nonsense but I didn't understand.

I did hear, "Try it old woman!"

What he did next was unexpected. Grandma was seconds away from dialing, her finger was almost there and then with two hands Louie ripped the whole boxy unit right out of the wall. A molar couldn't have been extracted such precision! Multicolored wires were hanging, exposed. Who would've guessed at the colors of a phone's intestines? And then he grabbed the receiver from her.
Slammed it against the edge of the table. The circular mouthpiece flew off and spun up. Whizzed up into the air. We all watched that whirling mouthpiece. Even Louie, with his gun hanging loose in his hand, saw it come down neatly.
It made a wet splunk!
It was resting in Mommy's cold coffee.
It was that comical splunk that froze everybody.
Louie shut his raving mouth and he too was studying the mouthpiece half submerged inside the cup. I ran for the bathroom and soon after I heard Louie slam the front door. He
was gone.
For awhile.

So I went outside and sat picking at the old step and thought about cat overpopulation and the woes it created. I wondered if Rusty's body lay behind the picket fence; a bullet in his tummy. A shooting instead of a drowning. I wondered if Louie pegged 'em all where they stood or drowned some. Then I thought about people overpopulation. The world's problems weighed heavy on me.
"Time for bed Kimmy. Kiss Grandma," Mommy said that night.
I scowled at my mother when I knew she was looking. "Thank Aunt Hannah for the paper. She got it special from the racetrack office with you in mind," said my mother.

"Thanks," I murmured, without looking up.

Hannah harrumphed. "It's not right Carol. You know that? She never looks at me."

Mommy and I always shared the bouncy bed at Grandma's with the goose-feather pillows. The feathers I could pull out when they stuck through the pillow just right. In my head I recited the prayer that hung on a wall under a painting of clasped hands my mother had painted herself for Grandma.

God grant me the Serenity to
Accept the things I Cannot change,
The Courage to change the things that I Can,
And the Wisdom to Know the difference.

I prayed in my head as my mother smoked the day's last cigarette. Mommy nodded off into a snorey sleep. *She wasn't supposed to do that until I did!* I jiggled her shoulder with vigor, getting her slack upper arms to shimmying.

"MOMMY!" I said, directly into her ear.

"Wha? Who? I'm awake," she lied. I watched as her eyelids dropped closed over her ocean-blue eyes. I saw the movement of her lids as her eyes rolled beneath them. I shook her again and watched her eyes open wide.

"I can't sleep," I said into the foreboding night.

"Think of happy things," she replied.

"Like what?" I asked her eyelids. "Like...Valentine's Day." Her murmured words melted into snores. I thought of Valentine's Day and its symbols and rituals until sleep stole me away.

Chapter Seven: The Sarcastic Tutu

Starr adjusted her much-hated everyday glasses; the ones that turned up in points on the outer edges. Teachers in our fourth grade class and strangers alike went on about how cute they were. I knew Starr hung her hair in her eyes on purpose to hide her glasses. I liked her glasses too but didn't let on. They did look pretty funny when she wore the short curly wig.

The wig I was wearing was black, short, and curly. It was hard to stuff my own unruly black mane under its inner meshing. My long curly hair felt like a horse's tail until my mother had it all chopped off; but what remained was thick, wavy and coarse.

"Gerta that ain't the half of it darlin'!'" Starr was Myrtle. Myrtle said, "I hear she drinks and gambles at the track!" We gossiped about pretend people.

"Oh Myrtle child! Say it ain't so!" I said.

We ad-libbed and fingered the strands of costume jewelry we wore over the silky scarves and polyester shift dresses. Between the pile of stuff in my room and our mothers' jewelry boxes, we were never at a loss for costumes or props.

"I done heard it all right Gerta," Starr went on. "It's true--the mailman tol' me. It's true as sure as Maisie's hair is blonde!"

"Now girl, you're talkin' ta' Gerta! And Maisie's roots are dark, girl!" I said. I'd absorbed some lines from my mother's soaps.

"I do declay-er! Hand me that salad there, y'all," Starr said.

Dandelion leaves made fine pretend lettuce we 'washed' in the sink strainer we'd found. Rotten wood made chunky white 'chicken' for our stews. We pretended to prepare and then eat our feast over gab sessions.
Afterward we swept the lot beside the boulders with straw tied to broken tree arms. There was not another soul in my world save for objects with whom I could relate so well.
The boulder playhouse was a halfway point between Starr's house and mine. I was allowed to walk to her house, two houses away, up the hill.
Daddy sometimes surprised me by showing up on the ride-on lawnmower and gave me a ride home for supper. I enjoyed the

bumpy ride over the pot-holed pavement but always I ima-gined myself falling and slipping under the lawnmower.

Back home, I winced, as usual, as I walked through the pantry into the kitchen. The sequins peeking out from behind the charcoal briquettes bag on the high green shelf were always winking sarcastically at me, taunting me. The tutu was stashed up there until such time as I was ready to tell Mommy I wanted to start the ballet classes. I knew I never would.
I wanted to be a graceful ballerina like the one in the jewelry box. The one who danced with the smartly dressed man's hands around her minuscule waist every time I lifted the lid. But I tripped over air pockets.
I would never be her.
The tutu had belonged to one of Aunt Maura's kids. The day Mommy pulled it from the garbage bag she got all excited but I walked away even though I knew I wanted to be like the girl at school who bragged about *her* ballet classes. Her body was cheetah-like. I was a chimp.

"I'll make the ballet lesson appointment, okay?" she said on and off that week.

Eventually the sequined tutu was finally put on the pantry shelf next to the charcoal bag where I could not ignore the shimmering of its sequin adornments every time I walked into the house. That my soul could dance I was certain. I danced daily. I danced with kitties in Starr's blue bedroom, on Ilana's porch boards, on the biggest boulders, and beneath the pear tree under the stars.
But my recipe for a perfect ballet class could never be, and I knew it: One on one with an instructor with confectioner's sugar sprinkling down on us two as we danced. The latter part may be a bit much but if the ballet is a dream it gets to be *my* dream. My graceful legs leaping and twirling against a sea of vast shining wood with polished knotholes. Silken shoes tied round the ankles with long ribbons. An instructor with a bun on her brown head, a demeanor like Ilana, a patience and angelic beauty like Mommy, with much to teach me not only about ballet movements, but about the ballet. The famous dancers who knew the art. *Oh yes!* This is as I imagined. But one on one *was* a dream.

Group lessons were discussed. Other children. Classes. Talking.
I *never* talked in school. Or to my uncles. Or around Starr's
parents or most of my family. Words sometimes traveled up my
throat and stuck there; a logjam of ideas and thoughts forever
unexpressed. The reality of this made me very sad. Ironically, I was a
writer; filling every scrap I could with phrases, idioms and ideas. If I
did *not* write, I feared that the unexpressed letters may dribble out
my mouth as I slept at night. I imagined them trickling down my face
in times roman script.
When people spoke, I sometimes 'saw' their typewritten sentences in
the air, twirling, beautiful, beautiful words. Without creative
expression through drawing or writing to bring out the nut in me, I
was a shell with no substance.
It would be that way in any class, I knew. There were a half
dozen people I spoke to, and my parents were included in that
count. A half dozen more people I answered at least
monosyllabically when I was spoken to. There were times I could
talk formally, politely.

Whenever my mother went downtown I asked to go inside the
travel agency while she waited in the car.

I approached the bespectacled woman behind the desk and lied with
my practiced story: "Excuse me, I'm doing a report on Hawaii. Do
you have any brochures on that subject?" The report on Hawaii
would be written to myself and turned in to me.
My other rehearsed question, oft asked, was, "My family is planning
a trip to England; may I have a brochure?" I tensed, waiting to be
caught in my lie; and hauled off to the police station. I did not relax
until I was out the door with my information. I began to have the
idea that some things were so
worthwhile, like the gathering of information, they were worth
being arrested for. I imagined myself in the black and white striped
attire of the felon.

Sometimes I could lose myself at the neighborhood ninety-nine cent
matinee. I had seen a movie, a true story about the life of Hans
Christian Anderson. He was in love with a prima ballerina and gave
to her the most beautiful gift I had ever seen: A clever colorful
bouquet of soft ballerina slippers that he'd sewn himself; the ribbons

trailing down around his hand as he presented them to the dancer who seemed not to appreciate them.

Some parts of life were not made for me. I was not made for inclusion in *it;* I wouldn't be the dancer in the music box; the lid was forever closed. I was not like other kids. But I would've swooned at a bouquet like the one in the movie. If my left foot did not turn in, if I was not clumsy, if I didn't stare, if I could be promised mirrors were not in ballet classes
if,
 if,
if.

>Mommy told me, "If wishes were horses then beggars would ride."

I wished nothing would ever, ever change. One day someone thought the shelves in the entry hall needed a fresh coat of paint. Grimy cans with stuck-on lids, and old bric-a-brac were cleared away off the shelves to ready for the new paint. I never saw the sarcastic tutu again. The chosen color for the shelves was flat pea green.
The color was starting to scare me a little.

Chapter Eight: Green Girl
I avoided the realness of mirrors. A TV world is behind glass as was I.

When I watched dramas on TV, I couldn't imagine that the shows were fake long enough to put belief in the story line. I could not suspend rational thought with abandonment. What I thought when I looked at most programming was the facts I suspected to be true-- and nothing more. I wonder if the man who plays the doctor role, goes home to a wife and children. I wonder if the pronunciation of that medical term came easily for him or if he had to practice it a lot. I wonder what the people are like who chose the props for that hospital room. Does that child actor get breakfast on the set? Doughnuts or eggs?

Afterwards I could not say what the show was about. Part of me didn't filter the important from the non-important. Situational comedies with predictable outcomes were preferable. Visual stuff, physical comedy, slapstick movies, sight gags, and variety show skits were easier for me to 'get', and thus, to enjoy. When watching the TV, pretending was an effort as it involved work. A deliberate honing and concentration of every sense, and of the mind as well. A chore.

I usually watched TV while muttering a mantra:
"Pretend...pretend...pretendpretendpretendpretend."

When I looked at faces, sometimes the features jumbled up. Eyes could change shape into almond shapes or change places with noses, or realign themselves higher up on the forehead. Noses enlarged and shrunk, that kind of thing.

I never really looked into my own eyes. But one day I was feeling like expending the effort. The bathroom mirror on the medicine chest was up too high for me to see 'me' closely. I balanced my right foot's arch on the edge of the precious old clawfoot tub and I situated the knee from my other leg on the edge of the sink basin. I was afraid of course, that the sink would separate from the wall and I would be buried in toppled porcelain and pipes.

If I maintained my balance at least for a little while I figured I should be able to see into the mirror very close up for at least a short time. Being coordinated was no easy feat for someone who couldn't even do buttons. My knee slipped; I strained and nearly gave up. Then there was my face. I fought the blurring out instinct.

It was a learned protective response that I should've obeyed; my protection against features that tended to rearrange and swirl. I was up close, real close. Nearly touching the mirror with my freckled nose.

I needed to consider my eyes as more than wet marbles rolling, scaring. I told my self they were part of a whole picture, not individual components. I looked at eyes and didn't look away; in fact I spiraled into their pond-scum depths and lost myself. My eyes had light brown speckles around the pupil. But they were decidedly a lichen shade of green.

My fury almost tipped me into the tub. *They'd been lying to me!* In the kitchen I found her and I started in yelling.

"How come everyone's been telling me my eyes are hazel!?" I said.

"What?" she asked, trying to stir my hot pudding.

"My eyes! You never told me they're green!" I yelled.

"Your eyes are called hazel," she said and her face looked angry.

"That's a tricky way to say green 'cause I just looked and they're green! I hate them! I want blue eyes like you and Daddy and Starr. Or brown like the cousins even. It's not fair!" I screamed.

The word "hazel" had always eluded me but I didn't know it meant "green." *So,* I thought, it is an evil color which makes me different enough to notice. My inner tornado of confusion and anger turned into hiccoughing stutters which turned into hyperventilation. My eyelids swelled; became sore and I couldn't stop the crying stutters that shook my body and made my chest ache. Mommy turned off lights. She forced me into her arms and we sat in the rocking chair together. Instead of ripping at her face I went into a fetal position. I pulled my knees to my chin. Mommy's long hard fingernails raked over my scalp. I dissolved into the smell of her house dress. Nicotine and Ivory soap.
We did this a lot.
I always had fits.

"Stop now; you're making yourself sick again," she said. I became the rhythm of the rocking.

Days later, men in white clothes came to change the color of my grey house. I ran from window to window, inconsolable.
Adrenaline, untouchable and sensitive like the mercury I found in thermometers *rolled* through my veins in a rush of anxiety. A stout happy little man was spraying flat pea-green paint right over all our windows' glass. He was greening us in!
Mommy went outside to see if there was a mistake. It was getting dark inside. When she came back in her smile was still on her lips. She had one for every person she greeted. She said his method

was the easiest way and he'd be back later to scrape the windows with a razor.
I sat in the kitchen chair with the vinyl that disturbed my fingertips. Might as well lick cigarette ash, step on black torn linoleum and eat mashed potatoes and salmon too!

Daddy laughed when he got home from work and said, "Musta' had a sale on green paint."

I just shook my head from side to side slowly, glad the whole fiasco was over. I was staring out the screened door at the sandbank. They'd taken the grey skin right off the house.

A weird thing happened: a downpour. It was weird because the sun was high overhead and very bright. Perhaps the rain would beat down the leaning garage once and for all, I thought. It looked like I could blow on it and it would keel over. I played games of 'survive' by running over and over through the front and out the back window of the old garage to see if it would collapse before I made it out. People would save you even if it was only one kid trapped inside. I watched the rain and saw a startlingly real daydream during the sunny steamy downpour. I stood at the screened door staring, my hands limp at my sides. There next to my billboard with the happy gas attendant on it, what was that? Beyond the wade pool, a green blur at the top of the sandbank. A fuzzy blur moved and took human shape as it descended the bank, disturbing stones that cascaded sand in sandfalls down the sandbank.
The fuzzy green girl floated across the yard past the swimming pool with its floating green scum, the color of my eyes. She got close, greening toward me. She passed through the door, mindful of the nail there that caught.
She was my size. My age, she had no expression.
A doppelganger? She melted through the myriad of holes that was the screen and into me. I closed my eyes and smelled the wet pavement of the hot highway and accepted the green girl dissolving into me. I stood at the door a long while listening to the rain pelt the pool, the garage, the house, and I wondered how my daytime dreaming could seem so real. I *was* the
green girl.
My house and I were greened.

44

I think if my house
could've flown off the hill
to escape that paint, it would've.
And I would've helped it,
standing tall
on the hilly lawn
in my Halloween
princess costume,
waving a wand.

Chapter Nine: Eraser Balls

Its skin was burnt-red brick. Ornate iron hooks were its helpful
hands that held our coats like in the Willy Wonka factory. Each
radiator-lined classroom had a coatroom, a dark narrow hall-like
passage behind one of its walls.

I imagined lots of such hidden and useful crannies in my own brain. I
wondered about my brain's folds. What purpose did they serve? As
the only non-sensate organ I had, as the only organ that could
withstand a scalpel's plunge and feel no pain, I admired and loved
my brain.

The school fed my beloved brain and I loved my school. The water
that flowed through those radiator pipes; warming us in winter, were
my school's veins. The clanking of the radiators was its heartbeat.
The children and the noise in the school ruined my orgasmic
experience with my brain and my school. Can't have everything.

It became necessary to skip school on gym days. I would stand there
and balls would bounce off my face before I'd tell my hands to do
something in time. I liked square dance and the solitary activities like
sit ups but the group things had rules I didn't understand.
Gym was on Monday. The red-bearded fifth grade teacher told
my mother I must have 'Mondayitis'. The classroom was as
stressful as gym class that year. Maybe more-so. Fifth grade was a
year of awareness on many levels. I had to cut back somewhere to
preserve energy. It was a playful atmosphere in his classroom. Boy
did that spontaneity set me on edge!

It was the first time I'd ever had a male teacher. He was witty;
always making jokes. The kids; they laughed as if on cue; as if
they were supplied beforehand with scripts I did not have.

As if a sign flashed in the room that I could not see: *Laugh now! Laugh!*
They not only laughed at his playful kidding, but seemed to *enjoy* it.
I wished for canned laughter like on TV that I could operate when
the others laughed. His words were riddles I couldn't solve.
Although I sensed he was loved by all the kids, perhaps more than
any teacher I'd had thus far, I could not relate. I wanted the teacher I
had the year before: the lady with her black hair wrapped into a twist,
secured on her head. In *this* classroom, I did not understand why
suddenly we were to replace ordinary numbers with 'Roman'
numerals which were lines and not symbols at all. *I was not Roman.* I
resisted learning the
new replacements and for the first time ever I struggled in school and
was given an impatient 'tutor' to help teach me math during class.

I liked Jason. He produced artwork with a sure placement of
lines and he liked to wonder aloud, "Who's the best artist? Me,
you, Eddie, or Dawn?" He didn't get an answer from me. I didn't
believe in "the best."

"What's with the sweater?" Jason asked me one day.

I thought, *I got straight A's last year. Think of an answer.* I was
squinting, trying to be smart enough to make sense of the oversized
clock on the wall which had Roman numerals. I could cheat a little
because I could count to where the number should be and write down
the correct answer. However, when the assignment called for a
number over twelve, I was clue-less. This strange math is what Jason
was supposedly helping me with.

"You wear that sweater every day. Don't you have any other
clothes?" Jason said.
I nodded.
"Why don't you talk for cripes sake? This is great. Just 'cause
I'm smart, I gotta waste my time on a dummy who can't talk or do
math and wears sweaters every day in this weather. It's almost
Summer for cripes sake!"

No matter how many times he explained Roman numerals to

me, I sat with pencil poised over paper; frozen. My mind could not get it. He became angry with me and belittled my appearance instead. I couldn't fathom how I could provoke respect from him for my artistic abilities but also antagonism.

 "She wears that every day for cripe's sake!" he would say, and look around to see if anyone was as perturbed by me as he was.

I loved my white sweater. It was soft like a rabbit. Tiny buttons and feathery to the touch. I craved routine and structure, not informality and spontaneity. The sameness of the sweater kept me from disappearing completely.

Innuendo was alien. "Learning games" involved moving desks out of their routine arrangements. We often sat on the floor in informal groupings. How did one accidentally touch the other kids' limbs and not wince?

Since the teacher said he liked a neat classroom, I kept my desk in exceptional order. If it was crammed with papers and books with torn book covers, it would draw his attention on me. I wanted to blend in as much as I could, to prove I was "as normal" as anyone else.

One day we stood in the lunch line at the side of the room. I could look into the mouths of the desks, and I knew mine was the neatest.

Then he made a joke at me. "Kim, do you really think you're going to make *that many* mistakes?" He was pulling on his beard and he had that amused grin again. The others apparently 'got' the joke because several were holding their hands to their mouths or stomachs and laughing.

Oh dear oh dearohdearohdearohdear.

I cocked my head to the side. Shuffled in place in line. Should I laugh and pretend I 'got' the joke? Or did the joke have meaning and require an answer from me? Did the joke call for some action from me? I just couldn't know. He may as well have said, "Hey did you notice that the schmip was schmop?"

"I think you should take all but one of the erasers home. I'm confident you won't make *that many* mistakes in my class." He said.

Most of the class was shuffling and laughing like ocean waves
in sync. *Did he say "erasers"???* So that was it! They were clearly
visible from his vantage point; lined up uniformly in the front of my
desk. I stacked them three-high and four-high. Little eraser towers.
There was my six inch eraser I'd gotten from a souvenir shop
with "Niagara Falls" painted on the front in black ink. Stacked on
that big one were my small rectangular pink ones, seven eight or nine
of them maybe. One white eraser was in there. It could erase ink.
Propped beside those were my multi-colored ones shaped like
spacecraft. I had aliens too with eraser arms that I'd gotten from
cereal boxes. There were pink and green and blue ones too with
holes in them so you could top a pencil with them. How I loved
collections of things that were alike but different too.
Amid the staring eyes and laughing, the teacher, anxious to send us
all down to lunch, smiled and casually fingered the pockets of his
neatly seamed slacks. I scooped up the alien erasers up and stuffed
them in the pockets of my own pants. I crammed in eraser after
eraser into my pockets. I tried to force the six inch eraser, my
favorite, into my bulging pocket but it was not fitting.
Fresh laughter erupted from my 'peers' as I shoved and rearranged
my pocket and tried to force that big eraser in; but my pockets were
already bulging with lumps.

"I think you can put that colossal one in your desk until the end
of the day. Just don't forget to bring it home with you today,
okay?" he said, grinning. He gave his sideburns a rub.

Okay so now he tells me. I put the big one in the front of the
desk and one little pink one directly in the center of it. I returned to
the line pinching the bumps in my pants. Could he next demand I not
wear my sweater?

Pink and so soft, my erasers smelled perfect when I sneaked
them to my nose during classroom discussions. They came in *every*
shape and size. Various colors too, but pink smelled best. I'd have to
find a special place at home for them now; perhaps next to the pencil
shavings collection. I had boxes of shavings.
But then I'd not be able to appreciate the erasers in class, which was
where I really needed them.

Could I one day rub the sides of them smooth, working slyly with my hand inside the desk, until they formed perfectly round and soft pink balls of many sizes? Would they then bounce? Would it be easiest to rub the corners against paper until a sphere took shape? Or rub the corners away on the inside of the desk itself? Would some balls be easier to shape depending on the brand of eraser? Oh, how I'd planned on cherishing my eraser balls. I would even save the shavings. I planned on filling little yellow boxes with the eraser balls to keep forever. Now I'd never get the chance.

There were other fifth grade issues besides my high absenteeism. I learned to sit at my desk so that both my legs faced the aisle. So both legs could get kicked evenly. On the home front, Mommy had been asking questions about the bruises on one leg so I found the solution. By putting
them both in the aisle, Holly could sashay by me to the front of the classroom to sharpen a pencil and wallop them both instead of just the one. She was one of his favorites, the class athlete. On her way back to her desk she would kick my shin. Hard. I tried to poke the other leg her way.

Please kick both evenly. *Kick me evenly* my mind begged, *or don't kick at all.*

All the while she smiled her prettiest smile. I concentrated on the smells of paste and paint from the cabinet in the back of the room. Sometimes I thought Holly invented reasons to pass by me. I smiled back; lips pursed together, eyes blurring out static movement in the room. I knew Holly, like Uncle Rodney, thought that mean-spiritedness would solve me. I was a riddle, a challenge. Holly would solve me if she had to kick the answer out of me. But the reaction she evoked was my typical serious, polite logical self. This was me. Holly didn't know that even people like me who did not express much with their features can have their pride-and flesh hurt.
        Some people need *so* much feedback.

Chapter Ten: Transitions

On the brink of being teens, Starr introduced me to the world of mainstream music. She had the album of the musical "Tommy" that we'd seen at the movies. We got together when her new friends were not around and re-enacted the movie in her blue bedroom as the songs belted out on her record player turntable. It was never discussed by either of us but it was naturally me who got to perform the part of Tommy, the deaf, "dumb," and blind kid.

She enjoyed playing all the other roles. She liked jumping up and down on her bed with an imaginary microphone, playing the role of Tina Turner the acid queen who tried to cure Tommy of my mute indifference to the world. No irony there, right?

Starr played her part, I played mine. Eyes unfocused. Hands held straight out. My face expressionless but telling plenty.

Our music attracted Wes, a neighbor in close proximity to Starr, to bob his head up outside her bedroom window. I mentally willed him to leave so we could continue our Tommy game. But Starr lifted the screen and hung her upper body out her window, laughing. She was already so busty my father had a nickname for her: Lumps.

She chatted with Wes. "Why won't Lena show her face at the window?" He asked.

Starr laughed. "Because it ain't Lena, it's Kim!" she said.

"Oh!" said Wes. "Why do you bother with *that* shy bitch?" Starr just laughed; ever trying to be diplomatic, friend to most everyone.

Her mother was getting ready to ship her a million miles away to a far-away state to live with grandparents, all because her mother was worried that she and I were too close and that Starr needed other friendships. I was yearning to understand, to be fluid, to accept as is. I supposed if I were a car, I'd have been a lemon. No matter, since yellow was my favorite color. When Frank, my class-mate, had made a comment about me about needing to wear a bra; truth was I hadn't noticed any changes in me at all. I was who I was ever unchanging. That was just me. I did not know how to roll with the tide, follow the herd, fly with the flock.

Chapter Eleven: Knucklehead Billy

Starr chalked a hopscotch grid onto an unpocked area of pavement in front of my house and carefully numbered the squares with squat happy numerals. I was savoring all my time with her as I'd be moving soon to live in the empty apartment above the cousins and she was being shipped out west soon to live with her grandmother. I supplied small jagged sedimentary stones, delightfully striated with grey and white for tossing into the hopscotch squares.

We had a game going between us when the typical roughhousing hooligans tore past us, trying to catch the appointed 'it' person. They had all their games in the road; it being a dead end and all. Richard, Billy, Wes, Lil and the rest, didn't ask us to join in their game of tag and I was glad for it. Billy jeered me every single time he whizzed by me with a sing-song insult but I did not absorb what he was saying.

"What time is it?" Starr asked, startled. "Oh, man I gotta get the contraption outta the tub and put it on before the madre comes home from work!" Starr said, and then she was suddenly sprinting toward her house.

She had scoliosis and was not supposed to remove the back brace unless her mother said so. She feared the repercus-sions from her strict mother. Of course she always did go without it when her mother wasn't around. She liked to conceal it behind the shower curtain; hoping her brother would not see it there and tell on her. I watched till she was out of sight and wondered what to do with myself. I bent over and retrieved my rocks.

Billy ran by me close enough to skid his sneaker into the back of my own. He was apparently 'it' and trying to avoid being tagged. I was paying attention now.

He stared me down as he ran. "Kim is a-DOP-ted! Kim is a-DOP-ted!" he called as he whizzed by. The others laughed as they chased him.

So he had found a new way to ridicule me?
Usually he just called me scumbag.

I smirked at him with a look I generally reserved for
stepping in poop.

Lollygagging up my driveway; I resisted the urge to sit and pick
at the crumbling sandstone in my rock wall that lined the drive. I
went straight inside. I was hungry. The kitchen did not smell like
anything yet and I wondered if it was one of those evenings we'd be
having spaghetti at the cousins' house. Indeed it was. My mother
announced to me that as soon as Daddy got home we were leaving.
I decided to share what Billy said. Daddy walked in just then
and so I expected they'd both get a good laugh. Mommy would
say, "What an odd thing to say! Kids today and their dream
worlds! Adopted! How ludicrous!" She'd laugh her throaty
Muttley laugh, the passionate kind that involved her whole face;
wrinkling the skin around her eyes and with no sound coming out of
her mouth. Daddy would chuckle, from deep down where his
diaphragm was.

He'd throw his hands in the air and remark, "What a knuckle-head,
that Billy!"

I blurted it out. "Billy said I'm adopted!" I smiled and froze the
bemusement on my face, waiting for them to follow suit.

Daddy excused himself as he said he'd been holding his water since
he got out of work and his teeth were floating. That meant he had to
pee. I repeated myself, still grinning toward Mommy. "Billy said I'm
adopted!"

Mommy repeated calmly what she'd said when I came in:
"We're going to eat at Aunt Nat's. Get ready. Don't you want a
chance to go upstairs and see what our new apartment will look like?
It's almost moving day, you know."

The grin slid off my face. I still had the rocks in my hands.
I didn't especially enjoy the pasta but my stomach was appeased for
now. After dinner, the four adults were embroiled in an engrossing
game of Pokeno at the kitchen table. I was left to ascertain whatever
cousin seemed to be the least cantankerous, and to devise a game of
my own with him or her.

My idea of fun at their house was to make a list of scavenger hunt items like "piece of paper with writing on it," and "piece of fabric," "bottle-cap," and "nail." Then I supplied the cooperative cousins with bags and waited to see who would win, dumping out the bags' contents for me to check off my list, things for me to secret away into my various boxes and enjoy later. Yes, I had clever schemes to get others to amass glinty things for me.

I was in the middle room on the floor on my back; supporting my hips with my hands. I was bicycling the air with my legs, observing the cousins. One kid was usually walloping on another one, leaving me to choose one of the other two cousins that seemed the most civil to be around.

Mommy called to me; "Kimmy, come into the kitchen."
She was using her Girl Scout leader voice with me.

The alarm bells went off within my head, as sure as if I had a warning system inside me that emitted danger signals on the same frequency as an internal dog whistle.
I stood facing the adults and none ever looked up; although Aunt Nat seemed fidgety; and about to burst; like she was strong-arming herself to hush up.

"What Billy said is true," Mommy said.

"I'm adopted?" I asked. I could've been saying, "Can I have a graham cracker?" because all the knots creeping into my sto-mach hadn't made it to my voice yet. "But how would *he* know?" I asked.

"Starr knew. I know her mother told her never to tell you. She kept the secret a long time. Maybe her brother told the kids on the street." She laid a red chip onto her playing board.

"Oh," I said, and skipped out of the room to find a cousin to watch a TV show with. "We didn't want you finding out like this," Daddy said.

It was a long ride home, or it seemed longer than usual, and

Daddy was talking-talking-talking! "We always meant to tell you at the right time, Kimmy. It never seemed like the right time. But you're eleven now."

I was twelve but no matter. He went on. "Your mother already had a lotta kids. She worked with Aunt May so she had the idea we do a private adoption. She said to the lady, 'Hey I got a brother and his wife in Connecticut that really want a child. Hey you should let them adopt!' Mommy can't have kids, Kimmy. She has two of every one of her productive organs on the inside. That's why she bleeds double whammies every month. If you have any questions, just ask," he said, looking in his rearview mirror to see me better. But I couldn't interject. He wasn't leaving me room to ask anything. I didn't know how he could drive and also talk so much. This whole thing had left him almost cheerful, happy perhaps that the whole sordid the secret was out. I just wished he wasn't calling some stranger
"my mother." My mother was sitting in the passenger seat staring out the window. It wouldn't really resonate with me that I had actual siblings somewhere, for many days.
"Your name was A-li-cia Marie," he announced. He enunciated the news as if he were reciting sacred words from a secret long-ago document. "Your *mother* wanted to give you that name on the conditions of the adoption. She wanted to be the one that named you."

"We didn't have a choice," my mother said.

" And we had to agree," continued Daddy. "I'll show you your papers when we get to the house…"

I had *papers?*! Like my poodle, Suzette? "When did my name change to Kimberly Diane?" I was leaning into the front seat, straining to hear it all.

"Oh Kimmy!" he said with much excitement. Great, he was going to ignore my question because he'd remembered some new bits of bombshell that hadn't yet been dropped on me. "Suzy is really a gift from your real mother-"

I managed to interject. "Mommy is really my mother; Daddy.

That means that Suzy-"

"Suzy wasn't from Aunt May like we told you. We pretended she was a gift from her. Your real m-"

"Birth mother, Joe," said my mother, in a weary voice.

"She wanted you to have the poodle as a gift. The birth mother, she raises poodles." said Daddy.

I said, "So when I decided on the names: Suzette if it's a girl, Pierre if it's a boy, everyone looked at me funny because they said that's the name the dog breeder gave to Suzy's dog-parents. So I picked the names *she* picked out for her own dogs." I was not about to say "mother" or "birth mother."

"Yup, yup. You couldn't have known. How 'bout that? You were on the same wavelength! Here we are!" he announced.

We were home. Mommy had a bath to take. A nightgown to get into. Daddy made an elaborate rite of stepping up onto the step stool to retrieve "the lock box" (which wasn't really locked at all) from the topmost shelf of the kitchen broom closet, where incidentally there was no clutter and we really did keep a broom! Why had I never snooped and found that box?
Daddy dumped its contents onto the table.

"Here's the paper when we changed your name," he said proudly.

"Oh yeah. I wondered how old I was when you changed my name to Kim," I said.

"Five. The school wanted a birth certificate and damned if Momma was gonna give 'em this one." He pushed a paper toward me that listed the names of my parents. It did not say "Carol and Joe." It read: 'Lila and Peter.' "We legally changed your name in…uh… '69. Went to the lawyer downtown. Whitehead was his name. Helluva nice guy." Daddy let a big wind rip and his chair vibrated with the sound! "Sorry Poopsie. Nat's cookin' does that."

"YOU should be called Poopsie!" I said. Daddy let out a funny little laugh. I said thoughtfully, "So my name was Alicia…? But you called me Kim anyway for five years?"

"Nope we didn't call you '*KimAnyway.*'" Daddy guffawed at his own joke. I smacked his arm. "We just called you our little Kimberly. Momma always wanted a Kimberly Diane! We called you Kimmy from the start, yessiree. Aunt May drove you to Connecticut. Coulda' had you sooner but you were born real sick. A hundred four temperature and a cracked eardrum." Daddy's whole body got into it when he talked. He made impromptu and unexpected gestures. He might adjust his glasses, twiddle the table with his big fingers, or rise abruptly to fart over in the corner and then return casually to the table because he figured I wouldn't smell it over there. My body was as focused and still as his was kinetic, moving at all times as he spoke. He was always that way. "You laid there on Uncle Sal's lap for the trip to Connecticut. Three days old. Longest two and a half hour ride she ever had, your Aunt May said, with you, three days old…When they got outta' the car and handed you over to Momma, we thought she was gonna' break you! She squeezed you so hard and she was bawling!
She's mine! She's mine! She's mine, Momma kept sayin'." Daddy laughed and when I looked his way he stuck his tongue under his bottom denture plate and flipped it up and down which he knew grossed me out. I ignored his antics.

A memory surfaced. I said, "I remember the day. At the lawyer's. I didn't know what a lawyer was but we got dressed up, and I didn't know my name got changed, but I knew it was an important day." I dropped my eyes to scrutinize my papers. I couldn't wait to call Starr in the morning!

In my new house, I took to mass ordering flower bulbs by mail, writing in page after page of journals, and trying to figure out how to get normal and live life sans Starr.
Out west, after a few runaway attempts Starr returned to our old dead end street to live again with her mother and brother. No matter, it was not even remotely in walking distance unless I wanted blisters on my feet. I tried walking there and that's exactly what happened.

We did manage to talk on the telephone albeit my side of the talking was like trying to re-befriend a stranger I thought I knew and knew I liked very much. It had happened.

She seemed like a...

stranger.

Chapter Twelve: Specks of Many Colors

I was paddling up from where I was stuck in a bogged down place. I kept going even though I was in quicksand—then I broke through to consciousness. My eyelids bounced. I saw a large black numeral 2, and it was floating. I thought I was dead and in a Dali painting that I'd seen in my library book! But no because aches and pains and smells were here.

I glimpsed my physical self. In a bed under good quality linen. I considered I might be dreaming but there was a clarity I could not ignore. You can't smell stuff in sleep. Can you? But that 2 was hovering like a space-craft and something was wrong with my eyes. Edges of everything were indistinct, blurry and every single thing was white. I blinked and blinked again. My eyelids felt like they hadn't been used in a while. I tried to command the 2 into focus. It was apparently on a white wall above a bed across from me.

A grey head stuck out from rumpled blankets in that bed under the 2. My peripheral vision was working. I looked sideways. Specks of many colors were there. I knew what they were and they made me glad. The specks were my mother.

"Really cleaned your system out," said a male voice.

"Do you recall getting your stomach pumped?" asked a wo-man.

I shook my head. It was like it didn't belong to me so I shook it pretty slowly.

"Coma-like state. One lucky girl," said the male. "Well you did get your stomach pumped. Do you remember vomiting?" he asked me. Jesus! I shook my head. Hah! There was vomit involved!

"You did. One question!" This from a happy doctor. "Who is John?"

They didn't need to know I'd went to the movies to meet with a boy... That I had a 'phone friend' and was 'going out with' a boy. My throat was scratchy, my voice hoarse, but I was trying to answer the questions, so many of them. I was only 13.

"I was on the phone with him, then I don't know."

"Well that's all we heard around here while you were under," said a nurse. "John this and John that."

"I would tell you what you said to the paramedics but it would embarrass you!" said Aunt Nat, laughing. *She's here too?*

"We never heard you say the F-word before last night. Shocked us all to say the least!" declared my mother.

"Paramedics?" I said numbly. I remembered none of that and shook my head slowly in disbelief. I was angry that a piece of my life had elapsed and I'd not been cognizant. Couldn't even get drunk correctly.

"Did she ever swear!" said Aunt Nat.

A white blanket covered my body, which was speaking to me in aches, telling me it felt fluish. Its suffering would not be ignored. It was wrung out, with a sore raw throat and woozy head. My brain reminded me of vodka and I did not believe it at first; that vodka could do this horrible thing to me but I knew it was true. I could taste the liquor, and smell it.
I turned my head to the left with concern. My head was really a bruised rotten fruit and would cave in. Smiling, dark haired Aunt Nat was really there and smiled even brighter. I looked to the right; to the person I knew was there, the woman I'd seen wearing the specks of many colors. My mother. Her eyes were moist and bloodshot, the skin around them creped with creases.

She was saying, "She's awake Joe!"

It was our shirt she was wearing. I tried to smile at its glorious presence. I wondered if she'd worn it on purpose. On one shopping excursion that we'd had, we'd bought identical shirts in each of our sizes so we could dress alike. The shirt was white with vertical textural ribbing. Colorful dots were splashed all over the shirt. But if you looked closely you saw that they were bold multicolored threads tied in knobby knots. I inhaled deeply. Let it out mightily. I noticed then the two men. Aunt Nat's husband and my father, who were brothers, were talking to a doctor near some medical equipment. My father had a shining bald spot on his head.

He was bespectacled with black glasses that were taped over the nose. Oh that Daddy. He was always breaking them. His round, short stature and bow-leggedness was in sharp con-trast to his brother who was taller, broader, and possessed blond wavy hair. The uncle was a truck-driver. Nat and her husband were special people in my life. They all noticed my opened eyes and came at me- nurses and doctors with clipboards and pens, wearing glasses and excited faces; spouting their words. If they overwhelmed me I was apt to not hear their words at all. I would somehow need to stare and focus on a pattern or thing but there were none in this white room.

I shook my head no. Already the words were spiraling out and down my drain. They were telling me I swore. I didn't remember that. I breathed deeply the pillow's scent when my cheek brushed it. It was a more favorable scent than that of the clammy sweat and liquor that seemed to emanate from every one of my pores. I was still shaking my head.

"Oh yes you did," said Aunt Nat and my mother in unison.

Apparently my aunt had watched me being carried out on the stretcher. I was ashamed they said I swore. I was ashamed I stank. I wanted to brush my teeth and I managed to say so.

People said "Sure!" and laughed.

My wardrobe was scant: a hospital gown that felt open in private places.

I wondered with more than a little embarrassment who of these people standing before me had stripped me of my nightclothes and put me in this undignified costume.
In a few days they moved me to a wing for children complete with murals of Pinocchio and the like on the pastel colored walls. The deed I had done contrasted with all this larger than life tomfoolery meant to entertain youngsters who were mostly in there to have tonsils removed. I'd been on that ward a month prior to have my tonsils removed and John had come to visit me. Just because I was so different than the kids at school didn't mean that I wasn't the same on the inside, with the same wants, needs hopes and fears. Nat's kids all knew that and tried to introduce me to boys when they could. John and I had watched Jaws together, had a walk in the woods, talked till 6:00 a.m. on the phone when I could lock myself in the bathroom, curl in a ball and stare into the floor pattern: orange, green and tan swirly tiles. We'd kissed a few times. He wondered aloud how I could be vocal via the phone and mute in person. I had no answers.

This waking-up-from-the-coma hospital stay was different than when I had my tonsils out. This time they drew my blood often, and applied paste to my hair and stuck wires to my head to determine brain activities, liver function, etc. A doctor came in and a nurse suggested that I turn down the TV out of respect for the doctor who had something important to say. I did. For the rest of my life I would turn down the TV when I thought someone had something important to say and figured if I visited someone and the TV remained loud, then I was not important. The doctor said the alcohol poisoning had not done damage to any of my organs. There was no brain damage.
As I recovered in the hospital, I had the equivalent of a drunken high for days.
At last, some fun. The janitor who swept and mopped around my bed in methodical swipes looked at me with brown eyes when he adjusted the bedside trash bin. So I looked directly into his eyes every time he sneaked a look at me. I wouldn't look away. My features felt silly, like rubber, and they

were fun to play around with so the next time he had to sweep my room and sneaked a look at me, I raised my eyebrows up and down.

In my private room with Disney characters on the wall, Starr called me on the phone. "Are you still a little 'oozed from the booze'?" she asked. I told her about the janitor. She called what I did with my eyebrows "flirting."

I was surprised it had a name and that I had learned to do flirting without being taught. She wanted details. There weren't any. He'd ignored my eyebrows without one change in his expression. Then she wanted to know about the night I drank
vodka. I told her the details I recalled, and when I was through she was sad I hadn't waited and drank with her instead of without her. But we just didn't live near each other anymore.

I shivered when I sniffed the bottle I'd found in the back of the refrigerator. It had been there forever and I'd finally decided to take it and open it. Neither of my parents drank. It was a gift from some Christmas party and one or the other of my parents would probably figure the other one finally threw it out. My whole body quivered when I forced down the first stinging gulp. Drinking alcohol was an experiment. I'd redesign my entire personality even if it meant burning a raw strip down my throat.
An adventurous girl my age, with a tomboy figure and cas-cades of blond curls often stayed with Nat's family downstairs from me on a spare rollaway cot. She was feisty and outspoken and since she was a family friend she put up with my company. She had permission to sleep over with me upstairs on the night I drank.
It was her first time drinking too. I was gulping down my vodka and Kool-Aid concoction and pouring more because I wasn't feeling anything different right away. I was quite the bartender.
But I didn't know that Blondie was sneaking into the kitchen and dumping her drinks down the sink in an effort to make it appear that she was keeping up with me drink for drink.
(She confessed this later, bless her!) I did not know that a thirteen-year-old body that consumes large amounts of alcohol can reach an overloaded point, poisoning the body into a comatose state. If the body is not pumped free of the toxins in time, the body can die.

Dumping her drinks was saving her life. At our age how was either of us to know any of that?

This girl, Ginger, whom I really barely knew, had the idea to call John and his brother, twins she originally met on a CB radio. I was intent on mixing drinks and gulping them down quickly. I figured since I was extremely quiet I might need the *entire* bottle to change my self.

My bedroom walls became a spinning fun-house tunnel. My sleepover guest handed the phone to me. She apparently went to my bed to sleep. I opened my mouth wide to let go of some extremely witty chatty, outgoing words.

I remember nothing from the moment I held the phone in my hand until I saw the number two floating over that bed in the intensive care unit.

John told me later, "You should've heard the things you said to me! Man, I was shocked. I was laughing so hard, I knew you were wasted."

I told him not to tell me what I said to shock him. I vaguely recall words falling from my mouth and onto the bed; I mean I could see them and then I was sucked into a vortex of light blue that was my spinning bedroom wall. But I did not remember what the words were. I guess my body fell over but my mouth kept running. Maybe that's called a blackout. I just can't say. I've never had one since.

Sometime that night a 45 rpm record got put on the record player called "Two Outta' Three Ain't Bad" by the band Meatloaf. Weary from her sips of alcohol, Ginger fell fast into a deep sleep. My record player had an automatic replay feature. The phonograph played that smash hit of the day over and over and over yet again. That's when my mother stirred from her resting place in the reclining chair. It was easier for her to sleep sitting up. Dammit she was annoyed by hearing the same lyrics over and over. She stormed into my room to take it off the turntable.

She turned to scold me but I was not even in my bedroom. There in my four poster bed was Ginger, long hair splayed out across the pillow, my cat Timothy asleep next to her face.

Since my accomplice was so snug under my bedcovers my

mother smiled and tucked the blankets in around her. But where was I? She had to go into the next bedroom to find me. I was across the top of my mother's bedspread with my limbs splayed spread-eagle in an unnatural and uncomfortable looking manner.

My mother tapped me a little. *Get up kid and get in your own bed,* I could imagine her saying, *You look like a contortionist laying like that!* She said later it was like poking dead weight. She spoke my name aloud. She touched my shoulder, and my head moved, which was a good thing because the action forced red stuff to burst from my mouth in a violent rain of Kool-Aid and vodka.

If her adrenaline hadn't overtaken her, then perhaps she would've smelled the vodka but her first thought was that it was blood. She screamed.

My uncle worked a night shift and was walking across the lawn below the bedroom window. He bolted up the stairs, a phone call was made, an ambulance came. Apparently I was semi-comatose or something but cussing at everyone as they pumped the toxins from my body. I was put in the ICU till I awoke the next morning. Then came the lovely specks.

"So that girl saved your life by playing the record?" Starr asked when I finished recounting the story.

I said, "Or did my mother technically save my life by finding me? Or the paramedics who worked on me? But yeah, the record playing was so annoying that it made my mother check me in the first place. Hey, if you want to go way back you can say that whoever bought me the record player with the automatic playback saved my life. My father!"

I spent five long days in the Pinocchio room. My "friend" and accomplice Ginger broke up with John's friend Tom.

I didn't shed tears over that. Like most teens I knew of, she had other boys in line for her attentions. But I panicked. She'd been my boy anchor. Without her to double-date with me at an occasional movie, speak for me, or hand the phone to me, I wouldn't be able to be around John anymore. Ginger had been the one setting up the meetings at movies. What would I do now?

When I was back home, I told her to call John and tell him I wanted to break up with him. She was glad to be of as-sistance.

Before long, my white phone rang. "I hear you wanna' break up with me", John said, and I could imagine him flinging his long bangs out of his eyes with a toss of his head.

"Mmm, yeah. I said that," I said, biting my bottom lip. It's an afterschool special, I told myself. Please…I wanted him to tell me, "It's okay if my friend isn't going out with your friend anymore. I understand that makes you afraid to face me without her for moral support. But we'll take this slow. I'll be right over. I'll talk. You'll listen." Say it John. But he didn't.

He said, "Good. I was gonna' break up with you anyway."

I never told him I'd called out his name while I was unconscious.

A few months later Ginger introduced me to her new boyfriend. I didn't think much of him. His name was Howie. He smoked too much. I didn't have time for boys anymore. I had high school to think about. I'd gotten myself into a tech school with my good grades. It was my first school without Starr or one of the cousins in it and I had a chance to try out various shops like sheet metal, auto body and hairdressing.

It was going to be a big challenge.

Chapter Thirteen: Sensing

Sometimes I lay on the roof under the stars, just outside my bedroom window, thinking about my childhood which was disappearing fast behind me. My mother was no longer a Scout leader but we still had our coffee can crafts on a shelf. We'd once painted coffee cans black and punched holes in them with a nail and hammer. Then we put candles inside and she lit them. We put our creations on the picnic table. Night bugs chirruped as they partied in bushes around us, braver to speak, being concealed from us. We gazed at the holes in the cans. Light twinkled like real stars flickering in a black sky. Granted, a small sky but the key was the pretending, Mommy said. These vivid moments had an air of holiness to them.

Older now, I spread out on the scratchy roof shingles to watch the great bowl of sky and its stars. It was a time for thinking. Grandma was dead now and I wondered about *things* like my old cup. At Grandma's old house I'd had a yellow plastic cup, kept on the cup-board, the board for cups above the sink. I would smell it, get involved in its color. I'd put Vermont water in the cup, which tasted orange, and take it up the narrow stairs to the bedroom. The chenille bedspread greeted me there. I breathed deeply from the stained pillow brought from home. It could never be washed or the smell would've been ruined. The wallpaper in that bedroom I'd never forget. It was an aged splash of faded pink roses that I imagined must've been glorious when it was new. I knew every place in it that wallpaper that was tearing. I loved touching the brown water stain in the shape of a frog holding an axe. The white bureau had curly-cue scrolling around the mirror. In its drawers' were treasures: a tablecloth with a teapot pattern, embroidered handkerchiefs folded into triangles, and musty doilies tatted long ago by a skillful hand. If I checked, everything would be folded with crisp creases. The sameness of the old was comforting. My relationships with things were still as complex at nearly fourteen years old as my people relationships.

Transitions

With my body now taller, it was hard to remind myself that others were older too. I didn't get the fact they were the same persons in different packaging, in bigger bodies. The mud puddle connection with cousin Nan was gone now, the way we rolled mud-balls and lined them in neat rows like prize turds in a crap show. So cousin Nan was now a stranger. I felt tears fall as I mourned this. I was not clay as the others were, easily molded, ever-changing. My high school experience was terrifying for this reason. Over the summer, *everyone* changed. I didn't even recognize myself. Old beliefs were seen in a different light now, and in retrospect I could think up past dirty secrets and suddenly understand them. The daring, rebellious, lawbreaker that I was, I practiced J-walking when I was eight. With a stick, I would draw a letter J in the sand and then I walked along its lines. But I quickly scuffed out the letter with my shoe. I hadn't wanted to leave any evidence.

Sprawled on the roof, hands behind my head, I was at peace,

recalling other places I used to feel peaceful, like the rock in the woods when I was eleven. I closed my eyes and remem-bered, a smile forming on my lips.

"This is my rock." I would say aloud to ants on my knees. I gave each a careful flick. Each wee ant face was frozen, not unlike Munch's *The Scream* as I sent them flailing through the air, legs akimbo. The rock was *my* real estate. My legs dangled over the big rock. Pin-dot sized red insects mesmerized me, gliding over the rock terrain. I had super vision, so I could see them waving their flags and bagpipes. My legs and arms were limp things separate from me. Maple tree arms swayed overhead, rustling their leaves in a swishing chorus. I tried to catch sight of the wind but it remained invisible, a conductor to lulling leaf choruses, a cracker of dry hollow limbs. Tall solid trees creaked and scratched their limbs together, singing and at times quarreling. I expected a leprechaun with filthy knees and suspenders to hoist himself up on the rock beside me, using his odd curled pipe for a cane, and give me an earful of dirty limericks. I smiled at the memory. I wanted to burst out laughing.

I opened my eyes and counted the cars that passed in the night. The roof was a grand place. I thought of Starr, who had others to be with now in her high school. She was more adept at pre-teen pursuits than me. She even seemed to need re-lationships with people, in ways I did not. Now that I'd moved to the apartment above Aunt Nat and her family, Starr was miles away. I had insomnia. Again. Sometimes when I did sleep, I awakened to find myself in a standing position, drawing quick breaths, alarmed, forced to feel the walls with the palms of my hands, and trace a route back to my bedroom in the blackness. "You always were a sleepwalker," My mother would say in the morning when I told her about it. She liked to tell the story of how she awakened to see me rearranging furniture while I was still asleep.
Once I apparently had a bloody nose and to everyone's horror in the morning we'd arisen to see I'd tracked blood all over the room while sleepwalking. I used to sleep with my mica vial, my Pixie dust. I would burrow under my heavy blanket and shake the corked bottle. That broke it up. It turned the mica to sparkly dust. I thought it would

ward off night terrors that awakened me with silent screams caught in my throat.

Three cars had passed. The air was cool on my arms. I sat on my hands to warm them, ignoring the roughness of the shingle grit. Not for the first time, I wondered what made me so different. For example, I used to read Mad magazine when I was twelve. But I did not understand that something that is funny in one context, may not be funny in another. I noticed a running gag that always made me laugh out loud. Hidden around the borders of the pages, in margins, were tiny cartoon people doing little activities. They'd climb the outskirts of the pages and hold up tiny signs.
One little man held a sign no bigger than a buttercup that read *This Space For Rent*. Surely if I painted that saying onto a T-shirt, I'd be the hit of the neighborhood.
I was proud of my paint job. *This Space For Rent* in bold block letters across my chest. I casually walked my poodle Suzy as I passed a horde of girls with bikes propped on kick-stands. I felt their glare. I heard their laughter and disjointed bits of sentences: "I can't believe she-" and "Oh my God, so funny!" Finally I realized I was being laughed *at*. I went home that day and stuffed the shirt way, way down in the garbage.

In the winter, I liked to pad past my sleeping father and out the door at night. Under the street-lamp I crunched snow with the soles of my bare feet. I delighted in the texture. Deep inside, sensitivity clashed with *in*sensitivity like hot and cold air currents slamming each other. I was doing things like reading stuff that scared the hell out of me, or walking barefoot in snow, just to feel.
When the day came to move upstairs from my cousins, I'd started unpacking the box marked "Kimmy's Room" when I noticed my rocks were not there. My mother admitted to allowing that nice boy Wes to help pack my stuff. She said we could return to the old neighborhood and ask around.

I asked Lil what she knew about my rocks and she replied, "Wes threw those off the mountain." I never saw my shavings and Pixie vial again either.

For this memory, a fresh tear.

I was accepted to a technical high school to learn hairdressing. I still could not tolerate cigarette related things or matches. But I took to heating up lighters and burning half-moons into the meat of my arms. This made me relax, it made me smile. No one noticed. I lost friends because I "snubbed" them in the hall when in fact I hadn't been able to respond when I did pass them, in such a bustling setting. In most cases, anyone waving me down in the sea of bodies, I did not see. I looked through people.

I'd convince my self that boys had crushes on me, only to be crushed by the weight of their callous words, "Move your book stack. She's such a freakin' retard, carrying all those books everywhere all the time."

School was hell as usual.
Sometimes I did things in my tech school that surprised even me. Friday was a case in point. I thought it over, trying to make sense of it.

"Why'd you write in my dust?" someone was shouting. We were in the auto body shop.

Bespectacled Linda whispered to Renee, "Why is that senior picking on that freshman?"

A meaty automobile shop senior had a stringy-haired guy by the front of the Lynyrd Skynyrd shirt. He was trying to lift him right up off the floor. "Why won't he admit it? Everyone knows he loves Skynyrd," whispered Renee.

"Hey man," The freshman pleaded, "Like I didn't do anything, okay? And like if I did, you know, what's the harm anyway? It's dust."

"I'll tell you what, freshman. Lesson one: Never fuck with the seniors' stuff. Lesson two: If the dust is on the seniors' cars, its cuz' it belongs to the seniors," Said the big guy.

"Look at that!" Linda pointed. I thought her glasses would fall

Under The Banana Moon

off her pointy nose. She was referring to the windowsills which had a thick coating of dust from the work the seniors had been doing on the cars all week. The meaty guy went over to see what Linda was excited about. "He even wrote *Lynyrd Skynyrd* all over the windowsills. It's everywhere!" Linda announced, bobbed blonde hair swishing as she exaggerated every word.

"Look, it's in the dust on the floor behind the car," said the perplexed freshman in the Lynyrd Skynyrd T-shirt. "On the *floor!*"

The shop teacher sauntered in from lunch and the senior showed him the car, with Lynyrd Skynyrd written all over it; traced into the dust on the windows, the side panels, everywhere in the shop.
The teacher laughed and handed the freshman some towels and a push-broom. "Relax, Pete. No harm's done," He said to him, then slapped his beefy back. I watched the teacher ruffle the hair of Tom, the accused kid.

"Christ," Tom smiled. "I'll clean it up, but I can't be the only one who likes Skynyrd in here!" He looked around at the crowd of seniors and freshman and even met my gaze for a second. "Man, won't somebody help me out here? I was framed!"
Pete shoved him and told him to get to work. "Geez, man. I was framed," said Tom.

Earlier Friday, when the buzzer sounded for lunch, I took my time. Spray painting the lines on the car had been a fun lesson. I'd even learned the proper name for what we'd done: We'd pinstriped a quarter panel. I looked around the emptied out room and saw that a fine white dust covered everything. Alone, I walked around the shop to inspect things. The spelling of "Lynyrd Skynyrd" had intrigued me for weeks, and now today that kid Tom was wearing that same T-shirt again. Trance-like, my finger wrote Lynyrd Skynyrd all over everything. I wrote it in block letters, in cursive, in child's scrawl. As I looked around at what I'd done, the unusual name (I had no idea what it meant) rung in my mind like when you hear a song and it replays in your head.
My head was singing Lynyrd Skynyrd Lynyrd Skynyrd l - y - n - y - r - d - s - k - y - n - y - r - d.

The ride home from school presented a lesson in tolerance. "Are you Deaf? Dumb? Or just Stupid?" This was the most popular sign, held up for me to see.
The boys found me different. I stood out. It wasn't long before the school found me different, too. They sent me to look at ink blots and get some testing at a shrink's office.

One day, after the boys on the bus held up the typical signs at the window (from their bus, parked alongside mine, so I could see them) my bus driver Mary Ann turned around to face me and said, "Hey why don't you hold up signs back to them? Jesus Mary Joseph!" I just shrugged.

Stuff like that was minor. It had been going on my whole life long. I heard a fourth car pass and blinked back fresh tears. How come I could not always talk? I wondered. Sometimes not even to my parents. I wasn't getting any better. Just last week I'd desperately thrown a clothespin into the center of the room with a note attached, "Can we go get ice cream?"

The poodle Suzy sniffed the note and Daddy shouted, "Stop your silly throwing things!"

I closed my eyes, mourning my talc rock so much that just yesterday I found myself searching for a miracle box marked KIM'S ROOM. Even though I knew that Wes had seen to destroying all of my comfort things, I'd still yell almost daily, "Mommeeee! Where are all my things?"

"They should be in your box," She'd say. Apparently she believed in magic too.

I had to design new delights for my senses, things that made me smile, relax. Like these nights on the roof. Like running in the cornfield, which was used for hay in the odd years, until my knees gave out and I fell on my face onto sharp piercing stalks.
Closing myself in the hall closet was nice. Pinching my skin. Stealing my mother's little yellow pills, which blanketed me with a calm subdued façade to face school situations. Writing up elaborate lists and schedules and adhering to them. Hurting my arms. Putting

on music and dancing in the dark like a wild person. Filling more diaries. I wrote about Grandma's hospitalization and subsequent death. I stole yet more alcohol, meaning to be more careful with my consumption level this time, and
I proceeded to try for normal.

Chapter Fourteen: Movies

Starr was in a different school. If I phoned her, her mother said, "Kim who?"

Once upon a time she called me "Graham cracker kid." In fact I could remember sitting cross-legged in Starr's backyard among wee wildflowers and hearing a strange voice cry out: "Don't pick meee….Don't pick me…Ow!"
I'd looked up to the window and there was her mother, being the voice of tiny flowers. She was grinning. Now I was nobody. It was understandable. Starr knew other Kims besides me. Now I was a pretty prop when Ginger met boys. I was a decoration, a painting in a house with an unknown story behind it and you knew you either hated it or loved it.

"There's a seat over here Louis, we saved you one next to Kim," said Ginger when the boys arrived in the theater one night.

I was being fixed up with afro-headed Louis. Talking was not expected at movies. That could work in my favor and that point was not lost on me. "There's a seat here too," Louis said, and sat far away from me next to his friend Howie.

Howie was a large-nosed guy who wrote three page corny notes to my friend in neat cursive writing to proclaim his devoted love for her. Throughout the movie, Louis was horsing around with Howie, telling him private jokes as far away from me as possible. The seats on my right and left remained unoccupied. When the movie's credits began to flash, I thought Louis might walk me outside and maybe say a nice thing to me. He dashed outside ahead of everyone. Later that night, I was sitting on my bed next to Suzy my poodle. She peeled back her dog lips and revealed her small

pointed teeth; she always had a smile for me. I kissed her head.
Her breath stank. The yellow T-shirt I'd put on her was sagging
but she was still smiling. There was a flea in the corner of her eye but
I didn't care. Her health care regimen would start in earnest later.

I managed to say, "He didn't talk to me or sit near me or walk
me out of there."

Ginger said, "Sorry, Kim. He said he likes you but he likes
another girl better."

"Oh," I said.

"Can I use your phone to call Howie?" she asked me.

"Yeah," I told the blanket.

Ginger was twisting her salon curls with her free hand and
putting the receiver face down to relay what her boyfriend was
saying. Howie told her Louis was watching me through the whole
movie and that Louis said I was pretty.
After some giggling with Howie, she hung up my phone and turned
to face me. I had cracks in my exterior over the preceding months
every time I'd been hurt in some way. Now I feared an earthquake
tremor in me might bust wide the crevices. I would be in pieces soon.

I said to my grey poodle, "You don't know how I felt." Then my
head fell into my hands and I cried bubbly tears that shook me.

"Kim, don't cry. I felt sorry for you when Louis said he didn't
like you in 'that way' but Howie swears Louis thinks you're pretty,
so don't cry," she said and made to hug me, but I moved in time.
Wow, if this kind of sentimentality was what interacting, reaching
out, daring to care, and trying for relationships, got you, I wanted no
part of this huggy stuff. "Starr's mad," I said.

"She can't fit me in because she can't be with both me and the others
at the same time. I'm too embarrassing. I lost everyone but you," I
said to my one time drinking accomplice.
Ginger said something that scared me with the depth of its

emotion: "It's okay. I'm telling you, things are gonna be different between us. We'll be closer. Don't cry." She made to hug me again and patted my back instead when I didn't make to hug her. I sniffled wetly and froze up. Closer!? Yikes.

"What do you feel like doing after school tomorrow?" she asked me.

"Getting drunk," I replied, trying to smile.

She said, "Good idea."

I put some wine in washed-out jelly jars that my mother kept in the pantry. Jugs of wine and other bottles were all around, upstairs and down. Then I hid the filled up jars in my drawer and recorded the whole evening in my twelfth diary so I could reread and analyze it later. It was important to record every aspect of my life so as to gain meaning from my experiences later. I often did not grasp the meanings behind what people said or the significance of what they did and by rereading my notes, I could make an attempt to sort stuff. Whenever we emptied liquor bottles, we hid them in ruts in the cornfield. My parents had dusty liquor bottles everywhere. It seemed that was the number one gift at holidays.

I wrote the sentence "We'll be closer." in my diary to make sense of it. There was a tone I'd never heard come out of her. The tone was worth a few paragraphs of thought. It made me want to put distance between us, and not 'get closer'. I became wary around her, on guard. I knew most girl 'friends' did hug. I'd seen it on TV. I did not hug my parents unless they approached me. Their hugs left nerve receptors jangling and impressions in my skin that stayed indented for hours. The thought of being 'best buddies' was scary. Did I owe her that because she played the record which saved me? I did not have room for any more close people.

I looked at Suzy, whose claw was stuck in her T-shirt. She was smiling. Her big brown dog eyes were moist. No fleas that I could see, but she didn't seem to have any answers.

When people got close I created space. The responsibilities involved in keeping up a friendship with another person properly, in a real-world way, were overwhelmingly taxing. Best to nip this closeness in the bud before it bloomed. Friendship was like thinking you wanted a cute puppy but then afterward you realized the upkeep. At last I had had a night out with Starr. My mother pulled the green station wagon in front of the movies to pick us up afterward. Starr and I got in. But my Ginger and her boyfriend Howie were in the car and so was Louis.

I hadn't expected them to be there. "I'll take Starr home first. Then I'll get you boys home, okay?" My mother said in her sing-song voice.

Starr got into the front seat beside Louis. It'd been a funny movie. We'd laughed all night. I'd even peed a little; always a sign that something was very funny. Laughing felt like healing. What's more, I had managed to be 'on' with Starr. It seemed we were 'getting along' again, unless I was imagining it. Perhaps I'd make arrangements with her to see a movie the next weekend. I tried to lean into the front seat to say this. I was sitting in back next to Ginger, the friend who wanted to be close to me. Howie had his arm around her.
I felt a tap-tap. His fingers were knocking me. I tried to say something good to Starr before she had to get out of the car. I had to keep the "getting along" vibe rolling smoothly. I felt a tap-tap. Howie's fingers were knocking me again. I wouldn't look his way, not even peripherally. His arm was around Ginger, but his fingers were tap-tapping me.
Time was running out…a ball of yarn unraveling. I didn't have much time to preserve the friendship and who knew when I'd see Starr again? I needed to fire off jokes, invitations, compliments.

It's not as if my parents didn't try to socialize me in my early years. There was this perfect little family they especially liked. A tall dark husband with a blond blue-eyed wife. They had two fine little boys. We went to visit often. I was left with the boys in the bedroom at the end of the hall behind closed doors while laughing, smoking and card-playing ensued in the kitchen.
My father never smoked a day in his life but he loved to talk. When they retrieved me from the bedroom they remarked that it had gone so well--surely we would have to visit more often! Little were they aware, as soon as the parents were out of sight, I was shoved into the closet where I would stand next to a plastic Fisher Price garage until they heard the parents coming, then yank! they would pull me out in time, knowing I would not tell.

On our way to Starr's house, Howie kneaded my shoulder. I shook it off. He squeezed again. I glanced at him now and saw him grinning. After riding along to bring the boys home, I went downstairs to visit the cousins in their room, and Ginger was still living there on her cot. I was hoping she might call Louis and then suddenly thrust the phone into my hand. But I couldn't tell her it's what I hoped.
Talking to boys is what I was supposed to be doing in the natural progression of things. Starr and her girlfriends did it, and quite well. I wanted to do what they did even if I did not feel for doing it.
Ginger did call Howie. Louis happened to be visiting him. I stood by Ginger; eavesdropping on her conversation. Her swipes of sparkling eye shadow had faded to a dull matte blue.

She put her palm over the phone and said, "Howie said to tell you you're cute." I rolled my eyes. *Get on with the Louis part.* "Howie said to tell you you're pretty," she went on. I rolled my eyes again and added a dramatic sigh. Ginger looked annoyed for some reason. She was using that tone that everyone said was snotty and her lightly penciled-in eyebrows were furrowed. "Here. Howie wants to talk to you." She pitched the phone at me, I barely caught it.

Howie's voice was one of those deep ones. For some reason he told me that he quit school and got a job and that my friend was a real pain. He said I was beautiful. I thought Ginger told him to say nice things to me because I'd cried that night in front of her. Then Howie asked me for my phone number. He had something important to ask me. I recited it to him, de-lighted to be giving it out to someone. It had been a whirlwind few months between the coma and Howie. I had reasons to be wary of boys, of people in general. I'd gotten in plenty of trouble when I

got

in

a

car

 with a guy with a friendly voice twenty years or more my senior. What he did to me in his car was always in the forefront of my awareness. He followed me to my house, saw the name on my mailbox, and got my name from the phonebook. He was stalking me and no one knew.

Sometimes the man called me to tell me there was a picture of his penis in my mailbox. He would call and describe in detail what I wore that day when I was out riding my bike.

It was far safer to meet boys through other girls. Sometimes I think "naiveté" was written on my forehead when I was born. Only the perverts could see it. I had begged for a second phone line when we moved in to our house, and for my name to appear in the phonebook. My mother told me young girls should not have their names in phone books but eventually she gave in. In the end my mother was right.

Howie hung up the phone on his end, and Ginger and I went upstairs to my room to see if my white phone would really ring. She was unusually quiet, staring at her lap and not sorting through my records at all. I began to think, for the first time, that he'd squeezed my shoulder because he liked me. I wondered if someone else might've figured that out a lot sooner. And the white phone rang. It was a rather odd turn of events when I thought that someone other than a pervert was calling me. Or maybe he was a pervert. Time would tell.

It was Louis! He said, "Hello?" when the phone touched my ear; before I had a chance to say anything. Howie's voice in the background was saying, "Tell her I think she's a good lookin' chick!"

I may have had a bit of distaste in my mouth for the slang word "chick" when I said, "What did Howie want to tell me?"

"He likes you and he wants to ask you out," was Louis's throaty response.

But that's against rules. I was irritated. "Then don't you think he should break up with his girlfriend first?" I asked Louis. I was perplexed. Ginger gasped and stormed out of my room. She adored short cut-off jeans which showed the barely-there curve of her bottom when she walked. I was much taller than she; more robust and sturdier. I watched her leave the room. She'd worn those shorts with holes in the seat for so long. Now finally I saw she'd ironed on two large red patches, one on each buttock. There was something I found endearing about the patches and I enjoyed watching her walk away.

It was like when I used to have to have at least one pair of red shoes every year as a kid. I heard her stomp down the stairs and wondered why she made such a racket about leaving. I'd been stating a fact. You can't ask someone out if you are going out with someone else. Wasn't that the rule? She knew
more about that sort of thing than me.

I hung up the phone and I heard a ring through the register in the floor. *Ring!* He was breaking up with her. A minute later my white phone jingled and it was Louis's voice as soon as I put it to my ear.

"Do you like Howie?" Again I didn't have to say hello!

"I don't know," I told him. It was true. I didn't know him so how could I know if I liked him?

"Do you or don't you?" Louis raised his voice at me.

"I don't know," I replied, equally irritated.

"Would you go out with him? He dumped her," Louis said, after covering up the phone and then returning to it.

Now I was angry. How did I know if I'd go out with him if he hadn't asked me? "If he likes me so much why doesn't he tell me himself?" I asked him. That was a reasonable question. It could all be a cruel joke.

"Bitch!" Louis yelled into his end of the phone and it sounded like he dropped the phone on the floor.

It rattled and then came a shuffling and Howie's steady voice. "Hello?"

"Why did he call me that?" I asked Howie, with my hands holding the receiver in a white-knuckled grip.

"Oh, he's stoned and he didn't mean it. Really, I promise you that. Don't worry about it," Howie said. He sounded straight-forward and kind. "Do you like me?" he asked.

"Yeah," I replied. *Well I didn't dislike him.*

"Will you go out with me?" Howie asked.

"Yes," I said. It was sort of like when John asked me out after the movie.

When Howie visited me, he brought along Louis or his friends Martin or Hal and I was content to listen to them talk. They kidded a lot, shoved and wrestled; in good fun. Their boy smells were not always unpleasant. I did not forget Louis had called me a terrible name. He apologized and I enjoyed his presence in my room. They didn't grab me by the cheeks and demand eye contact or belittle me for not keeping up the conversation flow.
Not unlike the notes to Ginger, Howie showered me with long handwritten notes, all promising to take care of me the rest of my life. Louis often shampooed in my claw-foot tub; then fluffed out his afro with my blow-dryer and the pick he kept in his back pocket. Howie asked me if I would shampoo his hair over the side of our tub with the hand attachment sprayer. I didn't mind. It got so he asked me to shampoo his head every single time I saw him, which ended up being just about daily. His friends affectionately called him "grease head" and "zit-face" so he made an effort to get clean. If I said I was busy with homework or had to clip my poodle's hair he pouted until I gave in and shampooed him instead.
Howie lavished attention on me and brought his friends to the house almost daily. Ginger disappeared from my life. The boys sat on my bed, played my records, pet my animals and drank coffee with my mother. I laughed a lot. I enjoyed Louis's grin and lazy eyes but Howie was winning me over. There were times I went to the movies with Howie and several of his guy friends. They accepted me as is. Louis laughed at our piles and dust but no one chided me for it. Howie was sixteen, two years my senior, and he started to drive. As for me, it never ever occurred to me I might drive myself one day. I didn't talk in person those first few weeks. Howie asked me

things. He told me I could answer him with notes. For a long time we stood side by side, me being too keyed up to sit.

He'd say something like, "What's your favorite color? When's your birthday? How many times have you seen *Star Wars* and *Grease?*"

I'd grab paper and write the equivalent of a preface to a book, leaning on a cluttered bureau top for support, handing him scraps as I finished, with my scrawl heading downhill. I always added questions in my notes for him to answer aloud. I had selective mutism. I didn't choose it, I simply was mute in certain situations.
Howie couldn't know it, but my Grandma, who had died a month before I met him, shared a similar note-writing bond with me. He accepted my ingrained quietness as something that was not my personality, but rather some "thing" to be dealt with that showed through my personality. It gave me dignity. I stood fidgeting, jotting on scraps of envelopes or lined paper from the disheveled bureau top. I wrote in an almost illegible handwriting that I did not recognize to be mine as I was shaking and could not form letters.

I'd write: "When is your birthday?" or "What is your favorite color?" He answered me aloud nonchalantly as if I'd spoken the words instead of written them. He was patient. I wished my grandmother could have known him.
That winter we went for walks and Louis always walked a few yards ahead of us. Howie and I were hand in hand. We were walking to their friend Patty's house. I liked her. I was Kim who was quiet and that was fine with Patty.

"Can I let go of your hand a second?" Howie asked.

I nodded.

He let go and scooped up some snow which he rounded and threw at Louis. Louis threw one back at Howie. Snowball throwing had always scared me. I had never participated in the activity and wasn't about to. At least they weren't throwing them at me.

"Give me back your hand. There," Howie said softly.

He asked me for permission every time he wanted to let go of my hand to throw a snowball. I couldn't believe my luck. I was spared being reduced to a ducking quivering mess because they'd had sense not to throw things at me. Not only that, but he was preparing me as to what was about to happen: no surprises!

Chapter Fifteen: Not a Word About My Smoking Thing!

I was 14 and had never touched cigarettes or anything to do with smoking in my entire life, save for the lighters. I feared that if Howie and his friends, who all smoked, discovered it, Howie would break up with me for sure.

One day, around the kitchen table, my mother started in to laughing that silent, breathy Muttley-the-cartoon-dog laugh and Louis, Howie and I laughed with her. She loved the company of the boys. She loved that I had company. "I need a cig-arette," she said through laughter-tears.

"Good idea. Kim, toss mine." Howie said.

I was clean. I looked at my mother with telepathic intenseness as if to say, *Not a word about my smoking thing. Don't you embarrass me by telling him*. I touched a cigarette pack for the first time ever. The smoothness of it against my skin sank into the depths of my pores like skunk stench. I passed it in Howie's direction and saw my mother's eyebrows go up. No one saw my hand under the table, frantically smashing the odor off me and into my jeans. I decided I would never do it again. He would have to be told. That night my mother bragged to my father about what I'd done and later she bragged to Aunt Nat.

"Howie's changing Kimmy! She handed a cigarette pack to Howie! Show them, Kim! Touch an ashtray!" she told my father.

"Don't get crazy Mommy. And don't go telling him about my 'smoking thing' either. He doesn't have to know," I said.

"She really did touch it, Joe. I'm not kidding," she said to my smiling father. Daddy winked.

We kissed a lot and it was nothing but a smushing of lips. Kind
of ridiculous. I wanted to laugh.
It had been the same with John and also with a boy called Lenny who
had had the same color eyes as me who had met me for movie dates
a few times; another boy met through Ginger. Those kisses were very
intense and I got nothing from it, worrying I wasn't doing it right.
I ended up deciding I wanted to run. Howie was getting close,
or trying to, and that wasn't allowed. I broke up with him on the
phone. I was able to meet a boy named Michael Jeffrey with eyes the
same color as mine.
I was even asked out by a boy Ginger previously necked in a car
with, who remembered me, but I had to say no as Howie and I were
going out again. I would break up with Howie two more times but
every time he kept showing up again.
Howie couldn't borrow the family car so he pedaled his bike all
the way uphill to my house-five miles-and pleaded with me to take
him back. I did. I broke up with him again weeks later. Again he was
at my house and wasted no time talking with my father at the dining
room table about me while I cried in my room.
My father told him not to worry. I'd come around. I told Howie about
Lenny and Michael because I didn't like secrets. But it didn't matter.
If I took him back I would be loyal. Forever. I guessed we were
going out again.

Howie and I got our first apartment five years later when
I was 19 and he was 21. By that time our first son was two years old.

Chapter Sixteen: Expectant at Sixteen, A Life Set In Motion

She wasn't always freckled, she's a work in progress.
Comforters, afghan and sheet are let fall
from the Imagist rising this afternoon's winter.
White bureau's mirror, streaked and draped with necklaces
is faced with upturned chin again.
Cold-boned blue-veined hands are free verse raking black nests with
the brush antique

purchased from the Isle Of Clearance...
till they shine, curl at the split ends, and rise
from static. She smiles.
Tonight she will play with the patterns and rhythms of common
speech.
Her goal's the wrinkliest brain yet, the more the merrier, night
school's free.
Miss Bouveau, typing teacher sprite, before the showing-once
held the poet's own
hands warmly in hers and made known aloud to all of the class
anear to hear that
they possessed long tapered fingers of the kind
"...with good reach Kim, if you choose to play piano one day..."
Then as now, the expectant writer turned her hands in the air
seeing nay
the pigment there but rather all that they might do
and she stared then into Miss Bouveau's brown eyes
until she winked and walked away. Today she reaches...for
chenille cocoon robe, sash tied securely in a bow across the bulk of
stretched belly where the button protrudes.
Robe chilled from its place on the door that hides the rattic
stairwell nook
where it slumbered sentinel on its iron finger hook in drafty
quarters.
The parents and boyfriend (with strong work ethics) are drawn
when night is brisk and chill to orange heat that's fake. Around
quartz heaters they forsake
The blankets but not she-those gadgets fuzz her head.
Olde layers of cloth, batted thick, overworn, are cozier to her
than electric manufactured warmth. Almond blossoms fill her
head. With fragrant thoughts she flutters dizzy room to room in
slippers worn to bed. The "Study At Home" assignment is due
to be typed on the 'tag sale find' and sent
through the mailways
to the grayed instructor who offers constructive criticism, wisdom,
experience and praise.
The teacher's price is met; they've found a way to send the
payments monthly and never past due date. Refrigerator's dead
womb gets a pat.
A token of appreciation and respect. She never took its life for

granted.

In a black snakelike pile, its umbilical cord lays useless coiled,
long out of the socket that gave it life. Deep breath and she
descends thirteen stairs mumbling "...thanks for the snow...more
than You know...thanks for the snow..."

Milk, somewhat iced's retrieved reliably from the aluminum
bucket; functional, rusted that
in the summer held her mother's tulips and now just holds
below
in sand beneath the snow their bulbs in waiting there just so
beside the concrete porch's steps. With loud protests the hacking
emphysemic kitchen
faucet spits into the whistler kettle bursts of water.

Instant coffee crystals await their melting in the chipped mug
useful as any potter's fine hewn piece-the insurance company
slogan wrapped round its yellow form.

Before the whistle beckons pouring, time is wisely played:
words spiral
from the skipping Bic like cake frosting. She writes of the
almond trees' pale pink blossoms with the bluest of blue ink. Of
those trees that blossom quite in sync
with the awaited return in Capistrano of the hordes of inky
swallows.

"...and amn't I," her pen asks paper, "my own amen corner? At
sixteen, are not my alpha and omega as far from me as
predictability?

I'm somewhat in the middle and what's more if an angstrom of
madwort
or alyssum could cure this madness to write, well then I'd have
none of it!"

Alarm whistles from the stovetop where at night mice play
across its cold burners. Hot exaggerations of steam are pushed into
chill air, screaming,
'i am hot now! warm yer innards!' She does. The milk, she
decides, can rest uncapped on the faux grey marble tabletop of the
white swirls
great for tracing with thoughtful fingers and when
she's partaken in hot drink and then savored a second fill,
and blood sugar has begun to rise from bread and fruit
consumed

she will trek outside and put the milk home. And not until.
From one hemisphere of her brain to the other her thoughts
switch over.
Caffeinatedly alert now, the realist side reminds her of
the boy she loves
and her father who toil gloomily at the factory
with girlie posters for wallpaper assembling ship parts.
She has to wonder if she should've spent
the summer before last,
with the guys, her friends, every night you bet
in the trailer up the road, now overgrown with weeds,
letting
herself out periodically under the moonlight to puke beer into
the cornfield. And she and the boy at the end of the following
summer she remembers walked
stealthily the same cornfield and nearby farmer's garden (but it
seemed alright) stuffing corn ears and
potatoes from the mounds
down her maternity pants with the same moon
for a silent accomplice. Tonight the
calloused fingers of the men
will trace the swirls and weigh importance of not the moon they
hardly notice but a forty minute drive to work a half a day a couple
days a week with lay-offs promised soon
and little more than minimum wages.
How much to keep in-pocket? For bread and gas
and milk? She's thankful no one drinks.
Those damned miniature skyscrapers
won a debate over a load of oil and so were
retrieved with haste
dusty from the rattic playroom
where they were stored just in case
after finding them, among other things,
like the Royal typewriter-at
Mr. Bead's widower's tag sale last Spring.
A new used refrigerator! is circled she sees.
Or will a new used stove with an oven that really heats be
determined the greater of needs? Its underlined
in blue with the skipping Bic
and the Imagist is back to seeing details...

The pills, first fondled are gregariously gulped and pellets of
lead they may as well be,
not iron supplement at all-washed down
the throat with thick white crystals,
once milk. Now streaked with
tan from the remnants in the mug where shakily milk was run.
One cool swipe of purposeful fingers elegantly scatters lovely
French bread crumbs to the floor but upends the quart in the
process. The jug is righted too late to be saved.
Little milk remains.
Anemic responses aren't to be trusted. Suzy the poodle and
Princess the rescued are quick to lick.
'Thanks guys.'
The writer steadies for an unplanned rising
for the towel. Tears rise too. Neither fall. Soiling too much
today means a load of wash
not counted on. Hot water may run low. Or not at all. The
kindred dusty phone
reminds her in a glance they'll be no calling the teen mother
whom she sits beside
at night school hearing tales of childbirth. Silent ringless
decoration now but
they say they'll find a way before "Kimmy's time comes" for it
to ring again full-paid
and anyway if not there's the bowling alley pay phone at the
foot of the hill providing there's pocket change and gas in the car and
it hasn't thrown a rod or had a blow-out or plain up and quit by then.
Already she thinks of mac. and cheese secreted by her mother
from the cafeteria and what a splendid surprise that would be today
but wait the realist side reminds with anger come the summer lunch
ladies laid off don't qualify for unemployment wages but hey!
For now perhaps they'll use her pay-consider oil over
quartz? She'll bring it up today.
Swabbing milk puddles from the patterned linoleum
her cloth dabs up crumbs too- a travesty as sad as spilt milk. She
wanted the crumbs left for the mice who dare run the green and
orange kitchen at night
while she sits like a sphinx in the dark, her feet up on the chair,
smiling, holding the button in the off position until there! eyes
adjusted, she sees the skin of an onion examined with

tiny elflike hands.
Yes, this is high fine entertainment after night school.
While they sleep. Before she writes...She clicks !on! the flashlight
and then sees the elongated face
(of course she'd known they were rats)
of the mouse accepting, unstartled, his nocturnal friend. Tonight if
the cupboards are bare
she and her mother will gather the staples,
shake a little of this and that into their palms,
and if it doesn't crawl away it will go in to the fare fit to pass as
edible and she will give thanks.
They will eat as they have before.
Tonight they can sleep in their rooms with quartz heat around fake
orange glow up the middle of them like little rectangular windows in
a city postcard. She will pile comforters and afghans again
and sheet atop herself and unborn and until three or so of the
next coming morn
she will play with the patterns and rhythms of common speech.
Then sleep till noon.

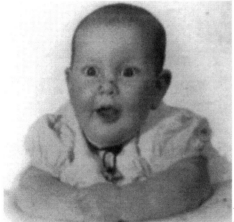 Baby Me.

My mother and I. That's the cellar door in view behind the old grill.

Ilana's porch entrance. That's me in Santa's sleigh.

Left: me. Middle: Starr's brother.
Sitting on my toy car: Starr
(in her cat's eye glasses.)

Left: Fourth grade me.

Starr, about   Me, about 14 yrs. old
14 yrs. old.   with my birth mother's
                 gift: Suzette.

Jeff, myself (age 29),
and Jeremy
(about 7 yrs. before Howie's diagnosis.)

One of my paintings of Howie.
Called: "Man In Yellow Shirt, Reclining"

Howie with Kerry;   Howie in driveway.
(photo taken by Amy Tuccio)

My parents,
Carol and Joe.

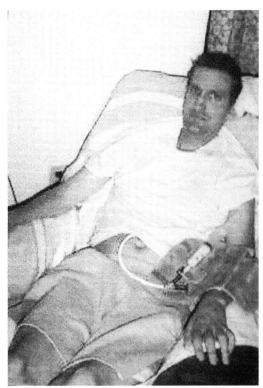

Howie, after feeding tube
insertion.

Kerry and I in mime. (photo taken by Amy Tuccio)

Good Ol' Pralphdog

Me, on a break from caring for Howie. (photo by Amy Tuccio)

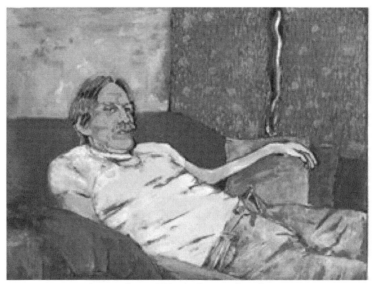

Another Howie painting.

Me in mime, posing for RIT student Amy Tuccio's class assignment in photography.

PART TWO
Chapter Seventeen: Meeting Donna Williams At Long Last
I was 30.

I had two boys: Jeff and Jeremy, and a daughter on the way; or so the ultrasound indicated. I did what I thought everyone did: get married and have kids. The phone rang, interrupting my thoughts.

"Hello?"

I was taming a steaming pot of wild spaghetti with a wooden spoon when the phone rang. It had been boiling at a mesmerizing roil. If I didn't stay alert, sometimes I had kitchen fires. I had fires a lot. It was commonplace.

"Kimbuhrley?" said an Australian accent. I knew immediately who it was.

I'd been writing letters to Donna Williams on and off for a long time. My brain had an inflated ego. It seemed it couldn't read enough about itself. I read anything about so-called disorders of the mind. I enjoyed memoirs especially. I was trying to figure out what made me tick.
One day I happened on Donna's memoir, *Nobody Nowhere, The Extraordinary Biography of An Autistic.* I bought it; figuring I definitely don't have that, but I'll learn something from it. I connected to the words in a surprising way and from the first fan letter, Donna Williams and I began our correspondence. Now she was on the phone.
Naturally I was alarmed. There were grease-like stains; the color of old tea, shaped like stalactites, that started at the ceiling and dripped stealthily down the sorry wall. *What must she think?* After a brief staring spell I shook off the panic. Aaah, she could not see them!

"Yes. This is her. Yes," I said into the phone.

"I am in your area," said Donna Williams.

My peer. My friend.
Howie followed the shorthand directions I'd noted down on an envelope and he drove me to the address of the house Donna Williams and her husband were renting while touring for her second book, *Somebody Somewhere*. It was a long impromptu drive. Howie was a roofer and quite adept at finding obscure locales as his work took him all over the Valley and beyond. The boys, nine years apart in age, enjoyed watching scenery fly by that they weren't familiar with. The little car was littered with fast food toys for them to rediscover in the cracks and crevices.

"Why the hell can't she just meet all four of us? This is bullshit. What do I do while you're in there with her? Drive all over a strange town wasting gas with these two?" griped Howie as he drove the car. He hooked a thumb over his shoulder toward the backseat where Jeff was fiddling with paper, shredding it and sprinkling it on Jeremy, who sat in his car seat entranced, holding his hands up to catch it. "I gotta be the biggest dick doing this," Howie said.

"No, you are the biggest nice guy," I said. "You know how I can't...be around a lot of people? She is like that too. She just wants to see me for one hour so you come and get me afterward. Besides, she did invite Jeff to meet her too, but he says no. Since dinner flopped we can take the boys out to eat after... Look, a Burger King! And right there, a playground for you to waste time in. It's meant to be! Just watch your watch and be back in an hour."

The house Donna was meeting me at was a saturated rich blue, the color I'd painted the doll's house I took eight weeks to build. It wasn't some wimpy pastelly washed-out muted excuse for blue and that was a good sign.
Now, they say you should throw daffodil bulbs and plant them where they lay. This makes for a scattered natural-looking setting. Not so this house! Prim uniform daffodils; each as vibrant and healthy as the one in line before it, stood deliberately in single file along both sides of the walkway in precise furrows. Soldiers lined up, daffodils saluting me, *come this way ma'am.* My lips curled up and it was more than just hormones from the pregnancy.

I became mindful of a line from Edna St. Vincent Millay's, *Afternoon on a Hill*, "I will touch a hundred flowers and not pick one'. Yellow flowers, another good omen. Yellow was my favorite color. Her husband Ian drew open the door before I could knock. A phone was adhered to his ear and he babbled into it about wanting to visit the Grand Canyon whilst in the States. He gestured for me to enter without ever making eye contact or acknowledging me verbally. This guy had Asperger's? *Hmmmm. Have to read about that.*

A faux rug was ingeniously painted onto the hardwood entry floor in a *trompe l'oeil* style. I wanted to get on hands and knees. I wanted to kneel and lay hands on the paint strokes to persuade myself that the series of yarn weaves were combinations of highlights and paint dabs and not real. But I could not do so in his presence.

I situated my rump on a piano bench and wanted very much to make the piano make a sound. I could only ogle the expanse of keys, longing to plunk one down with a fingertip, or shrink to their level and pirouette across the ivories. I had told Donna in one of my epic eight pagers that I would love to hear her play one day. I knew she wrote piano arrangements. Two plates on a nearby dining table had food-piles and askew forks on them. I did not comment on it.

"Where is she!?" It was Donna, bounding down the stairs. She looked the part of a mischievous sprite in an over-large tie-dyed t-shirt.

I stood before her in my maternity jumpsuit sensing that I'd grown to a preposterous height of seven feet tall in comparison to her petite frame and thinking myself an Amazon.

"Hi," I said, shifting the full to bursting paper grocery bag on my ample hip.

I am preposterous. I am simply preposterous. She handed me sparkling glass she'd collected on her trip around the U.S. I examined her array of crystal souvenirs, mostly sparkling things, rotating each treasure in my hand near a lit window so an ornament or some object could react with the sun.

As an Avon salesperson I'd been in a lot of houses. By comparison this house, with its rich textures and areas of interest, made those houses look as insipid as bland soup.

I was still lugging my paper shopping bag around on my hip, when we ventured outside. She'd asked me to bring my favorite things so she might get to 'know' me through seeing my things.

I handed her a miniature piano with a penny stuck inside, preventing it from winding up; a silenced instrument. For some time she shook it, but the penny rattled and never came loose. Next, I pulled out my African American figurine, Moe. Then I showed her some petrified mushrooms with smooth white surfaces large enough to be elves' awnings.

The hand tatted pouch from Grandma's bureau lay lumpy in my pocket. I had put the red strand Donna had sent me into it, to share space with the crosses and light bulb pull-string from the grey house by the corn-field. I slipped my hand into my pocket and caressed the tiny drawstring baglet but could not pull it out and put it upon the table. How could I explain it and its contents? Could I lay out the smudged pull-string upon the table?

No. It was from the house where once upon a time I had had to steal corn and potatoes because money was tight. The pull-string was all that was left. Three grey houses left behind, including one I lived in briefly by a river with Howie. In fact I was living in a fourth grey house now.

Donna plucked an exquisite errant weed from a crack in the patio cement for us to inspect. After we three had fully appre-ciated its intricate splendor close-up, she gently nestled its wee roots back into its cranny. We spoke of 'things'. Of objects, until a lawn mower reared up in a nearby yard, chasing us inside.

I marveled at the harmonious joining of things in the house. An aged map of the area was framed in the living room and I perused this piece of history, (I didn't know, but the child I carried would one day develop a love for maps). Crisp tender flowers and drying herbs were bundled in groups and hung with ties from swarthy profound beams above our heads. We tried to name the various flora.

Food still lay in nondescript piles of color on plates on the dining table. It did not occur to me right then that I'd interrupted their dinner and they did not offer that information. I sat in the wrong place in the living room and Donna redirected me as to where to sit while she flipped through channels, settling for a bit on Oprah. I found that Donna was most comfortable when I set things back where I got them, and sat where she felt able to communicate in the most effective way with me. I could not imagine tweaking my environment to make myself more at ease. It was an enticing idea - a brave new possibility.

The hour passed quickly.

"Well I'll use the bathroom now and then I guess Howie'll be pulling up outside to get me." It had taken me a full minute to plan and execute the phrase.

Lingering in the wee cubicle of the wallpapered bathroom to savor its Grandma atmosphere, I washed my hands and inhaled something akin to lavender or potpourri. That's when I heard the rise and fall of music. I paused before the antique sink basin, cocking my head and closing my eyes, listening. The piano was in full-play. I could relish the music from the bathroom, but maybe not in their presence. This house received Donna's music joyously, which thrummed on in a calm then harried pace and finished out neatly. I counted to ten to be sure it was done, and opened my eyes.

Back in the piano nook, the piano bench lay shining in the five o' five sun, empty. I saw Donna then, perched a few stairs up on the staircase that led to the upper floor. She was taller than me now, with the banister between us.

I said, "That was lovely," in her direction.

"That wasn't me playing. It was him." She sounded excited, frenzied, even accusatory. Ian bowed his head, frowning.

I told Ian, "It was very good. I didn't know you could play. You didn't mention it in the letters."

He shrugged. I went for the door.

"That's Jeff in the backseat," I told them.

I'd already told her the equivalent of my life story after I'd managed to get someone to forward her a letter. She was always helpful and forthright with her advice. She had told me things like: Be proud, be brave, be reasonable, be you, be on your side.

"I'll say hello to him," she said cheerily, having already surmised by my letters he may be an undiagnosed autistic person.

She'd even mailed Jeff his own signed copy of her book. It was rare because it had British slang. It was a copy only sold in the U.K. She peeked into Jeff's rear passenger side car window and said "Hello Jeff."

He rolled his eyes around like wet marbles and wiggled his fingers at her. He was thirteen. Jeremy was four, and sweaty from playing.

"Bye Kimbuhrley," called Donna Williams cheerily.

Chapter Eighteen: I Get a Kick Out Of Steak

Every Friday Howie and I and our kids went out to eat at a restaurant.

We had this thing about going out to eat every Friday, just because it was Friday. It *had* to be that way. It was a routine and any variation on the usual modus operandi was unheard of! The variable in this shtick was *where* we actually ate the food. Sometimes we journeyed out of the Valley confines and onto the great wide wonderful Post Road of Eating Choices! We'd cruise along past red, white and green pizza parlors wedged into strip malls, fast food emporiums that offered prizes in the kids' meals (our daughter Kerry always preferred the boys' toy) and numerous other places. More oft than not we'd turn around choiceless and head back through, discussing the same restaurants and the pros and cons of each.

The questions were always the same: *'Is anyone in the mood for diner food today?' 'Who's up for trying that new restaurant with the cartoon chicken on the front?' 'How about that hot dog place we went to last month? That was good...'*

With the three kids and Howie and I jammed into the sedan, we simply headed out- never seeming to have a destination in mind. We just let things happen and ended up where we ended up.

On this one particular night, we had my parents along. We followed them in our car and I watched as my father pulled his trusty little pick-up into a fish and chips place. I did not eat any fish, save for tuna (white albacore only) and the kids didn't eat fish either but we all loved the batter on the boneless fried chicken. Howie loved fish. The kids disbanded and ran ahead. My parents followed behind them. I was bringing up the tail end behind Howie. We went inside and the smell was what you'd expect from fried food specialists. It smelled like a frizzling grease-fest. It was Utopia! If the dog had been allowed in this place, he'd surely have blown his drool sacks as soon as he set paw through the doors. My father turned to face me as if something suddenly occurred to him. "Maybe Kimmy would prefer steak. I didn't bother to ask!" he said smiling. Now nearly everyone was looking at me.

At least we hadn't rounded the corner yet to join the line of customers. Jeff was darting his eyes about peripherally, scratching his belly-button and flipping his waistband. These were "stimming" activities, repetitive movements he used while acquainting himself with his surroundings. I often wished I could be so free as he was. Our middle son Jeremy was wide-eyed; absorbed by the pictures in the light-up menu. He calmly turned to see what I would say. Kerry, just five, was content to smile and hold tight to my mother's hand. She had ridden with them in their truck. They were agreeable kids; and it mattered little most of the time where we ended up. Maybe because by the time we usually decided they were famished!

"No, no. This is fine. I like their chicken here a-a lot," I stammered. I wasn't kidding! *Just move along!* That's what I wanted to say. But often the words I conjured in my head dissipated into nothingness; a mysterious eraser undoing my sentences as soon as I thought them. It had been a low cognitive day since morning and I was not improving. I was in a mental fog. I wanted to stare, to be alone, to sleep with a heavy comforter blankie over my face.

My mother was not satisfied with my tone, apparently. She didn't know that I was especially grateful at us having been able to pick an eatery so quickly! She didn't know that the ability to control my features 'felt' broken. I was uncomfortable at having been singled out. Not because we were eating at the Fish and Chips place. Uncomfortable. Just because.

"Do you want to go somewhere else?" she asked sweetly.

She had on her mauve lipstick. Her silk blouse matched her red sandals. She had on at least a pound of jewelry and her soft blond hair, so like her mother's (my deaf Grandma) was arranged in such a way that she was absolutely beautiful. She was smiling. It came easily for her to smile. She and my father, I calculated, (and Starr too for that matter) must've been blessed with gallons of serotonin (the feel-good chemical) coursing through their bodies at any given time!

"Let's eat here," I said, annoyed now by all the fuss. I *could not* make decisions for myself! Howie and I took a step forward.

No one else budged and we were forced to halt.
The floor had large muddy brown tiles. They were dirty around the seams and I physically winced. I couldn't look anywhere but down and the only pattern was the floor which had black places between the squares. Yukky black places.

"Let's go down the road. I know Kimmy likes steak and potatoes," my father said, winking. He patted my back as he filed past me, toward the exit door, singing a tune about a monkey and a lamppost to make Jeff snicker.

The kids and my mother paraded past Howie and I, so there was no use protesting. I sighed loudly, disgusted by the whole confusing string of events and also quite disheartened for not knowing my own wants. It must've showed on my face.
BAM!
It connected so sharply with my backside that I lurched forward, my arms flailing. The business end of his steel-toed work boot. I nearly fell. In a flash, I darted my gaze about the corridor. NO ONE had seen. Moist tears mushroomed up into the corners of my eyes and I held up my head, widening my eyes, forbidding tears to spill. This wasn't the first time my husband had lashed out; but it was the first time it had happened in public.

In the beginning of our time together, when we'd lived in the little apartment above the hair salon, he'd physically wailed on me and on the day following the attack, he'd said, "Get dressed. We'll go to the mall. You can buy anything you want."
I undressed in front of a mirror in the dressing room stall at a clothing store, intent on making him good on the offer. I had a pair of jeans and white blouse draped over my arm to try on. But I saw my reflection and froze before it; in dumbstruck awe at what I saw looking back at me. Distinct purple fingerprint marks on my upper arms and around the sides of my throat, countless dime-sized bruises all over my chest, and more purple splotches on my thighs. I was surprised to see dried blood across my knees. I'd run to the attic where Jeff wasn't apt to wake up from the noise and Howie had pushed me there against the floor-boards. That must've been how they got scraped up. Why, they must've gotten scraped right through my pajama bottoms! I had headed to the attic, you see because I knew the inflatable fishing raft was set up there where Howie was looking for leaks, patching holes. After being shoved to the floor, I'd crawled to the raft, a soft place, and let the assault continue there...I fought. Yes I did. But he was a roofer. A slim man, he was nevertheless hard bodied. This was from the daily swinging of the hammer and from carrying bundles of shingles that weighed nearly a hundred pounds; on his shoulders, up ladders...

"What's taking you?" he'd called sweetly from outside the dressing room. "Can't make up your mind? I'll buy them both."

How long had I been staring into the mirror? I dressed and rushed past him, dumping my selected items on the nearest rack. "We're going home," I'd said.

It was a twenty minute ride back to our place. I stared out the window, avoiding his questions. Completely mute. When we got home, I wordlessly showed him my body. He rose from the couch, opened an end table drawer where his rolling papers, marijuana, and lighter were stashed in a little box, and up to the attic he'd gone with the lot.

That was years ago; we'd had two children since, and I still couldn't remember what set him off that day. In the years following the attic incident, he'd punched my arm a few times, HARD, always catching me unaware. But to kick me in public? At least no one had seen. I continued to the car; hearing my father's song looping now-
"Oh the monkey wrapped his tail around the LAMP post! To kiss his ASShole! To get some CHARcoal!" The kids were holding their sides; splitting with laughter.

"Joseph!" snapped my mother, and I had to fake my best smile. "Enough already!" she told him.

"We have heard that one before Daddy," I managed. He chuckled.

With the phony smile pasted on, I pirouetted my head ever so nonchalantly to really *see* Howie's face. He was glaring directly into my eyes and I hadn't expected that, so I shud-dered and looked away.
But I would not rub my sore backside.
I would not limp.
I would not let my face seep.
He had a sneer like I was nothing but a bad smell. My eyes asked *why?* before I looked away; but the words that eyes speak are often unanswered.

The steak was tender. I cut Kerry's food. I helped her at the salad bar. I stayed as physically busy as possible while I forced the dirty shame and hurt deep inside me. I had a visual of stomping down garbage in an overflowing pail; to make room for more garbage.

Later at home, Pralphdog met us at the door with his fat bottom shaking from over-excitement. His tail whipped the air in a blur and yes, his drooling had already begun. How precious was he!

Two long stringy slobber strands hung from either side of his whining mouth. I had a bone wrapped in a napkin from Howie's TBone steak and he knew it!

I got the silent treatment from Howie for days. I went about my way in the house. Helping with homework, crocheting, avoiding the phone… It was like the time he pegged his shoe at my jukebox, shattering the plexiglass and lights that went off in blinking displays in time to the music. He'd ruined it. The best gift my parents had ever given to me, and given to me at a time in their lives when they could scarcely afford it. Because he'd been angry with me. But I can't remember why.

The jukebox was one of many of my possessions he had destroyed, by taking an axe to something, throwing it away, mocking my creations, or just plain selling my prized things at a tag sale behind my back for a quarter. The public kick in the rear was never discussed either. That was fine by me.

>I did not think ANY answers existed to explain away
>such acts anyway.

Chapter Nineteen: Jeff

Dear Kimberly:
Thank you for writing back so quickly. This type of communication is very important in our work together.
I am sorry the school meetings are difficult, but I believe they are very important to Jeff and his future.
I believe fully that both you and Jeff have an autistic spectrum disorder. From what you have shared with me, it is something that you have lived with for your entire life, and everything supports that you have done a tremendous job of coping with the difficulties these disorders present.
Going to the school meetings are not to diagnose Jeff (or yourself) as having Asperger's Disorder, or any other autistic disorder. I already know that this is true. The

*meetings are to get the school to support Jeff in learning
how to live fully as a person with this condition. Much of
the pain, confusion and suffering you have lived with can
be lived with in an easier way. It will not go away, but
there are ways to live with it more comfortably.
By getting help for Jeff now (at the age of 17) from the
school, Jeff may have supports in learning to live that you
never got when you were his age. I feel that he deserves
this chance, and it is by your bravery in facing these
meetings that he will get it.
When we set up our next meeting (you and I), I would
like to do some goal setting so we have a path to work on.
Relationships, as a friend, is a good place to start. I'm glad
you suggested that. Thank you for the comment about Ray.
He is a very good person, and a good teacher. He knows a
lot about teaching people how to overcome some of the
challenges of autism in the community.
I'm glad things are going well, or better than they were.
If you would ever like to schedule a family meeting with
your mother, please let me know. It is often hard for a
family to be supportive if they don't understand what it is
that a person is living with.
Thank you again. I know I do thank you a lot, but I
really am thankful for people who have the strength to
reach out to learn about living with a very difficult
condition. You are one of the strong.
Sincerely,
Dan G.*

When Jeff had started kindergarten the phone started ringing
and did not let up. It was the stout-and-quite-given-to-shouting-fits,
Ms. Johnson. I knew Jeff was like me in his way. The description she
gave, as I stared into the streaks in the mirror above the kitchen sink
(better to have streaks than to be stuck in the mirror itself), was of a
boy who meowed instead of answered questions, hissed when the
other students got too close, and licked the desks.

"Hmm, hmm, I see," was all I could muster, not at all bothering to feign surprise. "No, he doesn't have a cat at home. I don't know why he does it."

In preschool they had kept him back because his motor skills were not on level with his peers. Jeff had skipped his terrible twos, an absolutely angelic child. Just like me! The contrast between him and his brother, who was born when he was nine, were stark. Jeff had no use for people unless they served a use for him. But now that he was in high school, he wasn't handling himself well at all. Jeff's arms were crisscrossed in jagged scratches. He would break sunglasses and cut himself up with the lenses. He had scars.
Anything could set off the cutting- we couldn't afford the video game he wanted, he couldn't get a ride to the mall, etc. I was sure that like me, he probably had high opiates making him oblivious to pain, but the self-destructive behavior was destroying our family cohesiveness. I could relate, as I used to burn half moons from a lighter into the meat of my arm just to feel something; months after Howie and I had met. But *understanding* Jeff was not enough. He could not continue along this path.
At last I had a computer and I found an expert on spectrum disorders through an online autism spectrum group. Rec-ommended to me by Donna Williams, this newsletter started on paper and graduated to the daily email list it eventually became. A safe private space for autistics to discuss their lives. Someone on the list gave me the name of Dan G., a counselor. Dan started in on 20 hours of in-home observation with Jeff while we went about the stubborn matter of convincing the school he needed extra allowances for his condition if he was ever to graduate.
I would sit until 2:00 in the morning, working on the book. I had sixteen diaries for reference. It was not originally intended for publication. It was simply a cathartic attempt to make a footprint in the world. Every day I was moved, as I basked in the screen's glow, reading and responding to Colin, the three Davids, Ashley, and Kerry, a girl from Australia. I checked the list daily and responded to emails for letters from peers who *felt* like friends.
The cat always chose those moments to land splat on the keyboard and beg for attention, and the beagle Pralphdog was content at the legs of my orange roller chair; a fine chair my mother had found me

at the school where she worked. Suzy the poodle was long dead in a cremation box.

I printed out letters from Dan because they gave me an emotion I could not name. I sat and read them over and again, folded them into many squares and carried them everywhere in the seat pocket of my jeans. Sometimes when Colin was unusually witty and profound or Kerry, my Australian friend gave me insightful theories on her studies of autistics and malabsorption of certain vitamins and minerals, I printed those too and carried the papers around. I'd named my daughter Kerry after her.

Dan had a soft voice and a youthful face. I didn't even realize at the time he was older than my age of thirty four years. He wore a crisp white shirt the first time we met him; tucked into blue jeans and wore a necklace that I had to resist the urge to reach out and fondle. *Let me touch yer pretty necklace!* It was pewter probably, with cubes, pyramids, and various shapes strung along a string.

I would learn that he usually liked to match his socks to his shirt! Dan had his own style. He favored a pink vest quite regularly and also a green shirt worn with very faded green socks. Those made me smile! He owned what my mother called a brown bomber jacket. He admitted to bleaching his short hair, just a little.

Dan had been sitting on our couch, waiting for Jeff to show up. Part of Jeff's evaluation process consisted of many hours of in-home observation. After an hour, Jeff burst in with his beat backpack laden and clinking. Wordlessly, Jeff thunked onto the couch close to me, leaving me precious little elbow room, abruptly skidding the couch across the floor when he flumped down on it. I was taken aback to say the least. The couch just went skidding! Jeff's hazel eyes darted and ricocheted. He did not customarily while away time in the living room. He had a preference for the solitary appeal of his sanctuary, the back bedroom, down at the end of the long hall. The living room had *my* things, a decoupage angel on the hall entry door, my smells, tubs of paints setting on the entertainment center, and my dust, which most certainly was different than his. He was in black from head to toe, all six feet one inch of him, and his black eyebrows were thick clues that his hair was not really metallic blue...but naturally black like my own. He was a gothic panther.

I thought he feared that the red plaid of the couch may have arms that would envelop him, lest he not be fully aware, in this, his parents' dreaded room. *Damn*, I could almost hear him thinking, '*I am a full hour late trying to avoid this meeting and this guy is still here.*

"Whatcha' get? Anything good?" I asked Jeff. He nodded, staring at his backpack.

"Hello Jeff," Dan said. He greeted him so softly I had to lean in to hear him.

Jeff seemed to nod but not quite. Jeff locked into Dan's eyes and never looked away for the whole hour. He was in a word, intense. This was his natural state. Dan got out paper and scrawled a list in his horrible left-handed penmanship. Dan had once told me he had an "invisible disability" and I was beginning to think it was his handwriting.
He was not disabled, insofar as humanity. I had been handing him envelopes as pay for his consultations, with money in them; what we could afford. After a few visits he handed one back to me and said, "This has to be pro-bono. I want to help your family. I just can't...take anything for it."
He made points with Howie after that statement, who darn-near walloped with relief and gushed with compliments when I told him later. "Pro-bono, huh? Well if the guy *is* gay, who the hell cares?" Howie beamed.

"Firstly, idiot," I said, "he said he has a son, and any guy can wear pink. Secondly, what's pro bono?" I asked as Howie drove us home.

"Kim, it's working for free!" he explained to me.

"I knew that!" I lied.

Dan made up a list of things Jeff could do to make riding on the school bus easier. He could place his book bag beside him to discourage kids from sitting with him. He could bring a CD player with earplugs, even if it wasn't turned on, to block noise and appear distracted. He could try to position his body so it looked like he was looking out the window. As for school, why couldn't we arrange a PPT meeting to discuss arranging a way that Jeff could participate in oral reports separately, with a video recorder, instead of in front of the class, where he went mute? Why couldn't we suggest that he take gym class away from the stimulation of the kids, in the weight lifting room? And could they allow for an overload room for him to go if he felt stressed? It was all a start.

During one emergency meeting at the school, I was without Dan, and I sorely needed him. It was right after the Columbine shootings, and Jeff had alarmed freshmen when he jokingly remarked to a friend in the hall, "Careful, there's bombs in the rafters, oh no."

"But that's my son's stress relief," I told them when I got called in for the special meeting. "Why, when he was in second grade

a guidance counselor had to come to our home because he'd drawn Howie and I holding clubs and weapons, with fierce grimaces. It's just his sense of humor. School leaves him so pent up that at the end of the day he bursts through the door and paces around the coffee table emitting moose noises!" No, I wasn't helping our case at all.

Jeff liked sitting for hours, digging in the woods at foundation sites and around stone walls. He would come and unzip his torn sack and put bottle upon dirt-encrusted bottle upon the coffee table while I ooohed and aahed.

"What year do you think this is from?" I would ask as I turned over a medicinal bottle in my hands. I talked of his previous finds to Dan. The notion bottles, tin signs, license plates, Christmas ornaments, hand blown brown bottles, soda bottles, and countless other glass wares and canning jars.

The school meetings were difficult for me, even when Dan was there. School was not my best place to be. I liked the empty corridors. Ran my hands along the lockers on my way to the conference room where I would meet Dan and talk to school teachers. But the buzzer sounded off like an explosion. Kids burst from every door in the hall and surrounded me, so many living fireworks. I wanted to stop, drop and roll to a safe corner with my hands over my head.

I found a waiting area in the office, which was where I saw Dan and Ray, his friend, who would also speak on Jeff's behalf at the meeting. I fell into a seat, my eyes darting. I was pain-fully aware they'd never seen me like this before, like a vet having war flashbacks. School was a sensory memory of fear and confusion.

Copier fluid from somewhere in the small office smelled as intense as embalming fluid. Really, it seemed to *permeate* me. I moved my mouth to greet Dan but failed to create sound.

I remembered previous meetings at grade schools when Jeff had mooned the class and ate the crayons and licked the desks. I had not had Dan beside me back then. Jeff was an amazing, interesting person who took apart clocks, gadgets, and found items and assigned new uses for them. He often cut off the arms of action figures for example, and made elaborate robo-arms with special powers. He was in high school now studying electronics. Dan told me that if I was overwhelmed in the conference room, I needed only to jot HELP on a slip of paper and pass it to him and he would do what he could. I nodded.

Dan recommended a certified psychologist. Howie and I met her in New Haven. She reminded me of the Magic School Bus lady on PBS, but less frenetic. Her dark cave-like waiting area had a radio tuned to a soothing classical station, and her dusty walls of psyche books appealed to me immediately. There was an unraveling braid rug too. She wore a flowing skirt and had a soft voice. Don't all shrinks? I think they practice in shrink school 'til it comes out soft.

Chapter Twenty: Mosaics

The flea market guy said, "Let me give you a discount on those. They're chipped."
I said, "It doesn't matter. I'll pay the full price."
Howie gave me a laser beam-eyed stare. "Well I plan to break them anyway," I said. Oh, Howie gave me hell for that.

I bought chipped plates from a flea market table. They were imperfect and colorful. I smashed them to bits and put the different pieces into groups. If one had a yellow fleck, into the yellow container it went. If a shard had greens in it, into the green bits container it went, and so on...I bought some grout and built mosaics on everything from remote control holders to plant pots. I learned from this that each 'broken' piece had a proper place in the scheme of things, no matter how seemingly insignificant, and could be tolerable; even lovely as part of a unified whole.

I used to feel like a piece broken off a person and not a whole person at all. I saw ALL details and accepted the world as fragmented. Mica winking within a stone wall; dust motes swirling in holy light beams at church. These were my whole happy world.

It's amazing I ever did manage to apply color to my face. I can thank my brief stint in my high school's hairdressing classes for that. It was required. Filtering out what's important, what's not, that's what's tough. I could idle the car at the stop sign when Howie was teaching me, but I would count the holes in the stop sign pole. They varied as to whether there had been a storm. There were less holes if there was snow on the ground because snow would conceal some. And so it was. I could check to see if the parting in my hair was straight, if the liner on one eye was approximate to the other, and the like. I saw bits. And I walked away from mirrors before I got stuck in them.

I dropped out of hairdressing because I didn't like touching the people. After Jeff's evaluation came in at high functioning autism, it was *my* turn. I told her up front I was not looking at inkblots! She said it would not be necessary. The last time I had had that opportunity, they had all looked like insects. Just to throw in some variety, I had told the tester that the last ink picture looked like a lone wolf looking over a canyon.

I had a series of visits to Lynn, the new shrink while Howie waited ever-patiently in the car, sleeping, recovering from his fall from a roof. He could even drive with the cast on! Lynn's office was narrow, oblong, with a small bathroom I could visit before I went in, just before its entrance door. I went in there whether I had to pee or not just because I did for the first appointment.

Since her office was in the city, she had to give me a code, a series of three numbers to put into a system so the front door would open and no unsavory people could wander in off the street. I tried at each visit to follow the order of instructions on the sign on the door: Put in the code, turn the dial, pull the door, etc. It all had to be done so precisely or one would be standing there fiddling for an eternity.

I know. I was once quite late for an appointment. I told Lynn that the sign had one step out of order and also it should read that the thumb should depress the button *while* turning. Each and every time I tried to get in, I encountered the same problem.
One day I brought a black marker to the door. After I got into the stairwell, I would change the sign and then tape it back up; and then I would never be late again. Such errors should not persist! But Lynn took to meeting me out front and the plan never was set into action. Once up the stairwell, past foreboding locked metal doors and down the hall and into her narrow office, I was thankful there was a window to my right, and a wall for me to face. This meant the window was behind Lynn and she was to my right. It seemed preplanned to be me-friendly. I took tests, solved puzzles, played with words and did math within one of the oldest buildings in the city. These buildings had gargoyles on the tops of them.
Now I know gargoyles serve a purpose, redirecting rain from buildings, but they have so much more mystique than ordinary gutters. Besides, they are alive on the inside.

I invited my mother for the final results. Howie refused to come in the room and waited amongst the books and classical music, both which he had little use for. I was surprised he bothered to hobble on his walking cast up the stairs but he wanted to do it.
There was an extra chair brought in, a simple one, nothing fancy. Lynn asked again if Howie wanted to come in but he declined and so one extra chair would suffice for my mother and the door was closed shut as Lynn gathered her papers, my diagnosis. The place smelled delightfully old, and smart. Lynn thought it best that I not know my IQ. She could mail it to me, but she said it was not a true indication of intelligence anyway, and I declined knowing. So there were peaks and valleys in my brain. I did learn from her that I scored above college level in writing, and comprehension of words, but there were so many blacks and whites.
My math for instance was at fifth grade level...That was not surprising! Wasn't it fifth grade that I needed the damned tutor? My mother was visibly shaking and stammering; smiling and laughing like she did when she was unnerved. She and the doctor, Lynn, sat near to each other, facing me, and I was alone to view them and the window with its occasional pigeon fluttering by.

Apparently I was "dysthymic," had a flat mood state. I was nonexpressive and as my mother confirmed, "She always was..." Her crepe paper eyelids were getting pink.

I handed her a tissue box. I was elated. I was being explained! Lynn told her I fell somewhere along the autistic spectrum, specifically Asperger's.
Smiling deep dimples into my plump cheeks, I told my mother it was not her fault that I never wanted any interaction with other kids.

I told her, "You had me in Brownies, Girl Scouts, camp; even became my leader. You had me take catechism with nuns, and you put me in the 4-H club and even had me riding down Main Street waving to people in the annual Christmas parade. You brought me to your Dutchmaid, Artex, Tupperware, and food demonstration parties where the man set the dessert on fire at the end! You sent me to go with Betty to watch her square dance, brought me to PTA meetings with you and became the lunch lady at my school. You did all you could to 'socialize' me, and it hasn't failed. I'm just differently made-up. But it's normal, for me."

It was a revelation, a beginning. Now that I knew what I'd always suspected, I could perhaps incorporate what Donna Williams did to cope: tool my environment to suit me. That's what we were asking the school to do for Jeff, and it's what I needed to figure out how to do in my own life. My mother accepted Lynn's tissue and dabbed her reddening eyes.
She asked Lynn some questions as I sat, grinning. In the words of Steve Martin, I was thinking, *Things are going to start happening now!"*

At home later, Howie sat smoking, with the game on. It was the *important* game, the one that really mattered. I hated to ask, "What do you think, you know, about what I told you Lynn said, Asperger's; about what I've read to you about it?" but I *did* ask it.

I had to have a healthy diet, and mostly made things from scratch which meant there were a lot of dishes in the sink at all times. I dumped the last of the homemade chicken soup into the massive garbage pail (with the purple stripe sprayed up the front from when I couldn't bear to just keeping washing the crap off so I painted a streak over the crap), filled the crock-pot with water to soak, and sat in a chair alongside Howie. Easier to be alongside him than to face him. I had to half-breathe, by partly hiding my mouth under my shirt-neck because of his smoke. I'd been holding my breath all my life. Nothing new. The sight got him riled but I was bordering on ticked myself. He hadn't given me any feedback about my appointment with Lynn.

So I clung to Pralphdog, who nearly ruptured my insides, rebounding onto my lap, and I tried to get good breaths around the toxins of his cigarettes and asked him again what his take on the matter was.

Without hesitation, he replied in a melancholy tone without ever turning away from the action, "I always knew." I studied his face a long time. His features swirled and mixed up.

Nothing much changed, except that Jeff graduated from high school. Howie told us to stand in front of the maple tree. Everyone had one tree in front of their house, out front, a Maple. This made our little dead-end avenue more attractive. Every house was alike, save for the colors which were pastels and grays. Ours was grey vinyl siding, moldy on one side like everyone else's. We were living in the very same neigh-borhood I'd moved into briefly as a child. Only this time I was two houses away from Starr's mother.

She had long since married, divorced, and become re-involved. I wore my only black dress, and Jeff had on his black suit. As soon as we'd gotten home from the graduation ceremony, he had run his green cap and gown down to the basement and thrown it over some junk pile. We tried to lean, "family-like," into one another for the photo, he at six feet two, and me five feet, eight and a half. The picture was snapped as we moaned and then the diploma, held in front of us for the snapshot was put away in a book.

Chapter Twenty-One: Day In An Orchard

My head was stuffed with polyester batting.

Technically it was mucous. Connecticut country scenery was

all about autumn, dressed in its ostentatious colors, the informal gig before succumbing to the great fall. Howie made a u-turn.

"Where are you going?" I asked.

"Did everyone see that orchard back there?" Howie asked the lot of us, *sans* Jeff.

"I *smell* it!" I said. "Isn't it lovely kids?"

"Yeah," said the two kids in unison.

"Are we going to see it?" asked Kerry.

"We're going to pick apples Kerry!" said Howie.

I beat a path across the bowed down grass to the gnarly trees, dripping snot. Somehow Howie had managed to wander far ahead of me despite his bum leg. Even Jeremy's asthma was not holding him back. No one noticed me lagging. I sniffled; dribbling discharge into the back of my throat, leaned my head back, and swallowed the cheesy lumps.
There was the family, picturesque as any Rockwell painting, gazing up at a tree so laden with fruit, that some branches bowed and touched the ground. I hurried to catch up, smash-ing soft apples underfoot. The four of us considered the
tree's splendor before touching it; we breathed its sweetness. We had to pay for the bags we filled. I looked around for workers in tell-tale green shirts. Then Kerry plucked an apple off a low-lying branch with a snap.

She took an enormous bite. "Do you think I'm a strong brave girl Mommy? Picking apples by myself and eating them?" She grinned, apple-skin clinging to her little white teeth. She looked up at me with the not so round apple in her little fist and her long blonde pigtails caught the sun; they sparkled with white light like diamonds.

"Yes Kerry. You are," I said and I laughed at her five-year old innocence.

I recognized joy for what it was. And gluttony. We were "in the moment." Someone remarked these were the best apples we'd ever had! I ate three. Howie had four. Jeremy had too many to count, as did Kerry. We walked from tree to gloriously gnarled tree and I smiled. We all did. Like gluttons we tasted and tossed partially tasted apples.

There were signs in rows to tell what type each apple was: Golden Delicious, Macintosh, etc. I would only eat the red ones. Golden apples or green ones, although fully ripe, seemed untrustworthy. (I'd learned early on in school that A was for apple and apples were red and all other apples were impostors.)

More fruit lay on the ground than in the trees. On the branches the apples resembled bunches of large grapes, laid one upon the other roundly and ripely, so plentiful that one couldn't see the apples on the inward side of the bunch. Such abundance! The ones on the ground laid in various stages of perfection and mush, lent a smell to the air almost sacred. This day would be a poem, I knew.

After filling the bag with ripe fruit and eating our fill, we were giddy. Like lollygagging drunks, we crossed the road to the barn *slash* gift shop, which showed off its fresh baked (you guessed it) apple pies. Inside the shop we studied dried apple wreaths, sniffed cinnamon apple candles, read apple recipes aloud and purchased apple cider, caramels, and apple cider doughnuts.

By the time we got back to the little Hyundai, I was salivating. In the car's trunk we found cups, conveniently put there by my mother some time ago, "in case you need them," she'd said. The kids were thrilled to use special plastic cups for the cider. We devoured the doughnuts, ignoring the stickiness and licking our fingers.

At home I warmed cheap, over-salted, over-processed chicken soup from the can. It had never tasted so good. We indulged ourselves in several bowls of the soup, which loosened my cold's mucous and put a solid warmth in us. For dessert, all of us, even Jeff, who was usually holed up in his room, ate caramel apples and apple pie that I made myself.

Only once on that fall day, did our circumstance intrude into our thoughts.

Howie voiced his concerns to me as we'd left the gift shop to cross the road to the car. "Look at it," he said.

I'd looked at his arm, though I'd been avoiding doing so all day. "I see it," I said.

"It's really humming now, huh?" he said.

"Yeah, humming." I hated when he said it was humming. Humming meant emitting sound. Humming hardly described the mad rippling of his arm, like the rippling on a lake after a disturbance in the water. We didn't know what the disturbance was. We knew that from forearm to wrist, the muscles rippled or twitched.
The night before we went to the orchard he'd asked me to lay upon his arm, to "please try and stop this goddamn twitch," that he "might get some sleep if I stop thinkin' about it, ya' know."

So I had laid upon it, there on the mattress on the floor, which was how we slept. I used the weight of my neck to try and still it. This was not a success. When I thought he was asleep, I rolled off. The constant movement of it bothered my mind. It was almost an omen. I lay in the dark, staring at the tan ceiling, the color of fawns, for an hour or more, afraid to get up and pee. I now feared the flushing, again, as I had as a child. The fear appeared again as a teen. Went away. Now it was back. I couldn't pull down the lever again. When I did I would bolt; petrified of the guttural sound that would suck at me.
His twitch even worked while he slept. Like there were knitting
needles under the skin.
Neither of us slept
the night before the big U Conn. appointment.
We tossed,
turned,
hoped aloud, and I
cried some.

Chapter Twenty-Two: It's Probably Nothing
I sat on a plastic chair at the party for Starr's daughter; in her backyard.

It had been years since her M.S. diagnosis and she was looking great, save for a limp. I was glad for that. Why do I accept these invitations? I wondered. Because the guest of honor, the birthday girl was my goddaughter, that's why.
The sun was bright. The light was stark. Everything gleamed at once. The shine on people's cheeks, the glare off the tablecloth, everything demanded I look. I darted my gaze around and tried not to stare too long at anything. Things and people were not distinguishable one from the other. The six girls in the outdoor Jacuzzi nearby me demanded as much of my awareness as did the kratillions of blades of grass, each single blade wanting my focus, shining with droplets of splashed Jacuzzi water.
The backyard held adults outfitted in summer colors that I couldn't visually partake in for long stretches. Adults walked their casual summer walks and practiced their measured cook-out banter as they meandered from house to deck chair, holding wine or other drinks. The folks at my table conversed about such inane topics as how to fell trees.

I muttered under my breath to Howie, "I am the Lorax," and he did not appear to understand the implication of my statement.

He furrowed his brow, and talked about how to remove those nasty stumps once the trees were out of the way. They talked about how best to kill ants. I drifted.

"You're quiet today Kim." This from Starr's boyfriend, who knew very well I was quiet in my natural state. I offered him nothing more than a nod for stating what was most nonex-traordinary and in fact most normal, for me. He knew that. Your point?

At home later I cried snot into Sweet Pea's cat-fur and bawled silent tears until I slept. I cried because I accepted me as-is but I realized there were those who never would and at the time it seemed to matter. I have only ever longed to blend into the background, without comment, to be ordinary, without being the subject of curiosity or remark. I wanted to be scenery, not have a supporting role in the action but I knew things were about to change. Howie had trouble sleeping too.

"Hey, what did Starr's mother say this was again?" Howie said aloud, studying his twitching forearm. Starr's mother was a nurse and Howie had shown her the twitch.

"Probably a pinched nerve. Leave it alone already. The doctor says at the worst, maybe a tumor. Forget it," I said.

Chapter Twenty-Three: Let's Hope its Cancer

There were a few deaths in the family.

Aunt Hannah was struck and killed by a garbage truck. Louie had a heart attack a week later. My parents retired to their trailer in Vermont. I don't think they would've gone if they knew Howie was going to get sick. But at the time I thought it would be best financially for them. Stupid me, I talked them into taking over Aunt Hannah's place so they ended up two and a half hours away from me and I ended up with no family in Connecticut, save for one aunt. Even and all my cousins moved out of state one by one.

Oh well, that's the way it goes. I was a loner anyway.

Grandma's white house got sold to Aunt Maura's son and painted a navy blue like my doll house. My father had to ream out thirty-something years of living in Connecticut, and make dozens of trips to Vermont, lugging their possessions up there. I couldn't even help him move because I wouldn't leave Howie. The kids needed me and had schooling.

I could barely discuss Howie's problem with Starr. After all, she was debilitated in her own way: she had three kids and the M.S. was weakening her limbs. She knew all too firsthand what may lay ahead for Howie. It seemed wrong to discuss my fears about him to her. I couldn't even discuss my fears about *her* illness, *to her.*

As for Dan, he got in an accident and dislocated several vertebrae in his back. Could be I was bad luck on people. It was entirely possible.

Jeff got his first girlfriend and got much support he didn't have before. He got help. Dan disappeared completely after making off with a comic that I loaned him. But I forgive him. In all fairness Dan

loaned me a book too, not nearly as fine as the comic but I guess in Dan's mind it may have been an even exchange. I will never learn not to lend possessions. Once I lent a skirt to a neighbor but had to cut it up because it never did smell the same when she returned it. U Conn. was supposed to impress me with its giant sprawling buildings nestled in autumn hillside splendor and it did! A child giant could've plunked down those chunky blocks that were
105
buildings all over the hill and then neatly chalked in some lines for his toy cars to park. But it was real. The first consultation in the fall with people in white uniforms startled me. So much emotion was attached to life. So much seemed expected. They paused a lot. They *knew* something. Their smiles were careful. Where were the Dragnet doctors when you desperately needed them and, craved them? Just the facts, ma'am.
One woman with a sweet name (the name strippers usually get) was professional and kind and courteous. She had surveys.
She told me, "We ask that you fill this out every time you come please." Red flag! The surveys were condescending. *Does the disabled patient (Howie) ask things of you that are unreasonable? As caretaker, do you ever feel overwhelmed by his demands?* I thought feelings were personal. I thought *thoughts* were personal.
It wasn't long before I learned that these questionnaires were not protocol, turned in anonymously to the MDA for demographic data interest. No, on the contrary, they were indicators for the support person at the clinic as to whether the caregiver (me) needed psychological counseling. They don't tell you that. I answered them the same way every time. I didn't tend to change. Anything Howie asked of me was reasonable. He was entitled to anger, disbelief and to feeling sorry for his situation at times. We both felt that private feelings within a marriage should stay within the bounds of a relationship. Neither of us expressed emotions to the other fluidly; but we could express them to each other and that
privacy could not benefit from an audience.
The U-Conn. offices had the usual rollaway chair for the doctor, the framed print on the crisp white wall, the fluorescent lighting to offend you, the giant scale to weigh wheelchairs in the hallway. And not to be left out, the roll-out tissue on the exam table. The wheelchair symbols were everywhere. There was one blue wheelchair icon inside a solid silver square; sort of a giant square

button. You tapped it so it could automatically open a wide door in case you had a wheelchair that needed to fit through and your arms were too busy holding the chair.

One day we left the exam room yet again for the umpteenth time with no clear diagnosis. Howie's doctor was not in and a woman with a Slavic accent had to fill in for him. She had to honestly say she simply had no results yet and we would have to return yet again for a spinal tap...

She was a cancer specialist who needed to see his twitching. All she did was take a lot of factual information. It was the closest thing to the Dragnet-doc I'd been seeking as of yet. She walked us to the automatic door and we paused in front of the button. We were headed for that now too familiar waiting room where there were brochures about everything dreadfully terminal and some seats were made higher than usual, so people could rise easier from a sitting position.

Before I could grab the handle of the over-large door I saw her hand rise. The little woman thought she was a prize-fighter! Whack! She punched the wheelchair icon hard enough to break it. I turned to look at her, but she had pivoted slowly and was heading back toward the examining rooms, quite composed, hands in her white coat pockets. I thought of meeting Howie's eyes for a moment, but did not. Instead we were both mesmerized by the door because it was so slow. The little Slavic doctor's violent action had caused the door to slowly open. When it was wide, we walked through saying nothing. She knew something she hadn't shared with us and it had upset her.

Weeks later, we finally got news from the doctor who did the spinal tap testing.

He said to us, "I'm not going to pull any punches with you. I'm pretty sure we're looking at a motor neuron disease here. We'll hope for a benign form. Of course the best case scenario would be that we're dealing with...uh, hate to say it, cancer. There's treatment for that. I'll go over the tests and let you know the diagnosis December 17th. If there's a treatment we can offer you at that time, we'll discuss it then."

I'd seen him on TV, on the telethon. I trusted him. Even if he did try to wheedle the personal "How did you meet?" story out of us. And he had managed to do it too, because I had been relaxed when he was getting our history from us. Not once did he say how serious it could've been during that conversation. I would not have been relaxed enough to have practically spilled my life story and I wished he'd been up front immediately.

I like to know the facts, the suspicions. If there's a bug in the middle of my lollipop do tell me before I start sucking. Don't wait. Because I can deal with that. When times were tough in my teen years and the cupboard was lean on goods my mother and I would shake a little of this and that into our hands and if it didn't crawl away, then into the mix it would go. Sometimes we had flour and little else and kept our milk in the snow but we made do without complaint after my mother got sick with her heart problems.

I could handle anything. But that first visit was wasted on small talk. It made our story all the more tragic, and sad for him. I resented that.

It would be a waiting game now.

Chapter Twenty-Four: What Choice Do I Have?

We had suspicions about what it was since autumn but now it was winter and it was supposed to be confirmed. My parents even came in from Vermont. His parents and mine were at the house and we were heading home from the damned hospital with the news. I had the cell phone in my hand. I had never even turned it on by myself; because I wasn't really allowed to use it.

Technology was foreign to me anyway. If my computer wasn't a means for playing with words, I may never have had the incentive to learn its fickle ways.

It would take an hour to get home. I imagined my father, proudly sallied up to my computer, maybe engaged in PC solitaire. My poor mother would be sitting there in the kitchen, which was barely large enough to contain the small table and twin chairs, with Howie's mother; and I was quite certain the two were chain smoking. As for Howie's stepfather, Monty, he'd be holding Pralphdog on his lap, maybe looking for westerns on TV, with his eyes tearing up...at least that's how I imagined it.

Every time Howie stopped the red Hyundai at a stoplight, I was conscious of drivers directing their vehicles up alongside us, and the fact that their lives continued; cell phones stuck to their merry faces. It was the Christmas season.

Howie joked, "If I get to the point where I can't wipe myself, kill me. I mean it."

My head was a bag of wet cement, empty of coherence, filled with every scenario to face us in the coming years flooding in a maelstrom of torrents over my brain folds, even over the un-used parts. One cheek was wet and flattened against the cold glass. I looked through the people in other cars, oblivious to the sting of tears. Once carefully applied make-up was burning, it was snowing, and nothing and everything mattered at once. It was a game to keep tears inside. But oh, they fell. Betrayers.
And snow came tumbling, rolling all around the car as it maneuvered the highway. Like the peoples' faces, and their lives in their warm cars, the snow *was* the holiday season. But it was indistinct, the spirit was dead to me.

Back at the hospital, in the exam room, we'd received the news about Howie's fate. Which of course affected everyone. Every thing. Forevermore.
The doctor offered counseling. His eyes were moist. We politely declined. The first priority was telling the parents. Telling the kids. Being alone. A big woman in small clothing, a counselor, came in the room and adjusted herself to face us. It was then I realized that the doctor with the kind, teared-up eyes had been nothing more than a data collector; as he'd been when he wriggled my life story out of me, when we'd laughed and told him how we met, before we suspected anything serious.
There were no cures of course, not yet. That wasn't his fault. But during the previous spinal tap he pretended that he wasn't sure it was the terminal ALS, which we learned he had seen 250 times before, all the while extracting our cute story out of us about how we had been together for so very long. It made it all the more poignant for him to get us talking about those personal issues. Poor us. Lifelong sweeties now facing this! The story extraction made us seem pathetic. He had
suspected it was terminal the very first day.

I had thought that doctors took Hippocratic oaths requiring them to accept clients 'as is' while doing no harm. This doctor was a bad fit. He expected responses and emotions we generally saved for private. I surmised that spouses of other patients blabbered. I wasn't a blabberer. This befuddled him so much that he resorted to strong innuendo, incidentally hurting me.

Just because I didn't wear my emotions on my clothing, he needn't have assumed they weren't there. Just three doctor's visits later he would turn on me, and in the presence of Howie's sweet Stepdad say to me "You don't drive? Well you had better start. Howard is going to need a driver." It was as if this statement was defending Howie when in fact there was no situation needing defending.

We wanted to go home. I am sure some people welcome "professionals" into the room. We didn't want that. We had just said that. In fact they just told us it would always be "our decisions" and our choices as to the course of treatment. When the woman walked in, all of that was betrayed. It was her job to comfort but we only wanted each other and were denied that, lengthening our stay there by over a half hour.

At last we were allowed to leave. Howie drove with care through the snowstorm, holding the cell phone in a thin unsteady grip. I heard him say, "Hey Carol" which was my mother's name, "Put my mother on...Yeah, he did... We aren't coming home right away."

I imagined my mother, a Betty White look-alike, handing the phone over to Sue, Howie's mother, pacing from the small kitchen to the living room, and looking at my father, who would then look up from his solitaire.

"We're gonna' do some Christmas shopping. As long as you're there watching the kids, why not?" Howie said, smiling.

I turned to look out the window and focused into the snowflakes until they blurred from my tears. The flakes were nothing to me, nothing at all. Now I would have to go into a store.

"We'll talk when we get home... Everything's okay... Naw, I

don't wanna talk on the phone. Its gonna' be okay... It has to be, right?" Howie told the phone.
A pause as he listened.
"Joe," I heard him telling my father, "I told my mother we'd talk when we get back," I surmised my father was handed the phone and trying to get a straight answer out of him. *Did he have the terminal disease or not?* There was a longer
pause and then Howie said, "She *did*? See you in a while,"

Howie clicked off the phone and set it in his lap.

"What did she say, Howie?" I wanted to know.
"She wanted me to tell her *yes or no*. She knows it's bad. Your father said she's going for a walk," Howie said.

"Wow, around *our* neighborhood?" I asked. She had never done that. *What would she do*, I wondered. *Walk to the deli?*

Tears, the first of years of waterfalls to follow, came then. Incredulity was beginning to step in. In the ten years we'd lived on the dead-end I had never been in the corner deli. I rolled my wet face, chilled from the window, toward him. I froze the realness of the moment, knowing I would never forget his steadfast coolness. Both of his strong hands, scarred and callused from decades of construction work, gripped the wheel casually but deliberately as he turned the Hyundai into the mall lot.

"How are we expected to accept this?" I asked at him.

He said, smiling faintly,
"What choice do I have?"

Telling the parents was an emotional rollercoaster I'd soon forget. One of many to come. My father sniffled and went into the yard, came back inside and said that Howie would lick this thing. I told him it was the thing that baseball player had, that Lou Gehrig. He never watched baseball. My father didn't get into the sports. But he seemed to understand after I said that, that it was serious. He called that night after they got back to Vermont to tell me

Mommy had cried the whole way.

Howie's stepfather and mother, they cried a lot too, and the kids, we had to tell them according to their age levels. Jeff was Jeff. He could shrug and leave the room but he had to do a lot of processing. Jeremy at about ten years old, did hugging and tear shedding and Kerry was just a kindergartener. It was just the beginning of understanding for her. How could she understand what a life sentence meant?

I made the decision to stop selling Avon. There would be no mental time for that anymore. I phoned up an acquaintance I'd made through Avon to tell her the news. She seemed to know me so she was a safe person. During a previous conversation, she'd laughed and told me I sounded "Just like Rain Man for a moment."
If she only knew, I'd thought at the time. But I didn't go around telling everyone of my diagnosis.

I shut off the TV, to cut down on distractions; turned off the lights for the same and sat on the floor. Leaning back against the refrigerator, I dialed her up.

"Do you watch the MDA telethon?" I said after a while.

"No," She said.

The words poured. It was like the first time we talked about her Avon order and I saw fit to recount my entire life story to her in one phone call. "So Howie's going to see the doctor that was on the telethon. It's ALS," I went on. It's spreading. Now it's in the other arm. The other day, in the grocery store he bent over and his wedding rings slipped off and tinkled to the floor. His muscles look different- like they're less defined, or dare I say wasting. And he's weaker."

I fiddled with dry cat food tidbits on the floor, flicking them as my neighbor talked. I pulled lint-balls off my sweater and set to forming one larger cohesive lint-ball but it would not hold. I sent it away in the dog's fur. I told her no one usually lived past five years with the disease.

She asked if I'd like to go on walks with her. I said yes. "I'll call you," she said.

I wondered if she would really do it. Our former walks had become stressful, almost impossible for her. She would get attacks. She had to wear dark glasses. We never did walk together. I wouldn't have blamed her at all if she'd said, "Who the hell do you think you are? You put me down like knitting and expect to pick me up where you left off. It's like once you had no purpose or need for me, you set me down. Yet now when you need me, you expect me to be right here for you!"

All of that may have been in her mind, but she did not say those things. I did treat relationships like things to be discarded at my discretion.

When Starr went into the hospital now and again with M.S. problems, I couldn't bear the raw emotion of seeing her there. I resumed contact when she was home... and better.

Chapter Twenty-Five: Cause It's Friday

As Howie blew warm smoke into the air that day and fumbled for car keys, he'd said aloud, "I'm only thirty-seven."

Now we knew we were dealing with ALS for sure. We were all together and that in itself was a rare thing. Our nineteen year old son Jeff sat between his siblings in the back seat. Since Jeff's girlfriend traded his heart for that kid who sold hot dogs, we saw Jeffrey more. Kerry Annie, lover of classical music, kitties, and motorcycles, sat on one side of her big brother and ten year old Jeremy, our artist/poet/sensitive soul sat on the other. The younger two pestered all week about Burger King.

"How come we don't go out to eat anymore on Fridays? We used to go out to eat every Friday. We want to go to Burger King on Friday." They wanted it to be like before.

The kids had never known a time when I drove, because I'd never driven. There were times I tried. Like the school parking lot when Jeff was in grade school. He sat in the back seat, frantic, pulling on his ears. *"We're gonna die! Mommy's driving! We're gonna die!"*

Howie told me to turn the corner. He said "Cut it sharp!" I directed us into a snow bank. *What did "cut it sharp" mean*, I'd asked blankly?

I knew of so many autistic persons who did drive cars, but I also knew of many who did not; and their reasons were also mine. There were a lot of things my children had not seen, nor heard me do. Swearing, for instance. Not often and not very well.

You could not miss the things that communication impairment takes away if you have never had them, and such was my way. My children would not blink twice if I danced with the family cat Sweet Pea or snipped fringe from our sofa set (named Giddy Moonbeam) to sew onto an elf. I snipped fringe from small pillows, buttons from old clothing, and just about any old toy or cast-off thing was fair game when I got an urge to make an elf. Weren't all mothers elf-makers, dancers with cats, namers of couches, writers, poets, with eyes that were aptly hazel, you know, like the nuts? So we found ourselves, like we used to every Friday, just 'cause it was Friday, but some of us were a little taller now, crammed into the little Hyundai. He'd been getting worse.

We stopped going inside restaurants. He had this idea everyone was staring at him when I had to cut his sausage or if he couldn't tear open his sugar packet. Not going inside was fine with me! As my friend Colin liked to say, "Avoidance is not cowardly! It's a form of self preservation!"

I'm not advocating avoidance, but for people like Colin and me, sometimes it sounded supreme. And if my husband wanted to eat in the car instead of going inside, that meant no fluor-escent lights to hit me in the eyes 'laser-like' when I walked
into restaurants. No waitresses I didn't understand. No eye contact. No surprises.

Of course the drive-through window posed unique problems for Howie. His left arm was limpy. Some fingers were bent and stuck that way. The hand was weak. The muscle goes away and does not come back. There was a tremor. He had to over-reach with the right arm to grab the bag at the drive-through window, and then he had to keep his arms steady. Heck, lighting his cigarettes was a two-handed effort. He was especially miserable that Friday.

He was even snappy to the dog, who always meant well in his too friendly in-your-face-with-the-squeaky-toy-kind-of-way.

Pralphdog, the beagle he bought me for Valentine's Day, didn't even beg at the door to come with us after Howie told him to "Git and lay down and take your stupid toy with you and don't chew anything up while we're gone for Christ's sake ya' piggy chow hound!" Some days were better than others.

I pretended like I was that woman on TV sometimes when there was a mess in the kitchen. I crossed my arms, put my hair in a genie-like pony tail, and wiggled my nose and blinked my eyes once and twice. Predictably, this did not make little problems or big ones go away. Sometimes though, like when I pretended there
was magic in the world, or when I danced with Sweet Pea, the people around me laughed or started to believe, or seemed to believe there might be magic. A little twinge, a minute one, a little chink occurred like a healing. At least that's what laughter felt like to me when I heard it.

Sometimes Howie and I were allowed moments to be mundane. Ruts are the basis for roads. Back before any pavement was set down, the ruts were there, are there, beneath.

Sometimes, Howie and I were in our rut; so far in it that we forgot momentarily that doctor who said "...two to five years."

I didn't want to trudge ahead. I wanted to be stuck *right there*.

I had to say to that doctor, "How sure are you its ALS?"

"96 percent," the doctor had said. "By December after those last tests we'll know for sure."

"Oh, well then we have four percent! Good!" I'd said.

That day we went out into the parking lot with the news and we were slapped with the beauty of the perfect autumn day. That building was high on a hill! That hospital had such a picturesque setting; I thought, *My meager attempts at pointillism do not surpass this display*. But it could've been a piece of paper, that valley view laid out before us, filling me, inspiring me to dash home and paint one more matte page of a Fall scene. But maybe the trees knew more than we did.

Some days we were consumed by the stark reality of the 96th percentile...

Other days, like when we watched the MDA telethon, or learned about chromosome 21, the marvelous research, like the unraveling of the DNA genome, we lived in the ever hopeful 4th percentile. When we were blessed enough to be in a rut, to be mundane, like any couple with three kids and a dog and two cats, and a past and a present, we were simply living.

We said, "Shall we pick up crushed gravel to put in around the base of the tree?"

A plan, a project.
He could still drive and at the store the discussion turned mundanely to mulch. Yes! How lovely to have those topics in our minds. We would plant bulbs. We would watch shoots rise and break ground in the spring like anyone else. We were only 36 and 38 after all, and like many couples, we had three
kids and a dog and two cats, and a past and a present, we were simply living.

That Friday was not mundane. He'd been let go at work. For twenty years he'd said, *Roofing's backbreaking work. I do quality work. I don't drink on the job. Hell, I don't drink. I see these doofuses who break OSHA rules and throw houses together like cardboard. I gotta change my line of work. I got guys working on the crew who don't care about the product they put out. I care what kind of job I do. But what thanks do I get? A bad back? We don't even have our house yet. I gotta get out of this line of work. But it's all I know. And I'm good at it.*
He wanted to quit the business, but not because of a disability. Retiring at 38 wasn't in his plans. Before we left for the fast food place, he'd kicked the dog's rawhide toy. It had skidded clear across the unswept hardwood and hit the wall by the poor little guy's dishes. He slammed the bathroom door so hard we all sat crammed four to the couch looking at each other funny.
Since I had a hard time reading people, I was confused. He came out of the little bathroom after some time. What he could have been doing in there so long is anyone's guess, since it was barely big enough to turn around in without bumping yourself.

He announced to us spectators, "Let's get this over with. You only want to go to Burger King because you like the toys and you two damn well know it". We all weren't sure we wanted to get in the car with him after that but we did. He sputtered all the way to Burger

King. "They always forget to put my fries in the bag. They put on cheese when I tell 'em leave it off. And so help me, if you two act up back there," he said to the littlest children. *And what kind of threat is that*, I thought? He'd
never laid a hand on *them.*
We had to pull up behind a long line of cars in the drive through lane. It was dinner rush hour on a Friday. He thumped his left knee against the car door. THUMP! THUMP! It got attention but none of us said anything. Back and forth went his knee between the steering wheel and the car door. I glanced into the backseat at six foot- one Jeff. Limbs, hot breath, a weird twister game- we were all together! It wasn't even our car. It was my parents' car.
We couldn't afford one, and had to borrow this one on a permanent basis.
That was bothering him too. It was really small for this family of ours. I caught the penetrating gaze of my husband's eyes and didn't recognize him. He was tight-lipped and his stare went through my eyes-cold and hard. I copied his knee thumping, and started in to knocking my own knee against my car door, really hard-like. THWACK!
He slowed his thwacking down to a steady impatient roll. He gave me a disinterested sidelong glance but I thought he was interested in what my noise was about. I was only just starting. I wasn't angry. Far from it. He looked like a coil on a catapult about ready to fling into space. I wouldn't get him back if he flung into space. If he climbed into a black hole, there was a temptation to climb in with him. If I went in I wasn't coming out. If he'd unwind the coil, a little, he could be a charming guy.
Being like me means relearning for every situation. Copying. Maybe acting to get by. Nothing wrong with that. I'm as real as anyone. It means studying what people do so as to better fit because sometimes it is necessary to be in situations where I am required to play a role where I am the square peg for the round hole. Most normal (neurologically typical) people are chameleons. I was a chameleon who manually painted on the color, after I figured out which color it was supposed to be.
I started in to acting. I punched my thigh. I was a lunatic I'd seen on TV, a hyperactive, angry, tense person thwack-thwack thwacking
my knee! But I needed more.

The cars hadn't moved much. We were about two cars behind the ordering window. My voice, naturally soft, lent humor to my novice's attempt at cussing, and my results were achieved easily. I addcd tight lips and a cold hard stare for good measure! THWACK! went my leg against the door. There were bruises later on the side of my knee. "Those fuckin' whoremongers!" I said.

"Mom!" said Jeremy. "Did everyone hear Mom? What's wrong with Mom?" he leaned between the front bucket seats to study me, then sat back wide-eyed, stunned, searching Jeff's face for answers. Jeff snickered.

"Bastards making us wait for stinking food-I don't care how good it smells-they're gonna' screw up the order anyhow, always do!" I said. I was making like being real hyper, so I couldn't help but glance at Jeremy who was still searching his older brother's face for clues as to why I'd flipped.

"Jeff, do you hear Mom?" he said.

I swallowed hard, stifled a laugh and started in again. As for Howie, I saw his body go slack. His leg went quiet. Mine didn't. It started going locomotive speed. I decided flailing my arms would be a nice touch. He turned his head to look away from me; and rolled his window all the way up.

"Dirty sons of bitches!" I said.

"Mom!" Jeremy was practically spitting like Sylvester the cat now, the way he did when he was really frustrated. "I don't believe this!"
Kerry sat with unaffectedness, pinching the material on her jeans.
"Let me tell you," I went on, flailing and thwacking, "if they don't get our order right I'll personally go in there and open a can o' whoop ass all over their sorry burger flippin' asses! Sons of bitches! Move this fuckin' line! We're important people! Son of a bitch!"

Chink. I heard an escape sound come out of my husband's face, maybe out of his nose. Like he was blowing it. But I looked and he wasn't blowing it. Then another nose-blowing sound.

"Mom you're nuts. Dad, you're laughing," announced Jeremy.

Howie *was* laughing, then talking. "I'm not that bad, am I?" he said. Then he said, "Now shut up, will you? We're at the win-dow!"

"Mom IS crazy, guys!" announced Jer.

Howie pulled over near the big dumpster so Kerry might get a chance to see a train go by. The track tracks ran right behind the dumpster. Handy to throw our food bags in there when we were through eating. The oversized hamburger shook and squirted nasty stuff when he tried to grasp it. No small feat for the *non*-disabled! I unwrapped the tacos I brought with me. I did not eat ham-burgers or fast food chicken or French fries. He saw me looking at his unsteady grip on the burger.

"I'm *fine*," he said. I did not like the way he said fine.

A train rumbled by and Kerry leaned into the front seat to see. I figured she wasn't too damaged by my swearing; after all it wasn't as if she'd never heard the words before. Her father wasn't a habitual cusser but he sometimes slipped up.

"What's this extra bag?" said one of the boys.

"Did we order this many fries?" asked Jeff who was rooting in a bag.

"Mommy, am I 'posed to get *seven* chicken nuggets in my meal?" asked Kerry.

"They left off the cheese. I still don't believe they got it right," Howie said.
"What's with the extra chicken sandwich? We did not order this many sandwiches. Who wants this?" I asked, holding it in the air between the seats. Someone grabbed it.

"It's even plain!" remarked Jeff.

"Oh, gosh! You don't suppose they heard all my swearing?" I said, covering my mouth with a hand.

He was laughing then, they all were. I had a view of his hand, the lettuce, the fixins' all over his lap. I laughed. I *wanted* to be in a rut. I damned myself for all the years I'd wasted com-plaining what a rut we'd been in. Because what a road we had ahead. I had no idea if that road had working streetlamps on it for us to see. If it did, surely we were turning each one on individually as we went along. One by one. What's more, neither of us had any knowledge of how streetlamps worked, or of what was around each bend in the road. We climbed each lamp, by chance got it glowing, shimmied down, and happened along again.
That was our future. We lingered in each rut as long as we could flounder but eventually we had to trudge ahead. I was glad to hear us all together. A little laughing. I was glad it was dark in the car, what with my tear falling down. We tried to go out to eat every

Friday, just 'cause it was Friday.

Chapter Twenty-Six: Muddling Through

Sinus problems. Migraine. I dropped eighty pounds. Because of my Amazon-like height, I had always "carried it well" but now I looked bony. I was standing at the receptionist's desk of my doctor's office, viewing her through the sliding glass panel. She was gesturing to me to hold on a moment; she had someone on the phone.
She was talking as if to a child. I shuffled; and eyed the escape door. I wanted to be home with medicine. Then I heard Annie's name mentioned by the receptionist, Madge.

I said aloud, "I think you are talking to my aunt." She was just about my only relative left in the state.
Madge suggested I check on her. Howie drove me to her quaint one bedroom house; its bold primary red face a welcome greeting amongst its surrounding ivy ground cover like unruly hair. It suited

Annie. At seventy-something, Annie had rolled around on the floor with my kids and brought me home-made carrot cake for my birthday just a few years ago. Annie had given Howie sexy men's underwear just the year before at Christmas.

When I was a kid Annie brought me to watch her spin in her gay square-dancing dresses with a line of slaphappy partners at the ready. It was the Parkinson's that had her. I was surprised.
After an hour, Howie asked if she was feeling okay. She was unfocused and silent, her hair askew and her eyes shiny. I know she didn't recognize me. We were backing toward the door like wary crabs.

"You don't care anyway," Annie snapped. Howie's eyes widened.

When I reached the ivy, I turned and saw a horror at the window: She was clobbering her fists against the pane. Her white/black hair which was usually neatly dyed and coifed was now Medusa-like. Her mouth worked at a silent scream behind the window pane that I didn't hear from my place on the hill. Howie said, "You can't leave. I'll go home for the kids to see them off the school bus and I'll pick you up in one hour."

I took two steps inside her entryway and she grabbed me. Her hands were vises with the screws tightened. "Don't leave me...Don't leave me alone. They'll get me." I looked down at her beloved swayback mare statue, a flea market find.

"Who, Annie?" I asked, trying to take steps into the living room, enjoying the plush carpet under my feet but scared.

"They watch me," she said, wild-eyed.

I had a feeling she didn't mean her eclectic collection of kitschy statues of birds and other animals. Tears surprised me. Hers were streaming. Did not fall. I tried to coax her toward the flowery couch with its plump matching pillows. She broke from me and blocked my stride.

Police-like, she said, "Don't sit on that couch! The *people* are sitting there!"

I was flapping my fingers, over and over. "The ones that watch you Annie?" I asked. There was a measure of control in my voice.

She nodded hugely, her eyes wide, frightened. I talked to her a long while, willing myself to accept a spirit world. "I don't see 'em," I said. "But that doesn't mean they aren't there."

She seemed unsteady. At last we made it to the couch and collapsed on it. She drew in her body, a flower going in on itself, and put her head in my lap. I didn't know whether to touch her. My hands were confused things. After endless clock-ticking silence, she flung to her feet with enviable agility and disappeared into her bedroom.

When Annie emerged from the bedroom, ghost-white and searching, she was naked from the waist up. I led her back in with an arm around her shoulder as a guide and fit a dressing gown with flowers on it over her head that I'd seen strewn across the unmade bed. Her frail body wavered, silent amongst the staring porcelain dolls surrounding the bed in poses. Some of her "babies" had age-worn yellowing, cracked staring faces frozen in pouts, others were radiant, new with shining black shoes and prissy socks. More than one had only one good eye. I grabbed a handful of twisted sheets and blankets and started making up the bare mattress. I was mindful of my audience. Every doll was dressed to the nines.

At home I had on display the one she'd seen on the shopping channel and ordered for me. Her name, Kimberly, was scrawled in cursive on the back of her neck. With her dark horse-tail hair and light eyes, she was an uncanny likeness of me when I was ten before I had the lice. She wanted me to lay down with her.

"Come lay here, okay, Jane?" She patted the bed, calling me her daughter's name, the name of my cousin who used to wash her long hair in Grandma's brook. I sat down, but it was a ploy.

Annie was off like a shot to the living room.

We settled on the couch. She lay her head on my lap once more. I tried to fix her hair with my fingers. My chest was thumping with anxiety. I gazed out her window and thought of the Annie I knew, the one after she'd had her three children.

Her husband died. She never remarried. One of her sons, the only one to inherit her dark hair, was a sweet man who lived in a group home for challenged adults.

When I was a little kid, she granted me the privilege of calling her Annie. None of the other nieces or nephews had that right. They all called her Aunt Anne.

I'd never before touched or attended to her so personally. My fingers did not feel like mine. I disassociated from my sensitive fingertips as if they were stalk-like appendages that I did not recognize.

Studying her hair close-up, I was reminded that Annie once adored stylish hats and was known for her giddy get-up-and-go attitude. In her 40's, she went through a cigar smoking phase which thankfully didn't last long. My mother took me as a kid to Annie's house when I was sick and she would make me chicken soup. Annie had been host to many parties, some of them demonstrations. Jane, self-conscious of her pimply back, would serve as teen model at the clothing parties. Annie had a horse in the barn, pictures of elves she painted herself on all the cupboard doors at Christmas, and cats with names like Mortimer and Grasshopper.

But the horse and the farmhouse were long gone.

I didn't much like the view Annie was subject to all day long at this tidy little house with the ceramic songbirds and owl prints and sculptures on the floor. Big pines reached toward the sky but their limbs hung saggy-down. Such gnarled hands they had. Like the clawed hands of a Lou Gehrig's patient. I didn't like those types of pines that blew in ominous sweeps like that. They were foreboding. How come I had never noticed?

I would have liked for Annie to see those pines with attitude when she sat on her flowered couch. The pines with uplifted limbs, the ones that seem to lift a middle finger to the sky. I sat, reflecting on these things, amongst the alternate buzzing and humming of some unnamed appliance and the omnipresent ticking of an understated wall clock.

I began to think her 'people on the couch' were real. Maybe Aunt Hannah or Aunt Beverly or even good ol' Louie had come to keep her company, but she didn't seem to recognize them.

Beside the couch on a doily-covered end table was a large
'coffee table' book. I read it to the side so as not to disturb her
head. It was a hard-cover Time Life Civil War book with excellent
black and white photos of makeshift war hospitals and soldiers. I
marked my place with a torn corner of envelope I spotted on the
table and set it down. There was a smaller dog-eared Audubon bird
book too. I couldn't resist leafing through the worn pages. In amongst
the intriguing drawings of birds, I found a perfectly pressed four
leafed clover.

Annie stirred in my lap. "All those books are yours when I leave
here. I won't have any use for them," she said in a stern voice as if
she wasn't taking no for an answer.

"You aren't going anywhere," I said, a hint of annoyance in my
own. Her hands were crossed mummy-like across her chest. Her
knees were pulled up tight under her gown. Her legs were bent
sticks.
Her red-headed son Bill didn't live with her, but I heard he
stopped in daily after he got out of work. Sure enough, after some
time, he came through the door, greeted me and went for the
medicine bottles lined up on the counter, which I hadn't noticed
because we hadn't been in the kitchen except to walk through it. He
held them at once up to the light which was not very bright, one by
one. He seemed to think she overdosed on some pills or was
suffering some side effects. I was reprieved and Howie came to bring
me home.

Come Halloween, we all knocked on Annie's door, my little
dressed up family; but the inside light winked mysteriously off
after we knocked. I'd wanted to give her a bag filled with easy-to
make foods like Cup O Soup and tea. I threw in bath pretties, too.
I knocked on the door of her neighbor, and left the bag with a man
who answered the door. He promised to give the care package to
"Annie." I asked for a pen and paper and jotted a note: *Annie, we
stopped by. I thought you could use a few things. Sorry we missed
you. Happy Halloween- Love you. Kimmy.*

I hoped she would remember who I was. That weekend we
stopped to check on her and see if she'd improved, but she

appeared to be out, perhaps with Bill. The neighbor walked over to Annie's house and handed me the bag.

She said, "Annie was, I don't know, she gave this back to my husband the day after he gave this to her. She said you must've accidentally left it behind on Halloween when you were trick-or-treating."

I never saw Annie again, alive. Bill made the sensible decision to put Annie in a full-time care facility where "real" people could watch her all the time. The doctors said dementia had set in as a result of the Parkinson's. I hoped there were people there she could relate to, people her age, from her era. And better trees to look at. I thought of Annie, dreamed of her and woke up screaming a lot. In some of my other dreams, faceless forces thrashed my rag-doll body against the walls again and again like a hacky-sack.
The dream repeated itself night after night, awakening me wide-eyed with an unspent scream caught in my throat like a marble to the windpipe, my breath shallow and my heart racing.
The dream felt real. An unseen force with the strength of a tsunami tossed my helpless body smack against the wall. I would suspend there, terrified only to be hurled against the ceiling, the walls,

> again
>> and
>>> again.

Chapter Twenty-Seven: A Group Thing

We went to a support group at the hospital and sat at a long table amongst people with various stages of the disease.

One woman lost use of her hands and vocal chords, leaving her no means of communication, but she walked just fine. Others were in wheelchairs and in the throes of the "last stages," with machines all around their chairs.

A stubbly man rasped through his mask, "You're. Angry. Aren't you? You're angry right now." His name was Jack and every syllable was labored. He could turn his eyes my way, but not his head.

"I have three kids," I stated.

Jack was trying to smile around his face mask. A lawyer was introduced by a social worker. He rose and gave a speech on what to do with your assets in the event of your demise.

"I have three kids," I said to an open-faced woman with a bob haircut who glanced at me.
The room was bright, the table glaring.
The advice was practical. One man, who was there with his wife showed few symptoms. He too had a little muscle twitching and severe weakness of muscles but did not show outward signs, neither in speech nor mannerisms. Newly diagnosed, like Howie, he asked questions and he and his wife took notes.
They asked whether, if further down the line his insurance should drop him, maybe would it be wise to fake a divorce so they could qualify for more benefits? *Good, good*, they wrote down, yes, some people did that. It was a possible plan for them.
Next question: Should they secret their money, put it in the kids' names for protection? Oh yes...answered the lawyer, this disease often takes people for all they've got. The couple lit up, the woman taking notes, another possible plan.
At the end of the meeting we made for the door, me slowing my pace to match Howie's new pace. A woman who was very showy emotionally and was there to support her father, who was chair-bound, was blocking my departure to the outside hall. I got by her but she cornered us outside. Holding a doughnut shop coffee container and twiddling wadded tissue, she assaulted me with her wet eyes full in the face and told me her name.

"I'm Sally," she said, and smiled like a sad model. "This is my Mom and here's my Dad." The huge smile was a prosthetic limb being waved in the air for all to see, unattached from the rest of the body, yet waving there, boldly. Should I, too, learn to flash that artifice?

Howie smiled genuinely, I thought, and said, "Hi, nice ta meet you." He lit up his cigarette with two hands to steady the Zippo, all the while glancing around for a chance to flee but we were cornered.

The older man in the chair appeared to have no use of his lower body but his arms seemed okay. He said, "Look at me." We looked. He said, "I've had this monkey on my back how long now? Two years, goin' on two years and look at me, I'm doin' just fine."

"I have three kids," I said, my mouth tight.

They agreed it was nice to meet us.

"I have three kids, I mean *we* do." I reminded them, summing up the struggles ahead that my mind was reeling with, leaving much unspoken in my simple statement: *Jeremy may be a teenager when Howie loses his life. It is unfair to Kerry, just starting kindergarten, to go on in life having lost her father at a young formative time in her development.* All this, my statement didn't say but at the same time did say to them.

As for Jeff, he could not articulate daily life stuff, never mind loss.

"And my parents also have three, of which I am one," declared Sally.

"*We* have three, three kids," I told them.

At last they high-tailed it to the van and disregarded us. We headed toward the car ourselves. "Wait!" I squealed and turned to Howie who flicked away his cigarette. The act angered me as always, it would not biodegrade there in the gutter, especially the filter; it would dry out and blow around for an eternity.

I went back inside, down the short expanse of naked hospital and into the room where we'd been and there, on the table, was a pile of books. People were milling around the lawyer, still asking questions, and the matronly 'therapist' or 'moderator' of the group was beginning to take notice of us but couldn't immediately break from her conversation to say hello-goodbye. She was glancing our way. Howie behind me, I picked up a book, *Tuesdays with Morrie*, and held it for him to see.

"We liked this movie, I thought I should like the book even

better. She said we could borrow any book we want," I told him and I made to tuck it under my armpit.

"No," he said in the voice he reserved for Kerry if she was about to touch something hot. "Put that down. Let's get the fuck outta here."

"But why?" I asked, obeying him and following him to the exit. Even though he was weaker, he walked five paces ahead of me and I hurried to catch up. He turned to talk my way as we hurried outside.

"Because if we borrow that it means we have to come back."

On Valentine's Day, some people holding decorated cardboard boxes stepped out of a small van. From the kitchen window I watched a teenage boy scuffing about like a mad hen. Uh-oh, forgot to pick up Pralph's poops! I didn't know who they were, adults with children, putting boxes on the porch... Thank heavens they hadn't insisted they come in. A thank you through my doorway sufficed.

The ordinary cardboard boxes, two of them, were made extraordinary not because they were filled with food and candy, but because they were papered with pink, yellow, white, red and green construction paper hearts. I sunk to the scrungy linoleum floor in the kitchen.

Just when I thought there were no more reasons to cry, I found another one. I carefully removed every paper heart from the boxes with a kitchen knife to save in my keepsake box. "We care about your family!-troop 273" the messages said in crayon and in glitter and in colored pencils.

(Thank you Girl Scouts and Brownies, was the billboard in my head). "We love you! God bless your family!" and similar messages; I read on pieces of paper in frilly, sometimes illegible, always colorful, script. They signed their names too, in little girls' writing. There must've been a hundred hearts. I mean it, literally.

Howie faced the rush of ALS with swords raised.
He was courageous, beautiful.

When I painted him, I found I could not paint him in the realistic style I once painted in. My paintings of him were from then on done in bold rich color.
The patterns were surreal.
Certainly our lives had become such.
I was lucky enough to marry a poem.

If a cynic ever asks you if love exists
you can take my word for it.

Chapter Twenty-Eight: Fallin' Time

We were going through some bathroom renovations. Some men came from the Housing Authority and were widening our bathroom and putting in a ramp. The men who spent twelve hours a day in our house renovating were ruining my life. I was adhering more and more strongly to routine and it was impossible to eat. Pounds were falling away. The workers seemed to recoil physically; I could see their reactions when every day at precisely the same times, my decorating show would begin, then Howie's western, then this, then that, and so it was never varying. The theme show music made them insane but it was the only thing of sameness to cling to in a house being rearranged and filled with hammering, new dust, and men, men, men and stomping, cajoling and jokes.
When I rode to the bank or store I had to pass a factory downtown with a sign in front: *21 days without an accident!* The number in front of the slogan would change from time to time. If there was a fresh accident they'd go back to 1 and so forth. *1 day without an accident!*
I had a sign like that in my head. The first time Howie fell was on Thanksgiving. His parents drove to Vermont so both our sets of parents could have dinner at my parents' house. It went okay aside from me turning on the wrong burner and nearly setting an empty pea pot on fire. My mother didn't make a big deal about it after we figured out what the smell was and nothing got ruined, there was just a lot of smoke.
It wasn't like the Thanksgiving when I'd put the knife all the way through my hand and it had come through the other side and clinked on the pan. Blood everywhere that day!

"It's just cranberry sauce!" said five year old Jeremy at the time.
Poor clueless kid.

"There goes Thanksgiving!" Howie had said. He was right, we'd
spent that day in the hospital.

Back at the hotel in Vermont, we had a room next to his parents.
They were nestled in their room when we arrived at our room. The
kids were happily staying at my parents'. I went into the room ahead
of him to bring in some things. There was a thin black coat of
transparent ice in the parking lot. I thought he'd wait for me to return
and help him.
No sooner had I plunked the bags down on the bureau-top, did I hear
a thunk from outside.

And then came my name, weakly: "Kim..."

There he was face down on pavement; next to the driver's side
of the car. "What'd you do that for?" I snapped.

"Sssshhh. Just...just get me inside. Easy!" he whispered.

I hoisted him upward and pivoted him into a seating position
onto the seat. I figured I probably dislocated something in his
armpits, moving him so roughly. We didn't want his parents
peeking out their hotel room window and seeing this. Inside the
room, I helped him to swallow some Excedrin. Put a hot washcloth
on his head, picked the tar grit out of his scalp and patted the blood
off his forehead and out of his hair with plump white motel
washcloths. We talked late into the next morning with serious
undertones but this dissolved into laughter. It was too surreal not to
do both. After all, he was the same Howie in both our minds so this
was scary, amusing, surprising. He had fallen before, but that was
because the scaffolding broke or the ladder broke.
He was a roofer, a regular monkey! Why, there'd been times he'd
hung upside down suspended by ropes to do the shingles on a
church's steeple. He wasn't supposed to fall getting out of a car. He
didn't even have a fear of heights.

We made the decision not to tell the parents. I kept pressing on the forehead and saying, "Uh-oh. This lumpy bump is squishy; it will show, you know."

He had me lift his arm and place his fingertip on the bump so he could assess the damage. I held up a small compact mirror. "Yep. The forehead looks like a rug-burn, but at least the egg is in my hair," he said.

"I guess so," I replied, and touched the Silly-Putty lump in his hair.

"Ow!" he laughed. "I ruined Thanksgiving. They came all this way and this'll upset my mother. She's… you know how upset she gets."

"You didn't ruin anything, besides I've ruined Thanksgiving before." I said. "But Howie, this'll show. We can't *not* mention it." I warned.

I stayed close to his body, tossing and turning. He kept asking if I was awake. We talked until daylight came shining around the drapes until Monty showed up with Donut shop coffee.

"Ain't it time to sit down for good?" I whispered.

There was no answer. He hadn't used Hagrid the walker for long. (I'd named the walker after Hagrid, the giant in the Harry Potter films. In one scene he turns around and says, "What're *you* lookin' at?")
We had a plan. We told the parents that the bed was rather high and he fell out and rug-burned his forehead. They bought the story. We glanced at each other and exhaled. No one looked closely at the lump on his scalp or the blood under his hair. No one pieced together that he was too immobile to actually roll. He was always in the same place when he woke up as he was when he settled into bed for the evening. A paralyzed guy cannot roll.
It was amazing we were still operating the car. His legs were still untouched by the disease but his arms were quite limp which is why I did most of the steering. He talked me through every step of that process and it was 'high-anxiety' every time we got in the car

together to go anywhere. This accounted for my not eating, not being able to flush a toilet and the night terrors. The day after Christmas we'd gone *33 days without a fall*. So said the sign in my head. I could envision it. It had a square where the *33* was so the number could be changed out if another fall happened.

My parents came to Connecticut to sleep on our couch and reclining chair. It was becoming a holiday tradition. My father went to visit a friend, leaving the kids and me and Howie at home with my mother. Howie decided to go out to the car and 'start it up' because it was cold and he hadn't started it for a few days. He still figured he could walk pretty well. He only used Hagrid at grocery stores.

I was doing dishes when my mother said, "Oh Kim, Howie's calling you."

My heart leapt against its cage. "Where is he? Oh yeah, he's starting the car," I said. I dried my hands on a paper towel, paused to appreciate the sight of Kerry and my mother, playing with Christmas toys, and proceeded outside, bracing myself. *He probably needed help closing the car door*. Yeahyeah.

Around the corner of the house, I found him on his back. For some dumb-ass reason he was smiling. My blood pressure must have soared but I was as calm as a sleeping baby. I did what I had to do. I lifted the 160 pound guy.

When my father returned he found me bashing ice on the living room floor for Howie's head. He asked what the hell was up because he couldn't see the ice inside the plastic bag under the towel that I was hammering. My mother told him about the fall.

"Jesus, oh it'll be fine. He fall bad?" He was at a bit of a loss for words.

At six inches shorter than me, I cherished my father from his bald bespectacled head and Robert Mitchum good looks down to his bowed knees. I had already upset him during his visit and felt bad about that. He'd handed me a tape dispenser and as I took it, his finger brushed squarely across my palm.

It was just like when I ran the register at the department store where I worked five long treacherous years in the 80's. If people would hand me change and by happen-chance touched my palm, I recoiled and dropped the money. I didn't mean to. I'd learned to keep coins in my smock pocket to make the check-outs quicker.

When I pulled back from his accidental touch, Daddy had said, "What's the matter Kimmy?! I'm just handing you something. Has Daddy ever bitten you?" I was stunned and agreed that no he'd never bitten me.

Every day the sign changed.
47 days without a fall,
48 days without a fall,
now it had flipped over to: *1 day without a fall.*
I thought he'd at least wait until Easter to fall again. But no, I was dressing him when he lifted his leg, lost his balance, and tipped over backward. He scraped up his back on the metal edging of the bed frame. Not too bad. Some unwashed clothes broke his fall.
He had a good laugh over it and thanked the dirty laundry. He did, he thanked a load of bunched up smelly towels. From then on I dressed him while he was sitting down. You live, you fall, you learn to sit. You learn to dress a sitting person. You don't fall as much.

Chapter Twenty-Nine: Harmony

My neighbor Jill's daughter Harmony, 5 years old, didn't have what they term meaningful speech. I didn't feel too naked around Jill and harmony. I got down on hands and knees and looked up at her view from her angle, turning my head up, and she let me be near.

I noticed a vent with vertical metal grating. On the wall. It reminded me of the kind on trailer floors but this was on the wall; it was a really old house. I said to Harmony, "We can make music."
I put my finger on the grate and the resulting sound was
better than I'd hoped. I kept saying, "We ARE making music!"
Harmony put her finger along the grate; copying me. I varied pressure. Notes went up and down, fast and slow.
Their house was filled with interesting piles of things here and there and there again. Their yard had a typical array of tough

plastic toys: some to ride on, swing on, pretend-cook on. After a while, Harmony decided she wanted to be in the garage.

After much whining at the gate, Jill said, "She likes to explore the garage. The aides kept saying I should be stern and say no, and also she likes to sit in the truck. It's so hot in it. I don't know what she gets out of that."

I told Jill how I explored our old garage when I was little. All its shades of grey. It had looked like it'd blow over in a weak wind. Full of dangerous junk. So full of smells and texture for climb-ing. With a broken back window wide open. I told Jill how I made a game, a decathlon of sorts, out of entering the garage, climbing the wonderful junk, and exiting through the window. I did this over and over... I could understand the appeal. Also the danger. I remember clearly my mother's fear for my safety and her heeds to keep me out of our garage.
Referring to my neighbor "Jill" was difficult. Jillian was the first name she introduced herself as, but when she wrote her telephone number down on paper, she wrote JILL. It would be difficult to slang her name, but I would try. Personalization with anything other than kitties, dogs or my own kids was akin to putting an electric shock through my chest. I had never even said "Dad" or "Mom" or "How." (slang for Howie.)
I followed the little girl into the garage. Blessed things: rooms filled with things, things, things. I dreamed of delightful things. In some of my worst dreams, my recurring nightmares, I was trapped in horrid buildings, and wandered room to room lost; searching and blinded by the stark white of the walls but unable to find an exit. Sometimes a bear was in the house with me, grunting and seeking me out like a pig nosing for buried truffles.

This garage seemed to have a loft but Harmony didn't try to climb the wooden stairs. I moved a car battery out of her way with my foot. She didn't try to touch it. She squeezed between a motorcycle and a boat. Kittens appeared, reminding me of Grandma's shed. I knelt and discussed the boat. I knew she went on a school outing that day, on a real boat. Was that the attraction? To see this old boat? I wanted her to realize a connection.

"A boat! You saw water today! And a boat! You were *on* a boat today! Here's a boat," I told her.

But maybe she had made the connection herself. Here was a big solid boat beside us with cushions and junk piled inside.
She was staring at my hair. Was my hair jumbling up, scaring her? Was it my green barrette? Then she focused on my T-shirt. She'd liked the angel on my shirt the day before.

"Where did the girl on my shirt go?" I asked. I asked several times.

Back to my hair. Now that we were crammed in this dark stuffy place, she was noticing *me*. She was flapping her hand, humming, a wet sound coming from deep in her throat.
I touched my green barrette. Eh, forget the boat. Was she not used to seeing my hair in a clip? Suddenly she grabbed her short blonde hair in her fist, roughly. Her eyes occasionally met mine and I usually allowed brief contact but never lingered *in* hers long enough to be intrusive.
I didn't care for being *in* people's eyes too much myself.
Just what was interesting on top of my head? I might get a complex. I was still kneeling. She had her short blond hair knotted up in her little white-knuckled fist. It was dark in there and smelled of oil. Delightful! Her hand unraveled. She let go of her hair and gently picked up a strand of my hair that fell across my forehead.
She let herself experience it as it flowed through her fingers, examining it closely with intelligent eyes. "Haaaaaaaaaaaaa," was the sound in her throat. Was this her regular humming sound or could I believe that was an "h" sound?
I could understand how people could have misconceptions about autism in general. Here was a girl diagnosed severely autistic. Here was me evaluated with Asperger's. Outside was the boy named Greg, my cousin's son, with attention deficit so severe it overshadowed his moderate autism which would probably never be addressed because all anyone could see was his attention disorder, his significant inability to self control impulsivity.
But as hard as it felt for me to be touched physically, for Harmony to be in my personal space, it was monumentally harder for her. I knew that. I also knew there was hope for all of us. The stinging came behind my eyes as much for the invasion of my personal space as for

the triumphs I knew were ahead for Harmony, and for my cousin's son.

"Haaaa...," Harmony murmured.

"Hair! Hair! I have hair. We both have hair!" I said, not too loudly. "We'll go. We'll go in the sun. " With comic enthusiasm I said, "Come on!"

She followed me out into the gravel driveway where three vehicles were parked. The aides' former plans, so I was told later, to get her out of the garage, had been to repeat stern "no's" and demand she leave the garage immediately before she was hurt. As a result of that plan, she would linger, start to cry and end up being carried out screaming.

Out in the sun, I hoisted her onto my hip so she wouldn't take off into the road. For five minutes I carried her around so she could peek inside each vehicle parked in the driveway. I tried to tell her she could see her face in the truck's mirror but she wanted none of that. She cupped the sun out of her eyes and peered into the windows. I had never seen her expression so serious as when she peered in those windows! She wanted *into* those spaces.

She tried to form words to tell me to open the doors to each of the trucks and let her into them. But the sounds she made did not make actual words. I told her it was hot inside them. Then I lied, and told her they were locked. I stressed how nice the seats looked inside but so very hot. I carried her back into the fenced - in backyard.

She whined at the gate for another trip into the garage and I thought she might throw a little tantrum, but her curiosity having been sated a little, she gave up. She went away from the gate and sought out a place between the shed and the garage. A narrow space, with an old pool ladder wedged in there. She liked to climb up on it and stare up, up up at the tree limbs and everything that goes on in the intricate patterns they make. *Bliss. Yes, I know.*

I told Jill how I'd mistaken Harmony for being six when I first met her because she looked wise. But she was not, she was four at the time.

I told her how I'd moved the battery and how I disagreed with the aide who told her to say no all the time. No is important for big things, certainly, I told her. But if she's developmentally delayed, which is what being autistic is, then perhaps she should be allowed a baby-proofed environment and lots of exploration. She was very curious. And with stimulation, I told her, what gifts you'll both receive and discover!

With embarrassing abandonment, I said, "Harmony's so fun!"

Jill said, "Wow, no one thinks she's fun. They just think she's retarded." Her candor endeared her to me. She was becoming one of the truest friends I'd ever known.

"Einstein didn't speak till he was three you know." I said, and she said she had heard that before. She's really smart about what her daughter needs, and about a lot of things.

The mundane chores were diversions in my day. I was learning the names for some of my problems: dyspraxia, aphasia. I would hyper-see sometimes, tripping over Wal-Mart ads on floors. Why on earth would they put them there!? My depth perception was at times frightening. I would step over a crack and my body would react with a falling sensation as if I was pitching forward. I mapped and over-stepped; taking wide angles and big turns to avoid furniture. Plans for a future change if your spouse has ALS. It is especially challenging when the other spouse does not drive. If I could drive, I would. I believe I'm smart enough to know I don't belong on the road. Most people do not understand the scope of a condition like mine and the way it affects me personally. It involves perception, an integration of fluidly operating senses, cognition, communication, and processing to name a few. I'm seeing details but presently not pulling together a whole. I read an article in *Discover Magazine*, one of the dozen publications that come to the house, from The Chrysler Corporation which noted that driving is 90% visual...I suggested that if there were signs and steps taped inside the car, I might learn. STOP on the brake pedal. A sign with GO on it taped onto the gas pedal. Then I might remember which was which. During the summer, I decided to hang clothing on the back clothesline, to get fresh air, but also to save money on the electric bill by not using the dryer so much. It was seasonally hot and I figured the clothes would dry pretty quickly. I came around the corner of the

house. I couldn't leave Howie for too long unattended even if he was napping. The basket on my hip, I stopped. What the hell was that giant pile of shapes like the ones in Dan's necklace doing laying there? It was reminiscent of Picasso's cubist phase, balancing on the lawn. And it was pretty big. I attempted to blink the jumbles away there in the hot sun. I could make not a lick of sense out of this *thing* in the grass. I was frozen in place and staring at shapes.
And then, the pieces led one to the other: A bench, another one. A splintered series of thin slats of wood with my pink fingernail polish swirlies and doodles painted all over it. The picnic table. It was a picnic table the whole time. I stood on the back steps which had a door that led into Jeff's bedroom...
As I strung the clothes and clipped them to the line, I glanced at the familiar old table lovingly. How could it have tricked me?

Kerry flipped her bicycle upside down. "Hi Mommy. I'm playing!" Kerry said to me.

"I see that", I told her. She was spinning the tire of her bicycle as fast as she could. I patted my back pocket. Relaxed at the security and sense of belonging this gave me.
My e-friend David who, like me is an Asperger's autistic wrote this: *"As soon as I got in the car I started to feel that I would crash into somebody. When changing lanes, I looked in my mirror, but I didn't see what was coming. I also felt sometimes very numb. As if in a state of shock. As if it wasn't really happening. There were several incidents of near collisions that only my instructor prevented. I soon decided that for the safety of other people, I should not be a driver."*
It was his words I was carrying. I thought back to the time my uncle had complained to my father that he had talked to me and I had only stared, oblivious to him. I had had staring spells all my life. And my vision was always jumbling up. I didn't know why; I just knew it did.
Now, rifling through papers, I came across a legislative proposal that Dan had left behind. He had proposed it to create an avenue for services for persons who were on the autistic spectrum as they crossed over into adulthood. It had been signed by people like myself, and mailed to legislators, but to no avail and was the biggest reason, I assumed, that Dan left Connecticut. He wanted to help but felt so restricted.

It read:

For the past twelve years I have served a large group of individuals who do not fall into human service systems that currently exist in the state of Connecticut. They have diagnoses on the autistic spectrum. For the past two years, I have met on a Commissioner's level to try to find resolution and help for these people. To date, these people are still unserved, and in terms of existing services, have little hope for the future. In a meeting with the Department of Social Services, Medical Services Division, I was directed to you as one who may be of assistance in my work to advocate for others. I would greatly appreciate your review of the following synopsis of a very serious social service problem, a potential solution that can be made on a legislative level, and the rationale.

The People

Definition: The 'autistic spectrum' refers to people who have either autism, Pervasive Developmental Disability, or Asperger's Disorder. Birthrate: 1 in less than 250 births fall into the autistic spectrum (Dr. Ami Klin, Yale's Child Studies Clinic) Rate of other Disabilities: Most individuals with autism or related disorders do not have mental retardation, nor do they have a separate diagnosed mental health disability.

Nature of Disability: It is considered severe and pervasive.

Dichotomy of Disability: It is primarily a social learning disability, although it has many other features. It is common to be considered 'genius' in terms of intellect and work skills, but not understand how to wash and dress in order to get to work.

Availability of Services: Most people on SSI and Title 19. The Bureau of Rehabilitation Services will assist a person on the job. Most people cannot get to a job without some initial personal support. The Department of Mental Health does not have a mechanism to support these people. The Department of Mental Retardation will only support if there's coexisting diagnosis of mental retardation. Community agencies are not trained or educated about neurobiological disorders, and therefore cannot serve. As there is no money available to purchase services, agencies are generally not preparing to serve these people.

The Problem

Testing/Evaluation: Thousands of children have been tested and diagnosed with autistic spectrum disorder since the early 1990's. These children are now 'aging out' into the adult world, and have needed special services throughout school. Once in the adult world, they may never reach self sufficiency if services abruptly stop.

Adults: Thousands of other adults who have been misdiagnosed are slowly getting rediagnosed (usually from Schizophrenia to Asperger's Disorder). In the mental health system, they gained no skills to live in the community effectively. Now they are losing services, and are at risk.

Current Situation: Most adults who do not have an invested family, and one with resources, end upin complete isolation, and are at imminent risk in the areas of safety, health and welfare. Any social learning that occurred in school deteriorates over time, as does the person's ability to access the community and work.

The Solution

I am requesting consideration of the Department of Social Services to become the lead department by Statute in the service of individuals with autistic spectrum disorders who do not have other primary diagnoses.

The Rationale

The Department of Social Services has the greatest capacity and internal system components to implement services beginning in the home, rather than the creation of facilities in the community. Facilities do not work. If a person does not know how to access the community and has difficulty tolerating people, beginning with the opening of a facility will only create a building with few users. The Department of Social Services has successfully created the Medicaid Waiver for people with traumatic brain injuries. This type of waiver may ultimately be a primary resource for the people with autistic spectrum disorders.

Unlike other departments, the Department of Social Services is most directly linked into personal assistant services, educational services, and ultimately to return to work services through the Bureau of Rehabilitation Services. It is this continuum that has been used successfully in supporting people from isolation to self efficacy and self sufficiency.

Other Implications

This is not a rising crisis in the State of Connecticut alone. It is nationwide. Many states are faced with the same questions about how to serve this large group of people. Connecticut is the leader in the Nation in terms of research, testing and evaluation. Should it take a stand to build technology, infrastructure and services in the community, it will be the leading State in all areas of this arena. The National Technical Assistance Center and the Center for Mental Health Services are aware of this problem. With an investment in people's lives before the crisis, Connecticut may become a model state in the Nation for information, education and technology share. It may also stand out to the Federal Department of Health as a frontrunner in Human Services.

Thank you, Representative Handley, for your review of this material.

Daniel J. G., M.A.

Clinical Habilitation Counselor

Little did Dan know, wherever he was, that such a program that he had envisioned and petitioned for, really would come to pass just four years later, and I would be a participant in it!

I put away this paperwork in a manila folder in my desk drawer for later perusal.
I had lots of such folders, unlabeled and hard to find again when I needed a birth certificate or some writing notes. I knew I would be one of those people out into the world one day without my partner. Jeff would be in the world too.

Chapter Thirty: A Real Friend

One day I received an e-mail from Colin. He'd found the Expectant poem online. "You aren't the Kimberly Tucker who wrote that, are you?" he asked.
I'd sent him my writing in the past. He'd never offered much opinion. This was the first time Colin had ever said he loved something I'd written. I was beaming. Perhaps it was because he'd stumbled across this work on his own that he was allowed to love it. Or maybe, just maybe, even though I did not receive monetary compensation for *Expectant*, it was something worthwhile. The things that were getting stuck in my throat were coming out of my hands.

I was excited. It was spring. I had an amazing thought provoking letter from Colin, my pen pal and good friend, in my back pocket. I kept my eyes focused on the web of leaf patterns on the forest floor and the plays of sunbeams against tree bark. I was seeing every nuance in the woods, not the woods as a whole. Then I saw it!

"Howie! Stop the car! Owl balls!" I shouted, pointing into the woods. He stopped the car and I ran, scooping up chaff-like balls. "I've always wanted to find these!" I gushed as I sat in the front seat with them on my lap. "Owls can't digest bones and stuff from their prey. So they drop pellets or balls from the trees where they roost. If you pick apart the owl balls you get a clue as to what they ate. You can tell by the bits of undigested bone fragments." I picked at the material in my lap with much excitement.

Howie was grinning. I was glad he was as interested in the owl balls as me. "That's horseshit." He said.

"I knew that," I lied, flinging the crap out my window. "That was a horse trail in the woods. The manure, it dried in the sun like hay."

After we got home, I answered the questions in Colin's eight page letter, by writing him an equally long e-mail. I finished the epic letter with my take on the owl ball experience. Colin e-mailed me a response before nightfall. He related experiences similar to my own. Colin was in the process of completing the first autobiographical comic written and drawn by a person with Asperger's (to be published by American Splendor), and I was proud of him.
He walked long distances to mail me pen-and-ink drawings that came in groups of ten or thirty. When they arrived, I carried them around for days and they gave me strength. I felt I had a genuine friend, long distance though it was.
The first phone call from Colin was surreal. I asked him to speak slowly until I could grasp his Geordie dialect. Howie rolled his eyes and flipped through channels as I sat, knees up, on the floor with my back to the couch, twirling the phone cord and daring Colin to conform me to his beliefs. Sometimes I sat on the kitchen floor, in the dark, to tune out the game and I challenged Colin to see *my* points of view.
When I won a debate, I was damn well pleased. I learned about scotopic sensitivity syndrome, poor depth perception, seeing the part and missing the whole. Colin didn't drive either. "I'm a pretty unsafe pedestrian," he liked to say. "I'm sure I'd be an unsafe driver." It was wonderful to feel such a kinship with another person.
I noticed similarities between Colin and Van Gogh. They both talked lovingly of their ink pens. They both had a similar writing style and both chose to capture the images of the down-trodden. Van Gogh was a starving artist. Colin lived in an area he liked to call, "The armpit of the U.K." I painted a miniature recreation of Van

Gogh's *Crows Over A Wheatfield,* in homage to them both. I also hung a large print of the painting over my desktop computer.

Upon visiting me one afternoon and glimpsing the Van Gogh print, Starr joked, "Is that supposed to symbolize your feelings or something?" Sometimes she was flippant. She kept me balanced.

I was outraged one day when Howie smacked a fly right on the print, smearing its guts across the swirling sky. "What are you doing?! You know, the paint wasn't quite dry as Van Gogh lay dying of a self-inflicted gun-shot wound beside that particular canvas! Granted it's a print, but, you have such little respect," I shouted at him.

"I thought you liked it because you're obsessed with the Counting Crows music, so you'll hang things up just because they have crows in it," he said slyly. He looked at me with a grin.

"Shall I read to you some of Van Gogh's letters to his brother, Theo? Would you like to see other work by him? I have books," I offered.

"Not interested. Couldn't give a rat's ass," he replied.

He was right about one thing. I did have a thing about crows. Or did they have a thing about me? Just before Howie's diagnosis, I remember being at one of those parks with loopy streams and graffiti'ed picnic tables, and hiking trails that wound through woods, complete with footbridges over trickles of water that intercepted the paths.
I paused to count crows and looked up, right at one. A big inky thing hooked onto the utility pole with thick legs shimmering all purple and green in its feathers, making eye contact. It moved its beak and made an eerie sound.
The scenario repeated just a few days ago. I was in a super-market parking lot when I saw one lean into the air as if it
were committing suicide off the top of a parking lot lamp, with its beak wide open and an eerie *krrrrr* rolling out of its mouth. It fell forward my way for a mere second and then it ascended up.

I watched till it was a black speck in the grey sky. And this time I took this crow to be a harbinger.

Chapter Thirty-One: WTNH, April 2, 2003, 10:00 PM news

Each bedtime after the kids were snoozing we discussed the nasty mail from the state. Could they really take away our medical coverage? I needed my migraine medication. I could not care for him unless my head was all right. As it was I had to monitor every foodstuff that passed my palette.

"Look at the clock," one of us would say.

"No way. Not again!" Precisely at 11:11 we said goodnight. We came to think of it as a spiritual time but the troubles were mounting.

One day a news person phoned to say she'd be at our house in a few minutes, and would we give an interview? I stuffed dirty dishes into the oven, applied make-up in a ridiculous fashion, swiped deodorant on Howie's pits and changed his shirt. Jodi, the reporter, was animated and interested as she sat on our couch and asked questions. A few nights later, we appeared on the news at least six times; at various intervals. None of the abrasive, cutting remarks I'd had for our Governor made it into the series of clips used in the short, precise bit about us, which featured a shot of the Governor handing out stuffed Husky dogs to needy kids while a voice-over described the HUSKY program budget cuts.

"It provides health insurance to the neediest of families but budget trouble has the state looking to cut the HUSKY health program. Although a judge has halted the order temporarily, time may be running out for those who need it the most."

"He worked as a roofer pretty much until the hammer was too heavy to hold anymore and he just couldn't do it anymore,"

I say. A voice-over cuts to the various stickers of flags and such affixed to Howie's power chair, and he is shown, as the camera pans, chewing thoughtfully on the inside of his mouth and listening to what I say, eyes cast downward but half-smiling.

"At age 37, Howard Tucker was diagnosed with ALS, or Lou

Gehrig's disease. Now, three years later he's confined to a special motorized chair and takes an experimental drug twice a day to essentially stay alive."

"Makes me a little more mobile," Howie says, slowly but quite coherently. I was glad for that voice, which sometimes cracked and then faded.

"But they do say Rilutek helps to extend his life so it's important he stay on it," I say, describing the drug that costs a thousand a month and promises to extend his life by a few months. And that wasn't counting the other medications that made his disease a little easier, all experimental.

"The Tuckers, like 27,000 other Connecticut residents qualified for the state's HUSKY program, which provides health insurance benefits for working poor families with children. The Tuckers have three."

"This was our safety net. We didn't think they could take it away from us," I say.

"Earlier this month a special notice from the state came in the mail. The Tuckers and nearly 30,000 people, including 7,000 children, were being dropped." The camera shows a close-up of the notification papers splayed across the sticky coffee table informing us our medical insurance will be terminated.

"Lawmakers cut the program to save millions in a widening state budget gap."

"When we got the notice we were shocked to say the least," I say, turning to look at Howie who turns to look at me. When we see each other we look slowly away, frowning.

"The old HUSKY plan allows a family of four earning $27,800 annually to get coverage. Under the new plan families can only earn $18,400. The Tucker's earn just above that, which means their coverage will be cut and Howard's experimental drug will be tough to come by."

I say, "I certainly can't go down to CVS at the end of the month and give them 1,200 dollars in cash." There is a close-up of my face and I am aware of all the fat I have lost off my face. My cheeks are sunken in, my hair is pulled back lopsided. My eyes bulge and dart.

"A federal judge has issued a temporary restraining order allowing the Tuckers and others to keep their coverage, at least for now. The state says it's re-instating all the families cut off as of Tuesday, temporarily. The Department of Social Services says it's also working with pharmacies across the state so that if a HUSKY member needs to get a prescription they will not be turned down. As for the fate of the program, that's in the hands of the court." The spot ends with a shot of Jodi standing in front of our local pharmacy, CVS, in the dark, with a misty rain around her, holding a microphone and uttering those last statements. Jeff taped the spot for us because I didn't know how.

It worked. We got our insurance back. When I replayed the spot I was sure the weather guy was laughing at me. What a relief. The onslaught of machines, diapers, gauze, syringes and cases of formula hadn't even arrived yet! At the rate his health was declining it wouldn't be long. My hair was falling out in large amounts, splaying in tangles across my fingers and settling like a nest in the drain after I bathed or washed my hair.
There was an
ominous presence in the house as if the disease was a tangible thing. A monster. But we kept it at bay. We laughed all the time.
It hated that.

Chapter Thirty-Two: The Car
Gosh, Barbara Walters didn't drive. Neither did Picasso! He thought cars to be quite humorous.

I usually steered. He did the pedals, his arms limp on his lap. I was sitting close to him, steering all the time. To the grocery store and bank and even on long drives to Vermont two and a half hours away. Afterward I would be so keyed up, my nerves jumping with adrenaline, that I could not eat, speak or sit. I was catatonic.

He screeched "*Not that way! Cut it sharp!*"

So I stopped turning in the middle of the turn. We went straight for the utility pole. The car climbed up a grassy knoll, missing the pole by feet because of the incline of the bank. The car dug into the ground. The wheelchair in the trunk, I discovered later, went through into the backseat. Not all the way through, but it ripped a hole in the backing and also perforated the watermelon that was in the trunk.

So he said to me, "Put it in reverse! R, the R! "

So I changed the gear in a reserved manner. I did not look around to see who was doing the honking. I didn't want to know, thank you. A neighbor? A child's teacher? So we get backed out and finally I maneuvered home. *My* route. Less ornery than "sharp" left turning.

"You can't do that with steering wheels," he says later, after the event.

I say to him, "It's semantics! Specify if you want a follow through!"

Back at home, I got him settled in his chair and put the groceries away. Tears fell for a while as I sat wordlessly. He told me to check the car. I ran outside and noticing some neighbors on porches, I whistled a short tune then walked nonchalantly around the driveway alternately biting my nails and pretending to call a nonexistent cat over to play, all the while checking for damage on the car. Pretty smooth.

I ran back inside. "The license plate's bent," I informed him. He told me to try and unbend it.

I went out there whistling and tried the nonchalant business and ducked when I got to the front of the car. It was no use, I couldn't unbend the plate. I looked closely and I started seeing clumps of dirt and grass, and decided it was best to pull these out of the framework of metal in the front of the car. I ran inside to tell Howie of my intentions and then ran back
out to pull sod before he could chastise me too much. Pulling sod is useful, being lectured is not.
In the front grill was a shredded McDonald's cup, an ant colony, and a fat white worm. The bumper was rife with life! I was aware of sadness and guilt during this activity. I tossed the teeming sods of ants into my front yard. *Great. Now I started a war.*

City ants caught in the grill from the accident would war against
Project ants in my yard. I had seen enough documentaries to know I
had inadvertently started a war.
I ran in the house to tell Howie of the unexpected life caught in
the car. About the horrible war I'd begun.

"Yes," I sighed. "I relocated an ant colony, tons of them wiggling
through the chunks of earth. Now they will war with the ants in *our*
yard."

"Get me outside. You were supposed to be checking the car for
damage," he said.

A half hour later. "Okay, so far a hole inside the back of the
trunk lining where the portable wheelchair made a hole after it hit the
watermelon," I said, surveying the trunk.

He made me pull the hood release and check the blinkers. It
took patient commands to explain to me how to do these things.
They hide those levers in places only spies and detectives would
look.
He told me to pay no never-you-mind to the neighbors
because as far as they knew we were doing car maintenance.
People did that all the time. They didn't necessarily know I hit an
embankment. *Hmmm, did everyone pull shredded McDonald cups
outta their car grills?*
He made me pull, grunting at the hood release which refused to open
the hood. He said it was now misaligned. He told me to go around to
the front and to pull at it and it finally came up.

"Someone will notice," I wondered aloud. "What will we say?
There's a big mark we left behind near that pole. Maybe it's illegal,
the way we drive! Oh God, how do we go out to get food? We aren't
driving anymore now, are we?"

"We call my father to bring us shopping. I don't like depending
on him anymore than you. But this ain't workin'. We ain't taping
signs all over the car for you. And call your father. We'll tell him he
can have the car. As soon as your father can get down here to get it,
the car is theirs," he said firmly.

"And we beat their Hyundai into the ground, right Howie?" I said, repeating something I'd heard him say. "Know what? You said to turn and I did. I still could've gotten home on the road I chose, going straight."

"I never go that way. My way was shorter. You cannot turn suddenly back the other way in the middle of a turn," he said again.

I had a kitten in the house to distract myself from the drama, from the panic that set in over what we would do without a car. Jeremy named the orange tiger Mister Po. We took turns nursing it back to health with a little kitten bottle and formula. It looked like a dead limp bird when I'd found it at Jennifer's house. The mother had abandoned it, along with its look-alike. Its head was wet and limp and it was covered in fleas. Jen said that an animal had come in the night and beheaded the little guy's twin which had been an orange tiger too.

I couldn't help but think how fitting this kitten was to be Jeremy's pet. I 'lost' Jeremy's twin early on in the pregnancy and had had to scoop a little flesh colored fetus out of the toilet and bring it to the doctor's office as told.

Chapter Thirty-Three: Keeper of the Penis

When Howie could no longer type to his internet gaming pals or play a game without fumbling, an organization called Voice for Joanie came in and lent Howie his own computer, to find its massive place beside mine. It had a sensitive right-clicking mouse and even a program that made it easier to type, called EZ-Keys. When Howie could no longer use his hands much, Kerry sat on his lap and helped with the mouse while Howie poked at the keyboard with his long stick in his mouth. Peck, peck, peck. It was the phrase "lent him the computer" which bothered me. They would come to retrieve it when he…?

Without his income, our incoming monies were reduced not to welfare which we declined, but Social Security checks. Every time I visited the ALS doctor with Howie he reminded me that many spouses hired someone to 'come in' and the healthy spouse supplemented the income by working.

One woman at the office, a 'well-meaning' networker who set up our visits, suggested I had "something to prove" by opting out of the nursing care possibility.

I hung up the phone in shock, thinking, *Did she just say that I had something to prove...?*

What I needed was to gain independence, and to use my voice more now that his was weakening. Neither of us needed a disruption in routine that involved bringing a person into the home, a person with her or his own smells, ideas, and everything that goes with being human. We needed to maintain as much semblance of normality as we could muster; for our sakes as well as the children. None of us took to outsiders well.

I was now the keeper of the penis. It was like having a person in your pants, a little character! With moods. It morphed all the time. The time had come to help with bathroom duties.

"Guess I have to kill you now," I joked during our bathroom time, and I reminded him of his earlier statement.

He rolled his eyes and put on a stern face which was to be his mask, the "mask of ALS" as it is called in the newsletter we now got delivered to the house. The facial muscles were weakening. He had a no-expression face now. I related.

I would heave Howie up from under the armpits, and somehow hoist him from the power chair onto his feet. Then I pivoted him, stepping gently on one foot to hold it steadfast while I turned him. This was my method. Then I lowered him to the seat. Then came the gloves and hemorrhoid cream. And usually the suppositories. We were to be trying Colace soon, which was a liquid stool softener.

"Can't wait to try the Colace," he said. "It's...so...hard to go now."

"The lady at U. Conn. said maybe the muscle that controls pushing is...weakening now," I said, trying to be helpful.

"What do they know? Maybe I just don't get enough water," he said to me.

"That's part of it. We will definitely work on that. But it's common, the constipation, they say."

He was wobbly, never walked anymore, but he could still stand to pee. His hands were limp, and claw-like. I stretched his arms and legs in bed; trying to ease the stiff joints and muscle cramps brought on from lack of use. But the fingers, they could not be stretched out. He asked me to straighten the fingers on his worst hand, and I tried as he winced in pain. I dutifully followed his instruction to flatten and straighten the fingers and tape them down to a flat piece of wood, a child's block. He slept all night that way but in the morning when I removed the tape, they were already curled right back up like question marks, somehow having done so even under the restraint of the duct tape as he slept. I did this twice because it didn't work the first time, and I didn't have the sarcasm to say, *Told you so...a neurological disease is a neurological disease. You are at its mercy.* But I thought it, and the pain on his face bore into me.

I told him with wet eyes, "I would poke out my eye with a needle if that could make you well."
Looking at his traitor hands, where I'd arranged them on his chair arms, he nodded, believing I would. Clipping his nails always upset him.

"Shit! Forget the curled one already!" He'd say. But they were all curled.

I would pull his chair up to the bathroom sink and submerge his hands with warm soapy water to scrub them and then let them fall into the towel on his lap. It was important to dry them well, in between all the nooks and crannies and at this he would curse too.

"Get me outta this damned bathroom. Why can't you leave me alone? I'm not being shaved too. You did enough to me for one day!"

"I'm shaving you, then you can nap in the recliner. In your chair. I am not doing things *to* you, I am doing them *for* you," I stated calmly.

"Son of a bitch. Just listen to me." The force of his outburst caused his head to loll forward and he could barely right it again by himself. Soon, I thought, I would have to straighten it for him. "I am not! Not! Getting shaved right now."

I knew there was so much he couldn't control and he tried in a mighty way to control what he could. I pushed the button on his chair and it propelled forward. "Who turned this up so high?" I said. It was on *fast* and I crashed into the door-casing, then backed him up the opposite way in which I'd intended for the chair to reverse and he wailed about his hurt knee. The chair had careened backward like a crab backing under a rock, but instead of stirring up a dusty stream of silt, a stream of obscenities hurled from him.
"If you can't do anything right…! Now I got a fucking whacked up knee!" he yelled.

I screeched, "You want someone else in here? Someone who is not so stupid?" The threat of hiring a nurse always quieted him. Neither of us wanted that. We were a couple and the threat always re-minded us to reprioritize. "If you'd let me shave you, I-I- wouldn't have gotten tense. And you yelled! I should turn down the speed," I said, turning down the speed with the dial on the chair-arm.

"Just get me to my reclining chair. Hurry up. I need a nap now. I just- don't have any say. In when you do things to me." His voice was labored and quieting down.
Somehow I got him careening down the hall. Zip-zip. His hand had long since stopped being able to navigate the lever. Our days of charging up the chair and traveling side by side to the stores downtown were long over. Kerry would sit on his lap operating the control and I'd walk beside them. Oh we'd chat! Me on the weed eaten bumpy sidewalks, and Howie alongside me cruising in the road. The sidewalks were too bumpy for him. Sometimes the low charge light would flicker. We'd barely make it home!
Jill's husband Tim was a good friend to Howie. Once he carried Howie into their house and sat him down onto their sofa. We sat there awhile and acted like we were any couple whiling away time. Tim gave Howie a super long straw (two or three attached) stuck into

a beer bottle and we made like all was normal except Howie's arms didn't move.

After that night, he built a ramp just for Howie's use so he could come and go in their house. Tim put magnets on the chair that were so powerful they held up Howie's chair footrest which was always falling down and startling us. Howie's chair was his *baby*.

Tim had the idea he could customize the chair so he got glow-in-the dark day-glo orange stickers for across the back and sides of the chair for our safety when we ventured out at night. We even affixed battery-operated press-on lights to the back that I turned on with a tap when it got dark. They were like two big headlights. Two white full moons trucking alongside me when we were out late walking and they had made us feel safe. I peeled them off.

"We won't be needing these anymore, I guess," I said.

It was unsafe with his head lolling so much and his comfort level on the decline. His arms and hands and speech were just too far gone. We wouldn't be going out with the chair anymore. Not long distance.

So keeping the penis was one of my jobs. I had to hold it, glancing at the comics I had taped to the wall beside the toilet, the ones Howie couldn't turn his head to appreciate. I was in charge of urine output. He said it should be "shaken," after the pee event, but I used a tissue and made a big deal out of wiping it up. I had a problem learning when the proper moment was to shake. It sputtered and sometimes spurted. It was amusing when I thought it was through and then we got leakage on the seat.

I'd tell him "I'm getting the darn thing a washer, it leaks. A washer, get it Howie? Plumbing humor," I quipped.

"Hurry up so I can sit. Down. For cripes sake," he ordered.

"Okay chuckapoop, just a minute," I said, ignoring his anger.

I aimed it and put tissues in the toilet on purpose to sink them. All the while I'm wondering how far it'll pee, and I'm imagining how little boys get to experiment, as if discovering a toy in their pants when they're little. I wonder aloud if some men never

outgrow this, thus the term *pocket pool*. He tells me to shut up
already. I realize that I'm saying it all aloud; whatever comes into
my head.
I learned to be careful because once I pulled the waistband of
his shorts down but they snapped up while it was in mid-stream, and
the poor thing bent, closing in the pants while urinating. It sprayed
up, on the walls and everywhere. Even in my eye. I laughed and
Howie did not.
I asked questions as I stood there. How can it squirt in two,
sometimes three different directions at one time? Howie was at times
bemused at my questions and answered them thoughtfully and at
other times told me gruffly to get on with it already. Go look it up on
the internet.

"Oh my God no. I don't care to see anyone's but yours, dear!" I told
him. I got on his nerves. He got on mine.
We laughed every day. Which is good because when he sat down for
good he forgot his mouth still worked. He went through an annoying,
albeit short (thankfully short) phase that went something like this.
He tried head-butting when he felt cornered. I suggested he use
words, "*Tell* me you have your arm caught, damnit! Don't use
aggression."

We had a God awful time adjusting but he learned to
use words. He didn't hurt me too much with the head-butting but
because his arms didn't obey, he felt inclined to use what did obey,
his head, even though his mouth still worked. Ouch. A blow to the
psyche.

"Now what?" I probed, seeing a distressed look around his eyes.

"You haven't. Called me chuckapoop in so long," he replied.

I picked his arms up and placed them on my shoulders and
around my neck. "I'm sorry chuckapoop," I said, and meant it.

When I pulled back from him, he was smiling.

Chapter Thirty-Four: Choking

"Is that your husband sitting across the street in the car, watching us?" The matronly lady asked.

I sniffled, "Yeah."

"Should we go over and say hello?" she asked.

We all looked his way and it seemed his head was held oddly high, his chin stuck out. He had informed me that he hadn't wanted to be there when they came. This was as far away as he could get. My father hadn't yet picked up the car and brought it to Vermont. He was watching; sitting where I put him.

I was handed an envelope. Inside: A family gave us $300.00 in memory of their mother who died of ALS. Christmas would come to the children. While the children were in school, these people had come with wrapped gifts. This woman and a man in a military uniform loaded our living room with some assistants. I cried at the sight of them, busying in and out of the house with gifts of all sizes. They'd gotten our family's name from the school and suc-ceeded in filling the lists I'd provided them with. They even wheeled in a bike for Kerry. I hugged each volunteer woodenly because they came at me with splayed arms.

Knowing we were going to see the ALS doctor started a physical reaction in me that lasted at least two weeks before the actual visit. I would be ill and unable to eat, prone to crying fits and I'd beat up on myself; rattling a list of faults off in my head. I would bite my hand near the meat of the thumb. I would pinch my skin. I was too intelligent to blame the messenger for the message.

But I sense when I am not liked.

He sat in the portable wheelchair, in the sterile exam room, *bless him!* Smiling and trying to impress upon the doctor how very little this disease had progressed.

"I feel just great," Howie said every time, smiling as large as he possibly could and attempting some body gestures, such as moving his shoulder a little or trying to flex his upper arms.

Sometimes Howie physically tired of answering questions. He would look at me so I could take over. After a U. Conn visit he often couldn't talk for the rest of the day and fell asleep during his TV shows to regain some strength. He looked at me, pleading with his eyes, as his dad Monty sat stoically in a side chair. Monty had bought a van special just to accommodate us and take us places, including to this dreaded hospital.

I wanted to recall all the important things.

I said to the doctor, "I feed Howie now, I think I said that last time. He takes his time chewing; it tires him out. I always sit near him now, right beside him, you know, in case his body tips or he needs something...But oh! This smoking, he could set himself on fire if he's not careful. I don't leave him a second now."

The doctor shuffled some papers,
looked away from me, and said,
"What a pity
you have to rearrange your whole life
just for him."

If all your organs can fall down and settle into your feet then it felt like that's what happened. My eyes widened. I looked at Howie who was awaiting his respiratory therapist. I knew he'd ignored this transaction between the doctor and me. He could never relax in there until he knew he did well on the breathing test. He was maintaining a smile and looking toward the hall. I gasped and days later appreciated the cutting impact of those words.

What had I said to provoke that response? I asked myself, while adding tear stains to my pillow, *what was it about me that brought this out in people? What had I done? Was it a misread tone? Or arrogance? Was it hard for the doc like someone like me, someone who didn't act one whit like the other spouses of patients? Someone different...*
The Data Collector doctor assessed how far Howie had declined. His weight was 123 pounds. Since he was six feet, that wasn't good. I had been remembering, on a fixed routine to supply him with two potent multivitamins, C & E, and two Celebrex, also two Rilutek. I also mixed up Creatine into water for aid in muscle building, and prune juice of course. Robitussin orally, nightly, for the mucus production. To this, I was told that I should add four cans of calorie boosting vitamin drinks. He couldn't stand the flavor of the

drinks so his aunts, Sally and Shirley, uncles and parents started bringing us the fruit flavored nutritional drinks.

We kept a supply of boiled eggs on hand, and juice and if there's anything I know how to do, its gain weight. We were not counting calories, but I tried fattening him up. I knew it was imperative he gain weight, and soon, before he lost the ability to eat. Problem was, he tired after a few bites and as a result never cleaned the food off his plate anymore.

One night, I fixed dinner for everyone but me. Mine would wait until Howie was fed. Kerry sat doing homework in front of the TV, and I shoveled baby sized spoonfuls of beans into Howie's mouth. First his face seemed to be exploding, then he gasped and hitched, and shook. I patted his back, hard. He eyes were wide, his body tipping; his mouth was agape.

He was choking.

After I managed to get a straw into his mouth so he could sip ginger ale, he regained composure and with Kerry watching, and pretending she wasn't, he said, "No more beans. Ever."

He smiled.

The bean that shot out, we never did find it. Maybe Pralphdog got it. Back when he could still walk and had tried to cook eggs for himself. He fumbled for an eternity and drew my attention with all his cussing.

"What is it?" I came running. Smashed eggs were every-where *except* for in the sizzling pan.

"If I can't even break an egg…then…" He threw down the empty carton and retreated to the cellar.

As I'd cleaned up the mess I heard a primal scream from the bowels of the house. It was like an animal dying.

He had always liked escaping to the cellar. One day I was doing laundry when he jumped from the shadows and grabbed me from behind; his hands gripping my breasts in a vise-like grip.

The growl in my ear scared me. "These are mine," he warned. "Don't forget it. When I'm gone I will know if anyone touches them. I'll be watching from the other side. They're mine." He didn't release me right away. He let it sink in and then he skulked into the shadows of the basement behind some junk.

The night after he choked on beans it was a repeat of the same. Only this time he choked on chicken.

We made not only a doctor's appointment but a hospital appointment as well. He had a feeding tube inserted into his stomach. He would gain weight now!

As for his lungs, they were spiffy, considering the emphysema. They went from only 80 to 60 percent capacity. Of course if they were at 50 in April, we were told we would go home with a machine. The disease was now destroying the muscle that controlled breathing. And swallowing. And speaking. Pooping too.

I refused in-home nursing yet again, saying to the nurse on the phone, "They told us it would always be our choice as to how we handle this disease. I've been taught to use the tube while he was in the hospital. We won't be needing anyone to come into the home except the respiratory therapist once a month to check his lungs. That really is final. It's what we both want."

She said to me, "Well, whatever, you'll be calling us back. You'll need us eventually." She hung up the phone.

The fact that my body was now always in a state of shock made it impossible to eat. I was gaunt. The data collector would ask me, "Are you losing this weight on purpose?"

"Not really," was my reply. *I'm not your patient*, I wanted to say. I set up plastic containers on the coffee table. One container had Elmo on it and this was *always* for warm soapy water. The other had Big Bird on it. A yellow character, which would symbolize the clear warm water where I would rinse the gauze after dipping it in the soapy stuff and patting around the plug that protruded from his abdomen. Yellow for fresh clear water. Red Elmo for antibacterial, never to be reversed. A pat dry and then Vaseline finished the care, after a feeding. Of course before cleansing around the site, I would dip the tube and end-caps in the soapy water and then swish them around for a good rinse.

But I wanted to be sure the skin around the tube looked right. It would ooze, and the skin was so fragile looking, like rose petals. I wasted no time, that first day after the tube was put in, to ask Kerry to ask her friend to ask his mother, a neighbor, to come and check it. The neighbor had once been in a nursing home working as an aide with the elderly and had dealt with many of these tubes that were sturdy, white and about a foot and a half long. At the end, it branched into a letter v shape, with one flip-top red end-cap on each lobster-eyed stalk. I was to discover that if they weren't dried (with the sterile gauze) after each use, they would flip open and drench Howie's stomach; wetting his shirt and skin with stomach contents. Sometimes I taped the caps down with the tape I used to hold the tube secure to his skin while he slept. He learned to emit coughs as soon as I opened the tube.

If I didn't get the syringe, filled with his nutritional drink, into the tube fast enough, he delighted in making runny formula water filled with chunky bits come bubbling out of the end to warmly run down my hand, and over my wrist onto my sleeve. At least it made him laugh. I tried to smile after the appropriate "Ew!" He had five feedings a day and he liked to "get me" with a cough at least once a day.

Chapter Thirty-Five: Checking the Tube

My neighbor Keisha lifted his shirt. "Oh yeah this looks fine to me. You cleaning with anything other than soap and water, hon?" she asked.

"Uh, I wasn't told to," I said, panicked. I waited for the terrible news that the site was infected, that I couldn't handle this on my own. We'd have to get an aide. Maybe he'd have to be hospitalized. My inept care was making him die faster!

"You can, you know," she said calmly.

"Like what?" I asked, making a point to be 'normal', to look in her eyes, but squinting. The Abnormal do not get assigned jobs like this!

She lifted the tube gently and said, "Peroxide's okay once in a while. Watch for rashes, that's all. A rash always indicates a problem. But this looks good."

"Sometimes it oozes stuff." There. I'd said it. Stuff bubbled out around the site of the tube where it entered the stomach near the navel like a bizarre umbilical, branching into a V, with red caps on the ends, the forked tongue of a macabre snake, unbending and stiff unless it was taped down between feedings and even then leaving a telltale lump under shirts which now had to be a few sizes too big for Howie to avoid being pulled or tugged.
One red cap was labeled in white, *flushing* and one was *feeding*."
The nurse in the hospital had said I could use them interchangeably.

"This here?" my neighbor asked and pointed a lovely manicured brown finger at the skin around the tube which was tinged pink and thin where it hugged the tube. I was found out. His stomach was leaking and soon a strange woman would be here by our sides fourteen hours a day to do his care. I held my breath. "Honey, this ain't nothing," she said. "This is perfectly normal. Remember, this is a hole in his stomach with a tube coming out. Gotta expect stomach juices are gonna come up every now and then. See that's why it's important to keep it clean. Put a little Vaseline. They tell you that?"

"Yeah, yeah. Yeah." I exhaled.

"And turn it every day, you do that?" Keisha asked me.

"Yes I do. They told me that after the operation," I said.

"You all set!" she said.

Keep it clean.
Turn it.
Vaseline.
I could do that.
I did that, for
the next few years,
several times a day.

Chapter Thirty-Six: Men In The House

177

The cart was full of taped on notes. My step-by-steps and lists. I attached phone numbers in plain sight on his roll-away cart and posted warning dates as to when I was to call manufacturers and order replacement tubing and filters.

Overall, the kids were happy. They were not overlooked. I stretched myself beyond breaking to give them time and discovered I was more flexible than I'd first imagined. All sorts of people tried to keep their lives as normal as possible, picking them up for trips to happy places like the animal park, beach, aquarium, seaport and the like. I rarely left the house.

At night I studied the manuals that came with the machines and made notes as to how to clean them and with what. Some filters were allowed every few months and others had to be ordered monthly. I researched the machines and masks online and tried to pick up tips. In the early stages of owning the breathing machine Howie wasn't on it fulltime. Thank goodness! I used to accidentally unplug the machine to roll it into the bedroom for the night without turning it off first. The beeping continued until I unlocked it, and turned it off correctly. After awhile I was living and breathing machines, so to speak.

I took to standing before the bathroom mirror and shaving my head. Before long it was an inch long in places and down to the skin in the back and on the sides like a skinhead. Sometimes I bit myself. The machines came alive in my nightmares swinging their hoses with the sound of that labored breathing very ominous in the otherwise quiet of the bedroom when I awoke.

In-out. Wish-woosh.

I turned out the bathroom light, put a long housecoat over the one window to block yet more light, and curled in a tight fetal position on the cheap yellowed flooring that the men had put in the remodeled bathroom. It showed every scuff and droplet of hair coloring.

Blue, red, black droplets from Jeff's various shades.

Brown with an underpinning of purple from sloppy me. I held my hands over my ears. I lay there as long as I could get away with it, before someone knocked and said they needed the toilet or that Howie needed me. Sometimes I rocked. I rarely cried anymore. Although the church sent us food on holidays, I missed the experience of going. Given my state, if I'd had the opportunity to go I wouldn't have gone. I was a pressure cooker but I was getting life done.

Men came and fashioned a side ramp, but didn't do it ac-cording to code and after much ado with bigwigs in suits using measuring tapes; the men tore apart the ramp and small deck. Then built it again. They cut a hole in the living room wall for the new ramp's door. In the other wall they made a new door too so Howie could get into the bedroom easily with his chair. In all they made a larger tub, lower sink, and rails. The special handicap door levers and bath rails were a waste of time. His hands could not use them.

They did afford me something to lean on in the bathroom and the rails did act as a buffer in case he swayed while on the toilet. For months we stuck to the strict TV schedule of westerns, mysteries and home improvement shows, while people swarmed our house with saws and tools and whizzed up lots of dust.

When the power was off, we hid in the bedroom with the porta-potty and tried to have quiet time until they gave us the word that either we had electricity or the long-awaited new toilet was installed. I buried my face into his T-shirt, avoiding the lump that his tube made. He smelled like vanilla, the drinks that I gave him.

I hugged him lightly as we lay on the bed and we closed our eyes. When the men went home for the day, I visited the rooms they destroyed and behold! A bucket of grout! They used it for the drywall. I submerged my hands wrist-deep and brought up luscious white plaster. Ah that I could be six inches high that I could dive in the white stuff in merriment and have the sweet cloying scent in all my pores!

I slapped the creamy stuff as thick as white frosting onto the wooden fronts of the bunk beds and smoothed it on with a trowel the men left behind. No more knotholes. *Fun!* I scooped some out of the bucket and hid some away in stashes for mosaic projects, in plastic containers. Then Howie's voice beckoned me. He was pretty upset.

"Whatsa' matter, hon'?" I stood behind his recliner so he couldn't see me.

"Let me see your hands!" he demanded. He sounded kind of healthy. Anger could do that. Good thing he had *me* around.

"Jeremy told you?" I said, suddenly timid.

I splayed my beautiful hands out for him to see and I waggled them. Dried grout fell into his lap. "Oh, sorry," I apologized. I tried brushing it off and realized I was making things worse when I saw smears across his jogging pants.

"What the hell is your problem?" he asked me.

"They left a lot in there," I grinned. "They won't miss it. Gotta wash up!" I skipped to the bathroom ignoring his lecture.

Eventually it all ended. To commemorate their time at our house with such inhospitable people, one of the men left us a parting gift: someone stuck Kerry's bicycle helmet to the front of the house with gooey black tar.

Chapter Thirty-Seven: He's 40

Howie's 40th birthday. His mother made a big party here at the house. The highlight for me, was that Starr and her daughter Kassi came and of course Jill and Tim brought their three kids. I carried Harmony around for a time, introducing her to people.

Some wondered aloud why she didn't speak. I carried her to the edge of the party, where the telephone pole met the road and we touched it together and looked up, up, up. I told her about the birds that nested up there in the transformer flap. I was disappointed later, when Starr gave me the video she'd taken at the party. There was no footage of Harmony exploring with me. This had been when I'd been the most "me." The rest of the video, although it was well done, it was a collection of the events: the unwrapping of gifts, eating of cake, etc. etc. A lot of times the camera panned and I felt nothing.

Me, as I appeared in the video, was thin, tired looking, and draggy. Aunt Maura had brought bags and bags of fresh corn on the cob from Vermont. Unless someone offered to husk and boil these, I couldn't do it. I didn't. I was afraid I'd have a
fire in the condition I was in. No one offered and a lot went to waste but I appreciated the bringing of the corn. Very much. So that was the party.

Chapter Thirty-Eight: Mimic

"You're a strong person" He told me. I shook my head like a wet dog after a bath; with tears and snot married on my cheeks.

He went on: "I'll al-ways be there. Somehow I'll come back even after I'm gone. I told you that."

I was still shaking my head but with my eyes squeezed shut. His words were odd now. His voice was similar in prosody to the evil man that narrated the old black and white horror films I liked. I couldn't change the channel.

It wasn't his fault; I knew that. The muscle in charge of his speech was no match for the disease. When he talked, the stupid gold tooth in the back shone. The one he just had to have back when he "had money to burn, so why not?" As he liked to say. I stared at the arm of his stupid light blue recliner chair; daring it silently to be something other than pastel.

He said "If anyone meant our vows, we did. This is just the sickness part we got warned about, huh? Last thing we need is some bitch in here interfering with everything. We'll do this together. No round the clock nurses. Minor hitch in the way we do things. I told you, I'm one of those guys that lives with ALS for ten years. Or more...You'll see. We just… gotta get through the next…" He couldn't get enough air for a reasonable voice.

"Hitch." I said, with a lump so big in my throat I could barely get out the word around it.

The machines surrounded us. Memorizing how to run them, by rote was like being in school and acing tests. The type of learning that "gets you by" has a downside. It was a refresher course, a reminding, a relearning every time I looked at those contraptions. Amy, Jeff's girlfriend, was a break in this routine.

She drove seven hours from her college dorm to stay the weekend with us. Again. She said she liked my mosaic creation. I'd caught hell from Howie when I plastered stones and various glass and sand all over the entertainment unit. It made me happy. It made him spout obscenities. Maybe it wasn't very nice of me to play with grout and broken pieces in front of a paralyzed man who couldn't do anything about the situation; like maybe chuck my stuff out the window if he felt he didn't like it.

I enjoyed my projects, and I needed the visual saturation they afforded me. Anyway, I compromised by tolerating a massive Beanie Baby collection of Howie's and his baseball guy bobblehead. Both quite silly.

Provocation aside, I blamed his disease; and his tirades were stressful for all involved. I got a sedative from the doctor and gave it to him as needed. Oh, it wasn't like I was some mad scientist whipping secret cocktail concoctions up in my kitchen on the sly and then secreting them through his feeding tube to calm his nerves.

This won't hurt a bit cackle cackle... but I did threaten him: "If you keep up like this, you are going to take a happy pill!"

He didn't like the pills because they made him sleepy and if he was asleep he couldn't keep an eye on my actions and that was his favorite past-time.

He decided he needed to see the checkbook daily. I had never been allowed to carry or really touch the checkbook in all the years we'd been out on our own. The fact that I had to carry it around and do all the figuring, enraged him, both because he was losing control of so many things in his life and because he didn't trust I could do a good job. I'm sure he was right. But he had never let me try.

Amy came into our lives when Howie was newly diagnosed. Like the arrival of a new mole in an otherwise inconspicuous area of the body where it had not been before, Amy turned up, startling in her candor; but strangely alluring as if she was somehow exactly in the right place.

"Where do you go when you disappear with Amy? Where do you go; really?" he accused one day.

I said, "Yesterday you say I was down in the basement with the furnace guy for too long. Today I was at the bank too long."

I stepped behind his chair so he couldn't see me.

His face was slack, his color pale. He'd gained a tremendous amount of weight (a good thing) and we had a good routine going as far as his healthcare. I didn't know what he needed to be reassured that I wasn't the harlot he thought I was. *My T-shirt was too tight.* My jeans, which were frayed and battered, were decidedly *too provocative.* My shirts rode up scandalously (exposing my gorgeous, white as paper- slack stomach). He told me to turn in a circle so he could critique me before I left with Amy.

Who knew? We two derelicts, Amy and me, we could have a brothel on the side, a list of devious johns with names like Phat Joe and Sneaky Pete and a Swiss bank account apiece.

I was wearing my bellbottom jeans that dusted the ground. I'd previously spattered dabs of teal paint on them and so I'd painted yellow flower petals around each paint splatter to create something purposeful instead of a mistake.

That would attract all the hot guys for sure!

The argument started about one thing and turned into lots of other things. "Let me see that checkbook now, before you leave! You're not to spend… more than ten. Dollars, got it?" he warned me.

"You know what, I don't want to show you it, on principle," I said. Then I told Amy to wait in the car. She opened the door to the hall entrance and made a hasty retreat like a kid relieved to leave the principal's office. "Do you remember, Howie," I began, kneeling in front of his chair with the checkbook register in my hand. "When we first moved into the little pink house in Woodbridge? The bank statement came. The very first one? I had my calculator, and coffee, and pen all ready to balance the checkbook. You whipped the statement and checkbook out of my hands and said, 'I'll be handling all this from now on,'" I told him in a voice that mimicked his voice. The way it used to be when he was a tan muscled roofer. I was even seeing inside his wild eyes. I was daring to do that. The ceiling beam did not crash on my head for doing so.

"How many times do you have to bring that up?" he said in his weak voice.

"Point is, I never saw the checkbook again in over twenty years till now. I am only handling it because I have to. You never gave me a chance. "One day," tears sprang to my eyes as I continued, "I may have to do all that without your guidance."

"I'll never trust you," he said, honing in on my eye contact and meeting it with painful ice picks. His grimace was hurting my heart. People's faces jumbled up sometimes. It happened to my vision at times, like when I watched people sleep; their features spun round or moved places. But this was worse. It was one thing to understand that this was desperation/rage and some other unnamed "emotion" but it was another thing entirely to accept this change in him. In us. I stood up. I would retreat. Because I could.

"Are you comfortable, Howie? Jeremy!" I called for my middle son and he came quickly. I told him to change TV channels for his father, be mindful of drool and to wipe it and to sit with him until I returned and that I wouldn't be long.

"Go to. Hell. You and your little friend!" Howie yelled, in his strained, pained new voice.

I winced and addressed him from behind his chair. "Maybe I'm already there."

I would need to do pretending but I was upset. I would need to transform into a public face at the pharmacy; blend in and not show this hurt. I'd have to paint the chameleon when I got in there.

"You and me both," he said.

"I meant it, when I said if you think you should see someone, if you're depressed," I said.

"Just keep drugging me. I don't need no shrink!" was his reply.

When Amy and I got stuck in traffic, and it seemed we inevitably did, or the line was long at the bank; and it often was, my thoughts were silver pin-balls ricocheting in my head and devising ways to rack up point and thus dissolve his rants when I arrived home. Stress would not prolong his life. I would diffuse him with humor and health care. With massage, hot cloths, hand creams, toenail clipping, head-scratching, (he liked his eczema scabs plucked!) shaving (his beard got so itchy and flaky!) and maybe his happy pill as a last resort. Being with this nineteen year old, Amy was a respite.

I could not talk fluently with her but if she brought up school projects and assignments I was eager to hear about them. Like the essay she wrote, inspired by Oliver Sacks and also by Howie: She called it "The Man Who Typed With His Teeth."

And I could 'discuss' things via our long distance communication: our long e-mails when she was at her dorm. At the weekends she returned to us.

Amy wrote to me detailing a project she had to complete. She needed to use a person in her photography assignment. *Would I be her model?*

I read the e-mail and PPBLFTT! I made a noise aloud in the room like a balloon letting out air. I stared at the screen until my eyes blurred. Was it possible? This would be a challenge.

Time to consult my handy dandy manual again. It was one of my favorites: The Big Book of Facial Expressions. I studied the sketches of the muscles that are involved while assuming various "expressions" and "moods." I locked the bathroom and tried them in the mirror: anger, delight, surprise, happiness, indifference. Amy arrived on the Friday and set to work making a darkroom in one of our closets. She knew how to develop her own pictures and that was part of her grade. She drove me to a package store to purchase beer. I was mind-mapping through the aisles; taking pointy right angle turns. It was the first time I'd ever been in a place like that and bought alcohol all by myself. When I got home, I got lectured for something altogether new. All I'd ever got into trouble for previously was for splurging on books, magazines, hair color, and the occasional shirts and barrettes. When the armchair detective saw me go by him with that purchase, he really sounded off. I offered to put some beer in his stomach tube. I reminded him that his doctor had a patient who took a shot of wine in *his* tube on a daily basis, but he declined.

Our bedroom was the smallest in the house and could accept a black drop cloth behind the bed, affixed up high behind me with nails. There was just enough room in there for her special lighting.

It got so hot on my skin. She adjusted the white-hot spotlight to fall on certain aspects of me. This served to make me look annoyed. I knew that because I'd just studied my handy dandy manual and I was pretty sure that wasn't the look she wanted. But *annoyed* was what it felt like I was projecting, even after beer.

Amy told me that all her friends were working on assignments using nudes. *Would I care to do that?* We would have to postpone the shoot for a week while I considered that. Howie's face lit with a mischievous smile when I told him. I reminded him that Amy's teacher and classmates would see the finished photos but he didn't care about that. As long as he could store the nude shots on his tablet pc for personal viewing! He looked at me and wiggled his eyebrows up and down. I gave him a look that my handy dandy manual would define as "disdain."

All that week I wrote intense e-mails to Amy with "no-nudity" excuses. I told her I'd never undressed in front of Howie. It was the truth.

When we'd first started a physical relationship so many years ago, he'd taken me by the shoulders and shaken me. "Do you always have to be such a rag doll?!" he'd said. "Can't you show a little emotion?"

So I started studying people in soap operas and copied them. That seemed to suffice. But as far as the undressing, over the years I'd become as clever as the sitcom bosses on TV who developed props to hide the pregnant actress's blooming belly. I found tons of things to get undressed behind. My creativity knew no bounds! Oh and I could always turn off the light. Photography was interesting. I liked Amy's series of black and white shots of my daughter in the yard, painting a flag on a rock or just lying in the grass. She had an eye for composition. But the pictures she'd taken of me over the summer, I hated. I looked... *gruff.* That didn't match how I "felt." There I was in the pictures she'd previously taken of me in my white shirt and denim skirt, and I wanted to rip up the photos.

When she arrived the following weekend I gave her my decision. I would not do any nudity, but I would dress in something that would show the body's form, if that would be acceptable. When Howie found out that I may actually be shopping for something "sexy," he told me to take the checkbook and have fun shopping!

The sex place had themes. Animals. Feathers. That sort of thing. I picked out a short leather skirt and vest with matching whip in a very

petite size that I thought would complement Amy's mother's short red hair and small frame. I thought Amy should treat her to something she wouldn't ordinarily buy for herself. Amy was certain her mother would not wear it even when I suggested she only wear it in private; the way I was going to wear my new catsuit.
But no, Amy would not buy the outfit for her mother. My catsuit had nothing to do with cats. I had to go to several adult shops to find my tall size. It was a black lace head to toe stocking.
Before we left with my purchase, I wanted to look around. I liked reading the boxes with the outrageous puns for sexual innuendo but that got redundant real fast.
The place was colorful but I didn't find it titillating. "Amy, why would someone need that device?" I pointed to a weird object and Amy seemed to understand what it was. She explained things to me in concrete terms, so I would understand.
I laughed behind my hand. I made moon eyes at images of the human anatomy I didn't know I had.
At least I had never seen it from that angle. I was glad to leave. At home I realized the one piece "suit" was not exactly designed for tall people. I ran into the living room long enough for Howie to glimpse me, and then I hid back in my room. I sat slouched on the bed as Amy set up equipment; then I put on a robe and went to the bathroom with two cans of beer. I began practicing smiles in the mirror but I felt wrong. The stretchy lace was see-through. I figured I could get past that, but it was my face. I put out hands; feeling the air with my palms.
Would I always have an invisible box around me, preventing me from being fluid?
I asked my self aloud: *"It's always up isn't it? The mime's invisible box?"*
Then I watched as my mouth smiled. It seemed to have an idea. I took some white paint leftover from Halloween, the kind you make a clown's face with. It was on the topmost shelf beside the bathroom mirror. Amy called to me and I told her to give me ten minutes. When I stepped out of the bathroom, I was a mime.
Creamy red rouge made circles on the apples of my cheeks. With black liner I had made diamonds around my eyes. I topped off the look with a black beret Amy had bought for props.

"What the hell?" I heard Howie say as I scurried by his recliner in mime face and robe; and closed myself into the little bed-room.

The make-up was reapplied every weekend and we 'worked together' until she had at least a hundred shots. What great fun! I never felt more like me than when I was in full mime attire.
Art meets self.
One weekend Howie allowed us to go shopping to buy me suspenders and a striped shirt. I leaned against a pretend wall. I put up my hands and felt the invisible box. I liked those pictures of me clothed in a real mime's attire! Those pictures were not for her school. They were for fun.
After the photo shoots; no pressure to talk. Mimes don't do that, I simply stood alongside Howie-shaving him in full mime, suspenders and all.
Life interrupts art.
Sometimes my kids' friends Keith, Bill, Devin or Kevin were around. I might have to take a break and go do some laundry or fix them a snack. Funny thing is when I walked by the kids and their friends they never giggled behind their hands,
not even when I walked away. They didn't make fun of me behind my back. They accepted me *as is*. They didn't seem to raise an eye when I sometimes made an appearance to run to the bathroom during a shoot and they happened to catch sight of my mimed up face.
Ours was always a house of laughter and of unusual conversations. So why would this be *a novelty?* It wasn't.
Amy showed me how to load the photos from a CD to Howie's tablet pc. He scanned from photo to photo using his foot-mouse and the laser dot on his head. His face softened when he viewed the mime photos with his special computer.
I have favorite mime pictures. I like the profile mime. Where my back shows and I'm wearing the furry black hat. It makes me happy like I could be in the Benny and *Joon* movie. I also like the one where Amy forgot to edit out the pee jug. The wall behind me is supposed to be tan but it vibrates in blues and greens which are inside the tan. I am hugging my knees and my toes are curled because of course this whole process makes me tense and my body is not gonna let that tension get out; not even through my toes.
Amy's teacher would tell her that the oriental comforter in the photo was too "busy" but I disagreed. I like moving my eyes

around that picture. The earth-tones are pleasing. In fact I say there are never enough patterns and nothing is ever too "tacky." Amy said I developed a fan-base of students; male and female, curious about the model in the pictures.

Amy began studying models online part way through our sessions. Models apparently had elastic bands for limbs and I did not. Amy's idea was to get me to copy the positions she especially liked. Sometimes it worked and sometimes my legs got stuck and I toppled over and asked to try a different position. I was generally open to anything.

I'd see one of her ideas and say, "Ok I'll try!" and I would spend the next half hour arching my back, pulling up one knee, stretching out one long lacy leg, lifting up one arm, holding my head to the right, etc. etc. until I would say, "This is not working! Let's try something else…" or "Hurry and take the photo before I strain something!"

I became enamored of Marcel Marceau. I collected a huge cache of his stills. Amy and I set up a shot of me doing Marcel's rope thing (but not very well). The idea is that you're putting your hands in front of your face, with your wrists making as if you're holding a pipe, or rope. I didn't have the time to devote to study actual pantomime but I had a new perseveration. I read everything I could get my hands on about miming.

I watched TV in mime make-up.

I cooked in mime.

I had a new dream for the first time since I was a little girl and had wanted to be a ballerina.

I lay in bed entertaining thoughts of mentoring with someone who would teach me to mime. Mimes either annoyed or amused. I could relate to that.

One calm night, after my make-up was scrubbed away, I told Howie of my new fixation as the blue light from the TV flick-ered over the walls.

A calm smile made his face beautiful. He said, "You probably really will do those things one day."

Howie and I shared long talks of dreams, of mine and his. I told him
I remembered meeting a woman, a friend of his mother's at one of his
family get-togethers. It was one of the spare few we attended since
we usually declined invites. The woman had heard that I'd published
stories a few times. I told her I was writing a book of memoirs.

She told me, "Alright! You go girl. Go after your dream!"

Lying in bed, in the dark, I told Howie how, firstly her slang
had made me feel funny, but secondly I had wanted to say to the lady
that writing was no dream! Writing was necessary and if I didn't do it
then words would dribble out my mouth as I slept.
I told Howie how I'd wanted to tell that lady that writing was
ingrained. Writing really wasn't a dream for me. But being a
ballerina, now that was a dream! I told him all that. Now, I smiled
into Howie's twitching chest, I had a new dream. I was smart and I
knew a lot of dreams were attainable. Some were not attainable.
I was glad for lucid moments late at night after his computer
was put away and the lights were off. I could give myself a lame
neck by sitting alongside him in his power chair and putting my head
on his shoulder until he said he was cramped. And we would have
talks. I asked him what *his* dreams were. I was afraid to hear the
answer.
He said that he wanted to see his kids grow up, that's all. I told
him all about Stephen Hawking; the guy who lived so long with
ALS. He said he was glad I read science magazines. "I think you
really will be the guy who lives ten years…or more." I said, staring
at the entertainment center where I had smeared one whole narrow
section with grout and inlaid stones and colored squares of glass.
To fill in around the stones and glass, I had pressed in sand. Not
ANY sand. Sand from under the disability ramp.

Years later, when the entertainment center got unstable and wobbly, I
would bust it up, fine mosaic'ed front and all, and I would cart it
piece by piece to the curb for bulk rubbish pick-up. "Bye to you my
past. Bye disability sand," I would say.
But that was *years* away.

Every night I found peace in my artwork. I would blur out the TV
glare, the sound of the machines, his raspy breathing, and I would

lose my self in the mosaics outlined in sand, and held in place with pilfered grout.

Chapter Thirty-Nine: The Mime's Box

The elusive mime's box, with its allegories and invisible symbolism, is ever-present, having sustained me through all my days like Lynda Carter's invisible car. People were dropping in like parachutes and I faced them from the invisible box. Incoming!

In stolen downtime between feedings, as Howie napped, I closed my eyes and imagined that I was carefree. My head swam with the audible breathing sounds of the machines, and I mentally kept tabs on future appointments. It was life and death.

The methodical structure of the imposed routines, more every month, that involved Howie's care, took shape and become daily unvarying, rote, modes of action. The sudden drop-ins of the people, the interference of the phone and the doctor's visits all drew from me emotional strength I didn't possess. I couldn't even offer refreshments to visitors. I talked less than ever.

The ability to use an appropriate conversational tone with the respiratory therapists eluded me. What *was* an acceptable tone? I was clunky, monotone, not liquid. There were glitches. I couldn't change from setting to setting like the marvelous chameleon. I had to paint the chameleon each time. That's labor intensive.

Under the kitchen sink, next to the old Crockpot that catches leaks, is a creased tube of partially used wood putty. It's the color of flesh and dries to a hard knocking finish. I lay on the couch, alone for stolen moments, and I have an idea that makes me smile.

I think that I'll putty over my nostrils. *Yeah and maybe I'll putty over my eyes too,* I imagine. I dream while I can, as I am aware that when he awakens, he'll need the toilet or an adjustment, or a scratch to his stubbly face, or the request of a shave or nose-picking, which is an art I've gotten down to a science. I can pull out big long hawkers and then he can

breathe easier. We must nose-pick daily.

I could smear smooth flesh colored wood putty over my features. The putty would blend right in and if it didn't I would dab in some blush from my infrequently used make-up bag.

Long ago I learned to apply cosmetics so as to *go with the herd* and *blend with the mainstream* better. It was one avenue of conformity I had afforded my self and as of late my complexion was gaunt, my cheekbones prominent, my eyes big and staring with circles below them, my short hair shaven and unkempt.

Once fairly pretty, with long natural curls, I was called "sir" at the pharmacy. That did not even matter.

I'd sand the creamy putty smooth when it dried. Not unlike a wood surface, I would knock on it, right where my eyes were puttied over. Then I'd paint new eyes where my eyes once were, right over the smooth flat Pinocchio face. *But no,* I thought, I couldn't do that because once I puttied over my features, how would I actually see to paint new eyes?

My putty fantasy relaxed me and so did a visit to a special friend. Sometimes Howie said, "I'm so tired. Why don't you go visit Jill? Just put the catheter on me. I'll say something on the monitor if I really need you." I carried a baby monitor to Jill's house but that would have to cease soon. He was getting worse. We both knew it.

Jill had a secluded yard where I liked to sit, under the shade of a massive oak tree. I could hold her new baby and the newest litter of kittens if I could catch one. I usually could. But the yard on the corner posed problems.

I had to pass loud 20-somethings who stood in various postures, fingering cigarettes and boisterously vibrating to rap music in their falling-down oversized clothes.

One day I loaded my pocket with the monitor and headed out for Jill's fenced-in yard. People that had stayed inside all winter, were now drunk with the enticing warmth of the sun on their skin. Kids pedaled bicycles, men washed cars, and the boys on the corner leaned against cars and stared at me. I did not increase the pace of my stride nor did I slow it. The edge of the road was close to their driveway. I would not travel to the other side of the road just to avoid them.

I heard one hoodlum say, "I bet if you got, like right up to two inches to her face and like, *screamed* in her face she still wouldn't, like look you in the eye."

I suspected he was spot-on right about that.

Chapter Forty: Tanager On A Mango

Oliver Sacks' *Oaxaca Journal*. It was about ferns. I wasn't let down, not in the least. I would read, read and read when I could bide time. What interesting trivia Oliver went on about! For instance he crushed morning glory seeds, (just the blue variety) into a fine black powder when he was a lad and mixed it with ice cream, as it has properties similar to LSD and he had hellish trips, he says.

Here's the lyrical line that sung in my head when I needed the kiss and hug of words the most: It is lyrical and should be in a poem. He mentions it in a simple sentence, on his ride into Oaxaca to study ferns.

Oliver has a colleague who can label all the bird species...He doesn't just say he sees "a bird on a fruit," he rather sees "a tanager on a mango." I sang that phrase all week and it made me glad. "The gladdest thing under the sun!" to quote Browning.

Coming down from the socialities of the week, unable to answer the doorbell or telephone, or to talk with coherence or walk to the corner deli for milk, I set down the book and tried to imagine a *tanager on a mango.*

Unfortunately I do not know what color a tanager is and I couldn't imagine it. The computer with its amazing internet capabilities sat across the room on the antique desk. But the words were bell pretty and if I looked up the color of the bird the mystery would be gone. No way I was googling it.

I closed my eyes to the sound of Howie lecturing me sternly about the myriad array of phone calls I owed to various suppliers for reorders and on and on. I couldn't ignore life, he said. But he'd never understand what it was to have to take a reprise from worldly disturbances. It was necessary. I smiled, those things would get done in my time. For now I would have to imagine those musical words and wish them into an image to sustain my intellectual hold on all the slipping, changing nonsense.

Chapter Forty-One: Who Brings The Fat Man Doughnuts?

Somehow I had let a smoker into my life. All those years with him and I had avoided touching his cigarettes and now this, I was an accessory to his smoking.
keck: to retch violently
katzenjammer: a hangover
vermivorous: a wormeater

It's true, I saw smoking as a vermivorous type activity. Watch-ing a terminally disabled man partake in this habit made me keck inside. Burning filters were left to smolder in the ashtrays; he did not have the dexterity to crush them out and I could not put them out because the mere thought gave me a sickening katzenjammer sensation.

Every morning I woke and lit a candle so he could bow his head down and light the cigarette that dangled from his trembling lips. They were fanned out in the despicable white funnel in the jar and his hands never had to handle them anymore. I gave in to using the lighter but matches stunk and were out of the question.

I watched him bend forward precariously to tongue up a cigarette from the funnel. Kerry refilled it for him, removing the cellophane from packs, which I refused to do, and lining the funnel for the tonguing. I would latch Howie's seatbelt despite his grumbling protests because he leaned forward so much I feared he'd smash face first onto the desk just on account of lighting his cigarettes.

It was going on indefinitely and I told him this. His inability to try to stop smoking now that he could not even hold them in his hands reminded me of the story of the 800 pound man and I told him this too. I told him loudly, tinged with anger, as he rolled the cigarette between his teeth, Clint Eastwood style. He would smoke the whole thing this way; ashes amassing on the tip and then falling onto his clothing.

"Who brings the fat man doughnuts?" I screeched. When he got down to the filter he would lean forward and let it fall onto the ashtray.

"What, what...are you nuts?" He said between awkward ex-hales of acrid smoke.

"Howie, your smoking reminds me of the man who is so big he

cannot go out and buy his own food anymore. He can't leave his house! His body is so big, he's 800 pounds and he can't fit through the door frame anymore!" I yelled, near hysterics.

"This has to do with *me* somehow? I don't know the guy," he laughed. Then choked.

"You can't buy your own cigarettes anymore." I cringed on the word, cigarettes, still didn't like to say the word.

He had nerve to beg me to open packages of them and at times I *did the deed*. I opened them. I lined them in his little dispenser for him to tongue. Then cried while washing my self with the intensity of a woman scrubbing hard egg off a fry pan with a Brillo.

"You can't buy them anymore but you have everyone buying them for you! They all enable you. I understand them wanting you happy but…enough's enough! Only Jeremy finally gave up helping you in any way with smoking. By not opening them, or lighting candles, that sort of thing." I said this to him quickly, letting out the pent-up rage that was corked so tightly.

"I don't get the doughnut thing," he said casually, dropping the burning cigarette, half-smoked into an ashtray where I know it would smolder, releasing its fumes into the room because I could not bear to snuff it out. This fuels my anger. Burning filters are horrendous.
I once tried to wash an ashtray by wearing long gloves and swishing a sponge with soap around on it in the toilet. But the tears and retching were too much to bear. I never washed one again in twenty something years.

"HOWIE!!! Who brings the fat man doughnuts when he's 800 pounds? Who enables him at that point?" I go on, "You would think he'd begin to lose weight when he is in that room and cannot leave it, but no! And one would think his loved ones would stop bringing him the fattening stuff, but no...someone's still bringing him the goods. They cannot stand to see him complain, or see him sad, is that it? Everyone enables you. You are paralyzed and yet people are metaphorically bringing you the doughnuts. *When*, I say? When do you stop it once and for all?" I look at his stubborn face, shaking from my outburst.

"They love the fat guy. Wanna see him happy. Big deal. Maybe I'll get the smoker's robot..." he grinned.

"AAAAARRRRRRGHHHH!!!" I shout, banging my fists around in the air.
They actually offer, in a disabilities magazine, a device by which the paralyzed smoker can still smoke by attaching a tube to a lit cigarette which sits in the ashtray. The other end of the tube must be placed by the helpful caregiver into the disabled smoker's mouth. They need not move at all, save to inhale. Paralyzed though they be, they need only to be capable of inhaling, and with some assistance (enabling) from loved ones, they can still enjoy smoking, thanks to the keen smokers' robot!
I picked up the disabilities magazine and ripped it in half.
He laughed.

Chapter Forty-Two: Tablet PC

It had a contraption on it for his forehead with a laser dot and a foot mouse he could operate. We took out the tablet PC and he stated his wishes by painstakingly typing and saving each wish. Daily we worked on this stuff. After a few months, I started thinking of it as the porn computer. But I am getting ahead of myself.

One day he wanted to play a message for his parents. Monty and Sue arrived as they did at some point each weekend to watch a car race with him on TV. I set up the PC and he clicked on various recordings which boomed into the room in that robotic PC voice. He had me turn down the volume. They started sniffling.
The robot voice told them: "I waaant to be cremay-ted. I waant my ash-ess scattered in all our fay-vo-rite fishing spots. I do not want life sayving meas-zures. No tray-che-oto-meee tube."

Howie's mother went outside to smoke. Monty was crying and trying to appear as if he wasn't. I busied myself with unhooking the PC and thus ending the robot speech and then set up Howie so he was comfortable. I hoisted him up in the chair from under the armpits and

196

put pillows around his body. His arm had to rest on the chair arm with the fingers in such a way that they didn't feel too encroached. I wedged a towel around his neck so his head would not loll and wiped his moist mouth. I pulled the soft fleece blanket around his waist and laid it gently around the tube area. I couldn't offer them drinks. Jeremy came into the room at the sound of the machine talking. Ever the dutiful son, he fixed them coffee. He knew just how they liked it. Black for his grandfather. Light with two tea-spoons sugar for his grandmother. I knew too but could rarely ask them if they wanted any. I had trouble enough knowing and expressing my own wants.

After his parents would leave, his face fell. I knew it was work to maintain expression. Those muscles, which I'd studied in my Big Book of Expressions, were now affected by the disease.

It intrigued me, and I was interested in the way he worked to have a pleasant face on for visitors. I wondered if I'd have bothered. For his Aunt Sally, his parents, ex co-worker Danny, Starr, Uncle Bob or Uncle Bill. Even Priscilla, his former gutter customer, had come to eat a sandwich and watch some sports with him. And he'd put on that pleasant face.

When they left he relaxed his whole face. Then it became the face I knew from brochures and online, a slack non-expressive face. He was chock filled with emotions, and like myself he just couldn't express it. That didn't mean the emotions weren't there. While he had visits he thought it important that others saw him happy. I truly believe he was. Sometimes he watched people fishing on the TV while I read a book or prepared dinner. We had always shared fishing. Sitting on the bank at 6:00 a.m. watching beavers plop into the water from the opposite embankment, and travel upstream doing beaver things. We saw deer, appearing suddenly in twig-breaking sprints, four and five at a time, white tails bobbing out of sight into the

forest. We listened to owls hooting, laid out on the bank and watched mist rise off the water.

It was something I'd shared with my father too, years ago. We had tried to fish when he got weak but he had fallen in, and young Jeremy had jumped in and pulled his father out of the stream. Both of them limped upstream toward me and the car, bleeding. We all agreed we would not fish anymore. After all, Jer was too sensitive for that sort of activity anyway.

Chapter Forty-Three: Dreams?

I told Howie of my ballerina dream. He said he'd wanted to give up smoking.

We both smiled because he achieved that goal. One day he just stopped and never smoked again. I blamed a lot of his irritability on that too. He said one day I could be a ballerina because I was talented and could do anything. I knew he was wrong about that. I looked around at the floor, our hardwood floors, dusty, paint stained. Cat hairs all over the furniture. I kept the main things in check: the laundry, well-balanced meals and helping the kids with homework. But I often let the dishes wait and then washed them when we ran out of clean ones.

Trying to forever memorize his scent, which was both Keri lotion and vanilla, I cuddled into his shoulder and asked him if he was certain that he didn't want lifesaving measures when it came down to his final moments. He said to mute the game on the TV and I did.

"I saw that disabled comatose woman on TV. Look at me when I'm saying this."

I did.

"I don't want people having some legal tug-of-war over what to do to me if I can't talk," he said.

My face was real close and although I'd known him for so long, I was uncomfortable to be up in his face like that. I could smell his breath and I noted I needed to brush his teeth.

"You are a very strong person," he told me.

"I'm not," I said and looked away.

"I know you are. And if it ever gets down to where everything's paralyzed and I can't do anything but move my eyes and blink and think, with no way to communicate, I want to go. No ventilator, no trach-tube. That's not a life. That's my choice."

I relaxed into his shoulder. I would rather stare at the mosaic'ed creation on the entertainment center while my eyes blurred with tears that I thought were long dried up.

"I mean it," he said. "We're calling my aunt. She's a notary public. We have to get it in writing."

"Yeah. Yeah. That's the best way. Are you sure though? I mean even if you can only blink and you can't do anything else, at least with the tracheotomy tube cut in your neck, even though its round-the-clock care, to suction it and everything, it might, buy you time. Till there's a cure. Time to watch the kids grow up" I said through the lump in my throat.

"I'll watch 'em from the other side," he said softly.

I searched his face then to be sure somehow, to get a clue he meant it.

This time he was smiling *for me*.

Chapter Forty-Four: Another Kind of Movies

He told me the cat-suit was not enough. For weeks as I poured cans of formula through his tube slowly; barely awake; or as I watered the plant or fed the animals, he persisted. I told him that just because he was a dying man didn't mean I had to comply with every wish. He grinned and said if I loved him I'd pose naked for a dying man.

So what else is new? I caved in. Sort of. Who cared if our toilet showed as a backdrop? Only Howie would see these. Besides, Amy had fancy tools for editing out the background in pictures.
Then the light bulb above my head gave me an idea; as if on cue. I flung on my housecoat, zipped through the living room and zagged into the kitchen where I grabbed a small parcel from the cabinet and

made for the bathroom again; calling to Amy as I ran by: "I'll just be a few more minutes!"

The stark lighting in our little bathroom would really sparkle off my Saran-skirt. I opened a second can of beer, depositing the first empty in the toilet-side waste can. I sure was white as school paste. Wasn't the socially accepted color for legs, but I was smart for avoiding the sun and I liked 'em fine. Still, part of me hated my legs and it was this part of me that I was covering up with a see through plastic-wrap skirt. I wrapped and wrapped until I wore the plastic wrap so tightly over my hips and upper thighs I could barely see through. Fine fine mamma jamma!

One more slug of beer. I set the can down. Okay, a second swig.

"Come in!" I called. She was taken aback by me; fiddling with her expensive camera and trying to avoid looking at me.

I stood in front of the toilet and told her to hurry up and get ready already. "What are you wearing?" she asked.

"It's Saran wrap, see?!" I told her and I pointed to the oblong box on the floor with the food wrap roll in it, near the tub.

"Yeah I thought so. I uh, thought he wanted *nude?*" she said, avoiding looking at me.

"Oh well he should be lucky to get this. No mime make-up, just me," I said and I whipped off the robe; and stood there sha-king, naked from the waist up. From my excellent peripheral vision I saw her fidgeting with the controls on her camera, putting it up to her eyes to focus me in the shot, and then putting the camera back down and staring at it as if she'd forgotten how to use it. Her backside bumped into the towel rod. I hugged myself under my breasts and stood so she could get my profile in the shot.

When I moved I could hear the plastic wrap crinkle. The bathroom sure was a bright place at ten o' clock at night on a Saturday.

"Will you hurry!?" I yelled, trembling.

She turned her eyes away from me, putting the camera down

again. Then she turned to face the clothes hanging on hooks on the back of the closed bathroom door. "No. I'm sorry. I won't do it," she announced to my surprise.

He would be so angry with me! "Just do it!" I yelled but she persisted, stammering.

"I'll explain it to him...that, that you really wanted to and you were all ready but it was me. I'll tell him the truth that I was the one who backed out," she said and she left the room like a mouse with slippers on, leaving me to my self.
I put on the housecoat, collapsed and sobbed, hugging my plastic thighs. How I had a desire to please!
Sure was hard unwrapping myself.

From the other side of the bathroom door she spoke to me. "It's not art when you're uncomfortable. It's not right. I won't exploit you. It feels wrong. I'm not about that."
Howie lectured me a long time that night and later on in bed, and then he told me he had an idea. I was sent back to the adult stores for outrageous things. I lay beside him, rolling my eyes and sighed. At first he was happy with still shots of various parts of my naked body. He said I may be more at ease without Amy watching and that he still thought it was bullshit that she wouldn't do the shot when I'd been ready.

"Not explicit enough," he'd say and then send me back in with the digital camera, when the kids were at school.

He wanted movies.
We had long, heated, riled up discussions. I took to wearing looser clothing. I stopped wearing make-up altogether except when I did the movies.
When Amy arrived on weekends, he gleefully sent her and I out to the adult store, with the checkbook. I countered that I was reduced to being a collection of body parts and not a real whole person at all. I tried to show him a drawing I was work-ing on. I read him my poems.

"Well? You barely look or listen. You have a glazed over look.

You either want sex or you think up new ways to view me! Have you nothing to say if I ask you if I should use green or orange in a drawing?" I shouted at him.

"Everything you do is great honey. You're beautiful and tal-ented," was what he said.
I didn't need feedback but it was impossible to talk about anything other than sex! He was a man possessed. I told him so. He told Kerry she was his little squirt but he wasn't even looking at the children anymore.

"Someday I'll never have sex again. I want everything while I can," he said to me.

I tried to feed his insatiable ideas and delivered him the mo-vies, several cassettes worth.

Jeremy wondered about his father. "Why's Dad locked in the bedroom?"

I hated fibbing. "He's making a video, trying to talk on the camcorder." He was actually viewing the tapes.

With ALS, everything fades except the sexuality and the brain. Those two things stay sharply intact. Pretty cruel thing to have happen to a guy.
By that time, few people could understand anything he said. He was taking labored breaths between words and he stammered, barely able to form one recognizable word in a sentence. Because the kids and I and Amy spent the most time with him, we could interpret what he was saying 90% of the time and repeat everything to the doctors or to his company.
People brought him bobble-heads of his beloved Red Sox team players and T-shirts celebrating their victory. How he'd whooped in his recliner when they won the big game, the whole "Series."
But his breathing was so incapacitated; it could no longer be measured at U Conn. Hospital. Amy's mother recommended a doctor who made house calls. At last we stopped our frequent trips to the dreaded hospital! No more Data Collector! Howie was more than ever homebound. He spent his days 'inside his head' watching *The*

Warriors movie on DVD over and over again, night after night. The Coney Wheel at the end signaled time for bed.

It was one of the first movies we had seen together at a drive-in in the late seventies. He watched the Leprechaun movies and laughed, violent as they were. He adored his westerns with their suave heroes, predictable outcomes, and gritty ingénues. We watched so many Bonanza reruns that I caught my best parakeet Kramden whistling the Bonanza tune!
Of course there was one Bonanza episode that gave us both the chills. A guy in a cowboy hat strumming a guitar was singing a sad tune that went like this:

"Good ol' Howard's dead and gone!" He repeated the chorus over and over!

Howie said at last, "Change the channel!"

When they recommend Hospice you know you've got five or six months to live. Said no thanks.
The mask was constantly over his nose now, strapped around his head with Velcro straps. We all became accustomed to hearing the in-out-wish-woosh. It pushed air into his lungs for him. When the room was quiet at night, the sound competed with the tinnitus in my bad ear. I now had a duplicate back-up machine on standby in case the power went out. I would leave that one in the bathroom and when he had to go in there, I would race him in and quickly hook him to the second machine; but he didn't relish the breathless trip on the way to the toilet. It was decided he would never use the bathroom again. I resorted to bedpans and then diapers.
He made me promise not to tell anyone about the adult diapers but I'd always been honest with his mother who sometimes cornered me and wanted to know how "he really was." I left a box of them in plain sight one Sunday so she could spot them. Nothing was said aloud but I knew this was my way of being honest. She had seen them. I could tell by the way she raised her chin, sniffled, and excused herself to go outside and smoke.
The movies were viewed in the bedroom where we didn't sleep anymore. I would balance the camcorder in his lap and there he'd sit.

"You know I'm writing a memoir," I said. "What's ok to leave in or leave out?"

"There is. Nothing. I am ashamed of Gim, write anything you want."

At night, I positioned him hopefully, for a full night's sleep. Mask in place just so, I adjusted the feeding tube so it wouldn't cut into his flesh and taped it down. He was starting to skip feedings and I scolded him that this was not a good sign. He said he knew his body better than me and he did not want a feeding. I respected his wishes. He wasn't losing weight. His cheeks were full and his body fairly robust. His color was pleasant. A doctor would come in every few weeks to monitor his vital signs and listen to his weakened lungs. The doctor showed up one evening at 9:30 with an actual Red Sox winning celebration shirt, in navy blue. Howie was thrilled by this gesture. A shirt commemorating the World Series victory. Throughout the day and night, I rearranged his testicles so they wouldn't become pinched, until I realized that some of these requests were a lurid call for attention! (He could still wiggle his eyebrows up and down.) I had to be careful not to cover his arms. They had to be a certain way, across his lap, on the top of his fleece blanket. He couldn't stand for them to be covered. He was always afraid of accidental suffocation. A rolled up towel placed just so on the left side of his head prevented it from lolling forward of its own accord. Of course when he took to lecturing me about what little sex he was getting, then his head would roll and I would have to unfold and reposition the towel again. I learned to laugh at some of the things that disturbed him, but that could get him riled up again. He still had his nose hairs trimmed on a regular basis by me, and I also insisted on keeping those nails trimmed so they wouldn't dig into his palms. I liked undressing his feet, roughing up the calluses with a special loofah, and mois-turizing them with a menthol balm. I would take this time to massage his legs all the way up to the knee as I sat on the dusty wooden floor at his feet, and he protested, telling me I should be making more movies.

I should be having sex with him right then, in fact. I was was-ting time. He was obsessed!

I kept the cysts behind his ears squeezed, applied salve to his skin flare-ups, scratched his constantly itching scalp, and several times daily pulled long hardened snots out of his nose with wadded paper towels. I used a percussion vest on him to loosen mucus too. I was exhausted, yes, but I didn't notice. I was on a fast track. I had strict routines.

Machines to wash. Humidifiers to clean and fill. His fragile psyche to stroke with whatever soothing words I could muster.

Amy decided to get a job at a local hospital and move in with us. She said she wanted to help us out more, and could drive me places. I would not leave Howie at all anymore. I was his biggest personal cyst. If I needed anything I wrote her a list and gave her my debit card. I found a grocery store that would deliver food right to the house! It was wonderful to sit by the light of the screen and take my time with food selections. When the man arrived with the food on the pre-selected day, I never let him past the entrance hall.

I instructed him to drop everything in the front hall. When I returned to the living room after putting the food away, I could count on Howie reprimanding me for wearing something he deemed provocative. He would have Kerry read the itemized list of foodstuffs aloud to him so he could tell me what was an unnecessary purchase and how I'd overspent, *as usual*.

Along came January. The respiratory therapist checked out Howie's lungs and advised that we call for an ambulance if he felt worse, and she went on her way with the cough-a-lator in tow. Howie didn't want it. It felt like I was vacuuming up his lungs (and his life) right along with the secretions.

Chapter Forty-Five: Emergency, January 2005

Yesterday Howie had summoned for Jeff. Asked, no *begged* him to kill him. Jeff quietly left the room. Howie turned those wide eyes on me and begged with them.

"**No,**" I mouthed silently and collapsed by his side, my head on his knee.

Today he was still in a bad way. I could barely understand what he was saying to me. Tears streaming down my face, I demanded, "Say it slower! What do you want? Arms adjusted? A sedative pill? It will help you get sleep. Please, even I can't understand you now."

His eyes widened again with something I never saw before. Fear? Frustration? But I had no trouble hearing his strained accusation: "Yerrr. nawt!.......Lis...ning!" he accused.

I mashed a sedative, put it into watered down ginger ale and into his tube with a syringe from the bag-load I kept on the four foot high stack of formula cases in the kitchen. I used five cans a day. The soda 'cleaned the tube.' I cuddled near to him with no words.
He slept fitfully. The next day I asked if we should wash his hair. Starr was a hairdresser. I would use the marvelous dry wash shampoo on him that she'd given me. I wouldn't even have to move the straps on his mask. If I could freshen him up he would be all better, I reasoned. I offered but he declined with a weak shake of his head. He was barely talking now and he had a vacant stare. I sat beside him, rising to adjust tubes, the blanket, his head, the towel.

That's when I asked him, "Howie, remember years ago
when you met me, you insisted I wash your hair. Here you were 16. I was 14. You were capable of doing it yourself. Why do you suppose you wanted me to do it?"

He was still wide-eyed and his breathing was raspy and labored. I could see him strain for air. The tendons in his neck stiffened. His chest was hitching. He was trying to indicate something to me by pointing with the nose on his face. I asked him to blink if he wanted the TV off and he did.

"Well, do you suppose, that maybe your soul knew I'd be the one caring for you? Like this? Maybe it had to be sure, your soul. And so it was testing me to see if I'd physically care for you, even back then. I must've passed the shampooing test," I said. I stood before him, smiling. Not really expecting an an-swer. "What can I do now? You are scaring me," I asked him.

"Call. Nin. Wun wun," he said.

I went for the kitchen phone. A hand-held, and punched in 9-1-1. "My husband has ALS and he needs assistance now. He's pretty stable but please get someone here to bring him to the hospital and get checked," I said mechanically. I had practiced that line in my head and aloud in the bathroom for a long, long time, just in case. Tears stung and did not fall. I busied around the room, packing. "Howie, you'll need the battery back-up for the breathing machine! The cords, got to pack them!" I said and threw various notions for myself and him into plastic bags.

And then at last, when the men came barging in, it was time to unhook the breathing machine and get it hooked up to the battery for transport. I unplugged it incorrectly and wasted time resetting it after it made itself known with incessant beeping. Howie talked me through, as best he could, how to plug it into the battery. I seemed to have forgotten. We made use of the new ramp.

Chapter Forty-Six: Hospital, First Stay

Kerry, Amy, Jeff and Jeremy were ushered out of the ER room. Their father needed a 'procedure' and the technicians didn't want them to see.

They stood just outside the room, with Howie's mother who told me that Howie's sister and Monty were waiting in the waiting area near the TVs. I had used the cell phone to call Sue, his mother, from the ambulance.

I could only say into the cell phone, "Uh, meet me at the hospital, okay? And could you swing by and get the kids for me first?"

"Where are you?" she'd asked, breathless.

"In an ambulance," I said and clicked off the phone. These were the only words I had in me.
And now here we were and people were cutting a hole in his chest to help re-inflate his lung. It was collapsed. I had to show

them the papers from the Notary Public about not wanting lifesaving procedures but, yes, agreeing with this particular procedure. Howie had been cognizant enough to smile at the kids and his mother and then in a blink people were crowding around him; and cutting. Jeremy, fourteen, was asking questions about the machines. Jeff stood beside Amy with his head on her, no easy feat as he was six feet one and she was five feet six. Jeremy and I and Kerry were watching from the hall. I realized that I couldn't make a cell phone call in a hospital when my mother's voice started to crackle after I told her where I was. At least I'd gotten my message across.

We spent thirteen days and nights in the hospital. I didn't leave the room except to go down to the gift shop and purchase a newspaper, chocolate, nuts or gum. Kerry stayed with us that first night; curled up beside me on the cot under the thin white blanket and sheet. The nights to follow she spent at home. Amy got her awake for school and brought her to the hospital to see us after the school day.

Amy was a transporter at the hospital. A strong girl, she navigated patients to and from treatments throughout the hospital; pushing them through the corridors. Her mother sat in front of a desk performing various duties and she was also in charge of the dog visitation program and a Greyhound Rescue organization.

My cot was alongside Howie's hospital bed. It was a sea of white buoyant comfort. I kept my newspaper, magazines, mail from home, and pocketbook either under or on it. Those first few nights, since my body was trained to awaken every few hours, that's exactly what I did. Every time a doctor or nurse came into the room, I stirred. When he napped, I tried to nap. It seemed I no sooner would fall onto the luscious pillow, than company would come. When Starr or Sue arrived daily with their Dunkin Donuts cof-fee, sandwiches or doughnuts, I popped up from my prone position. When they left I fell back down. I was one of those inflatable clowns.

Howie's voice came back nicely. I was interpreter when hordes of doctors came in and asked him questions. A routine was established. My meals came consistently. Nurses came in to do his feedings through the tube. Not having to do that freed up a little time to read. After they left the room he knew they'd be back for his sponge bath and he'd try to rest because he knew that would tire him out a great deal.

The nurses commented to me on how "immaculate" his skin was and they noted there wasn't any skin "breakdown". Eventually he was taken off the heart rate monitor. I had to show the nurses how to work the breathing machine from

home, and some of them, particularly the ones who came in to take x-rays in the room with their hefty x-ray machine on wheels, didn't understand that he couldn't have his mask removed under any circumstance. I was his voice.

"Leave it on when you hoist him up. Let me help. His head doesn't have support," I told the various people who came in the room to take his x-ray or to boost him up or roll him over to wash his back.

The drooling was in full swing, and I never sat for too long as I was needed to wipe his face nonstop. I had read online about rich ALS patients going so far as to get pricey operations to

have drool slots incised in their lips; so as not to look socially improper-drooling in front of others.

A pleasant Jamaican man came in to administer breathing medication by bypassing the breathing machine and putting it into a cup that would turn into a mist and he could inhale it. I paid a great deal of attention, actually taking notes. I assisted the man with setting up the treatments. I was told I would have to start these at home as part of our new routine when he was discharged.

The man gave me a bag of hose attachments and cups for the medicinal solution. I asked lots of questions.

Outside a blizzard raged. Inside, a doctor came and put a brand new tube in Howie's stomach. Pop! No anesthetic. The doctor just plucked the ragged one out of his stomach without any warning and then set in a new one. Howie never flinched. Could he have?

Amy came to me one day and told me that her mother had fielded some questions about me. Some of the nurses had heard that she knew me and wanted to know why I was "like that."

Amy's mother told them it wasn't so much that I was de-pressed, introverted, aloof or standoffish; I was autistic. Asperger's to be more exact. The nurses said they hadn't heard of Asperger's and looked forward to reading more about it. I was glad that her mother explained me.

Chapter Forty-Seven: Home

A hospital bed arrived at our house and was set up behind the couch. He much preferred his trusty recliner which kept his upper half elevated so he could breathe easier. When he slept in the bed, it would take me a half hour to prop certain pillows and get him comfortable enough to lay there. He used it three times. Then it became mine. I hated the hospital bed too, even after I turned off the bed-breathing mechanism on the mat-tress, an inflatable system which was supposed to massage certain body parts at intervals.

One day I lifted Howie to make a trip to the bathroom for a hand-cleaning and head washing when his legs folded. He was down!

"Call for Amy!" Howie cried in his jumbled up voice.

I tried and tried to say her name, to shout it, but couldn't. *Had I ever said it aloud? Wouldn't it be easier to jog up the street to get Starr's little brother than to say her name aloud?* I had never liked that Amy's name began with a long vowel. For some reason it was so hard to say aloud.
Howie's body was sprawled over the chair and floor in an odd way. Try as I might I couldn't lift him. This was different from his previous falls. Instead of losing balance his legs had simply crumpled. He knew I couldn't say Amy's name, that the vowel didn't make sense. It was becoming a reason to ridicule to me.

I yelled, "Help!" No one came.

"Call hrrrr!" He insisted.

I jogged down the hall and paused in front of hers' and Jeff's room, saying, "Hey! Come help! Hurry!" I shouted at the closed door until I heard someone opening it.

Amy shifted patients for a living. She got her arms under

Howie's armpits and hefted. I barely needed to assist her; she was so mighty. He had a floor-contact burn on his knees and aside from taking a while to catch his breath, he'd be okay. From then on, I brought all the shaving goods into the living room with a cup full of hot water to dip the shaver in and a towel for mopping up stray cream. His head would have to be scrubbed with wet towels and the dry shampoo.

Jeremy introduced me to his new girlfriend Heather, a month after Howie got home from the hospital. "Walk around here, so Jeremy's father can see you" I said. "He can't turn his head so good."

Like Amy, her hair was dark. She was pretty and introspective, and very cute. She walked in front of the chair, gave a wave and a small, "Hello." She was quick to smile.

Later on Howie remarked, "Jer has himself a pretty nice girl there. Good for him!" It took him awhile to get the sentence out, but he did.

Our home sang with the laughter and cajoling of two kids who already seemed to be in love. Howie and I gave each other silent looks that bespoke volumes. His eyes were tender. On weekends when Heather came to visit, we heard the sounds of Jeremy tickling Heather, and her cries of, "Oh my God! Stop it!" emanating down the hall. I liked to think she had a laugh like me: sudden, unexpected and from the gut.

The kids went about their schooling. Kerry did a school assignment about muscle disease and plastered pictures of her father all over it. He wore a yellow shirt and was smiling. If not for the mask, he looked the picture of health.

Jeff didn't walk into a room, he ricocheted like the silver ball in a pinball machine; spouting witty euphemisms filled with curse words that surprised us but made us laugh. "Butter!" he'd say, for no particular reason. "Butter's better than margarine!" He was making an effort to talk to us and we saw it as such.

His face, while intense, would roll like Jim Carrey's. His rubber-like features made ever-changing expressions as he twisted his double-jointed body into contortions and he buzzed around the room, asking the parakeets and cats personal questions about their sex lives. He

particularly liked to throw his left arm over his own left shoulder and walk around with it hanging there. That was the position he found most comfortable when he sat in front of his computer.
Jeremy, now fourteen, was floating on a love cloud.

"I told Jeremy to loog after you," Howie told me one night.

"You said I'm strong, but I'm not," I said, yet again. *Why didn't he see that?*

"Oh yeah you are Gim sweetie. Don't for-ged I want you to geep my gold tooth."
I couldn't believe he was referring to that again and I had to smile despite the lump like a rock in my throat. He couldn't say the "K" sound. I was Gim now.

"Right, right. How many times are you gonna bring that up? I mean people don't just rip those out after a death," I said, sud-denly smiling.

"You haf to asg before the gremation," he said.

"Yeah, sure, or what? You'll come back to haunt me?" I asked.

"I already told you I'm doing that," he smiled. "Go to a psyghic. A John Edward show. I will go through him to talk to you."

Chapter Forty-Eight: Five Months Later

His voice disappeared. When he rasped and gasped for words and searched my eyes, I got out the trusty Yangour tube and sucked the depths of his mouth and throat for errant clogs and plugs. I really called it a Yangour now, which is what the nur-ses and doctors called it. I was learning way too much medical jargon for own liking.

I gave a chest beating to loosen stuff up. I put the right mixtures of medicines in his inhale cup and let him breathe his treatment. I adjusted his mask. I wiped drool nonstop, pulled snots that seemed

lodged all the way down his throat. Then held them for him to beam at.
I crushed pills and added the stool softener and put them down the stomach tube and called the therapist to turn the
breathing apparatus "up a notch" and check his oxygen levels.
After these routines, he had a voice. Maybe for a few hours. If we were lucky, a few days. And I did the health care that made him comfortable-the scab picking, the whisker-itching, the lotion massages, on and on. I never ever stopped doing a thing. I like to think he would've done it all-for me if the situation were reversed.

"I'm sorry son. I just don't understand what you're trying to say," Monty would say in his thick Maine drawl. It pained his mother and dad to not understand and more than once they had tears in their eyes.

When Sue left, she'd kiss his head and say, "Bye my son."
Come June for several days in a row, he had that big-eyed look and was talking less.
He told me to call 9-1-1 again. I packed up.
The paramedics would not let me ride in back. From the front, I craned to try and see what they were doing back there, warn-ing them, "Watch his head, his neck can't support it. Don't unhook that mask accidentally. It has to be on over his face real good."

To my surprise tension seemed to be mounting. One guy radioed in that they were pulling over. In the parking lot of the department store I used to work at, men spoke into his face, "Mister Tucker, can you hear me? We're going to cut an airway. Do you understand?"

"No actually you're not!" I said, straining to see back there and just seeing the back of Howie's head and his body under a sheet. "He doesn't want that. What do you mean cut him?" I demanded.

"Ma'am, to save this man we are going to do a trach right now. Are you saying he does not want us to do that? Mister Tucker, is that right?" The man asked him. No answer.

"He doesn't want that. He decided that a long time ago," I re-peated, louder this time.

"Unless you provide me with that in writing right now ma'am that's just what we have to do. Mister Tucker, do you want a trach put in?" he asked yet again.

"He has it at home on his talking machine. That's his wishes. You are not going to cut him," I said. "I left in a hurry…the papers are home." I saw someone trying to lift his head to speak more clearly into his face.

"It has to be in writing. That doesn't do us any good. Do you want the trach Mister Tucker?" the man said slowly.
There.
His
head moved!
It was just that little bit but even from behind I could tell. The driver must've seen it too. He said, "That was clearly a no."
They proceeded to work on him, saying things like, "We're losing him," and "Keep hanging in there Mister Tucker." At last he was stable enough for the driver to start up the ambulance and to tell someone we were finally en-route.
At the hospital his heart rate was very high. He was in Intensive Care for days and I slept in there too, on a cot. It was another collapsed lung.
Amy brought me the bills and when the second week in the hospital got under way, I sat on the cot writing out checks. He wasn't asking to see them to verify if I did them right.
I made a little cardboard communication board. I put the alphabet on it and he blinked when I pointed to a correct letter. We made sentences.
I wrote key phrases on the board like "Pee jug" and "Adjust mask" or "Get nurse." I went through the list of key phrases and if he didn't blink, we spelled out things with the alphabet chart.
One day Michelle, his main respiratory nurse came in to check on him. Kerry liked her short black spiked hair so much that she brought the Wahl razor to the hospital and had me shave her hair into a short cut just like Michelle's. I showed Michelle a small bloody thing resembling hard snot that I'd suctioned from

Howie's throat. I had kept it on a napkin to show her. Howie's mother was impressed with it and it made Howie glow to be rid of such a thing. Michelle oohed and ahhed over it too! I told Michelle that Howie felt blocked and when Michelle dug into his throat with the Yangour wand, she suctioned up huge mucous plugs that resembled bloody dead mice.
I thought I was sucking pretty deep at home when I used the wand for his drooling, but Michelle went even deeper.
His voice came back until he got restricted and she had to redo the procedure a few hours later.
While Howie's mother visited, and got up periodically to suction drool, I told her I was going down to the gift shop for something. I didn't get lost in the building like last time.

I had gotten lost just days before and wandered into darkened corners of the hospital where vacuums hummed and janitors busied themselves in empty offices. It was creepy. When I'd returned to his room I awaited a lecture that didn't come. Howie stared blankly straight ahead as if I had never gotten lost. I'd paused in the doorway, waiting for my usual lecture to begin but he was vacant.

After his guests went home for the day it was decided that they would go into his chest and try to glue the now re-expanded lung to his chest wall, which would prevent it from deflating again. They didn't have the glue they usually used but they had something similar and they didn't want to wait. I called Sue and she and Howie's sister arrived while he was being operated on.
Before the
procedure both me and Michelle had asked him, "Is this def-initely what you want them to do?"
He was able to blink twice for yes.
That was it and he went into surgery like no big deal; it'd be just like the lung surgery before that one.

Howie's sister and mother and I sat around him waiting for him to come out of the anesthesia. Michelle buzzed in and out of the room, checking his blood oxygen level with a little device that was on his finger. I was trying my best at small-talk. But I wanted alone time. I wanted to collapse beside Howie on the cot.

His sister said, "Are his fingers supposed to be purple?"

I lifted his hand. His nails were white; tinged with purple. The hand was cold and lilac. Howie's mother and I said "No," in unison and she went running for Michelle.

"Can you hear me Howard? *Howard?*" she called loudly. She took one reading of his oxygen level and threw the little gadget onto the bed, backing up and saying, "No that's not right."

A team of doctors poured into the room. Machines rolled in. We were ushered into the hall.
My cot was rolled out into the wide hall to get it out of the way.
I backed into the bathroom at first and noticed that someone had thrown my newspaper and milk carton in the sink. I sat on my cot in the hall and called the kids, and then Starr.

"This is it, he's dying," I said.
Both she and the kids arrived pretty quickly. Amy always was a fast driver. Someone mentioned intubating him, cutting him like they wanted to do in the ambulance. They thrust papers at me and told me to sign so they could intubate. I stared dumbly at them. At the bottom-most in the stack were the papers we had notarized about not intubating him.

Howie's sister spoke to me very slowly. "They are asking you what to do. Should they do this, is that what you want? Or not?"

"I know that. What is on this paper, is what he wants," I stated, staring into a space in the air where motes danced.

"Right now, Mrs. Tucker it doesn't matter what it says on that paper. You can override that and sign this, and we can start the intubation. That's his best chance," said a sympathetic sounding doctor.

"Yes it does matter. These are his wishes right here," I said and shook the papers. At last he walked away. I would not sign.

People started yelling, "Are we starting?"

"No, he's a no-intubate!" someone yelled.

I heard Sue fall apart behind me, telling her daughter, *"She's power of attorney."*

I stood at his head.
Michelle and the others got his heart rate up. "Atta boy How-ard! We got him back," she said. One minute later: "We're losing you Howard, where are you? We're losing him fast."

I looked at the ceiling, thinking that's where he was, looking at US. After this back and forth drama went on a seemingly endless time, Michelle turned to me and said, "Do you want me to stop? Tell me and I'll unhook everything. It's up to you. We've done everything we can." I stared at her hands a long time. In the movies they unhook things while the person is still alive. There are tender exchanges between the dying person and the loved ones as they inhale the last breath and move peacefully into death.
There were exchanges of tender words and then the last breath.

This was it?

Someone urged me to speak after a few minutes elapsed.
"Yeah," I managed. Michelle pronounced him dead at 11:13 p.m. But I knew better. He died at 11:11. I was sure of it. I spit on my finger and took off his ring. It was inscribed:

Kim and Howie 1977 to eternity

Jeremy was sobbing so hard his body shook. Starr embraced him. Michelle collapsed on me, apologizing that she couldn't do more. I patted her back, assuring her that "she'd done all she could, and more!" Jeff was in Amy's arms. I went out to the cot to hug Kerry, who was not crying but let me cry on her.
I sat on the cot and called my mother who was very brave. The cell phone had worked. No one wants to make a call to some-one at that late hour because the person on the end of the line hears the phone ring and thinks the worst. But I had to do it. I knew she'd have a hard time when she hung up the phone. We took turns saying bye to his body.

I wiped his mouth. It didn't strike me as my lasy physical act of caring for him. It was automatic. The sadness was a gaping hole in my chest.

Kerry finally sobbed.

After everyone seemed through having quiet time with what was now "the body," I sat on the cot in the corridor, which was no longer my cot. I assumed my pocketbook was tangled in the sheets. I'd had it last to write out bills.

Someone asked what I was looking for and I told her. "It's probably in the bathroom. I saw a lot of my stuff in there."

After a long search, my pocketbook never turned up.

Chapter Forty-Nine: The Aftermath

I plucked one, then two, then three, four, *five* clovers with not three, but four perfect little leaves. Mini shamrocks. How could it be? A whole patch full.

Over the weeks that followed, when Monty arrived to mow our grass for us I asked him to mow around the rare clover patch but I didn't tell him why. He obliged; preserving my newfound treasures. They made me think of Annie. It had never happened before and would never happen again: an actual

patch of four leaf clovers in one area no bigger than a hand towel; all of them had four leaves.

"Just mutations," said Jeff.

Yes, true enough but astounding to me who pictured elves bandying about with special four leafer seeds, tiny wheel-barrows and fertilizer when no one was about, just to thrill *me*.

Kerry and I slept pretty late the day after the death, or we tried to. Howie's mother Sue and her two daughters arrived to help plan the funeral.

Not having any speech, I excused myself to go out and get the morning newspaper. First I put Pralph on his chain to do his duties. Something had to stay the same in this new world without a mate.

Walking down the driveway and past Amy's car I avoided the

front door and kept walking. I walked by the side ramp, full aware that my guests may be wondering where I'd gone.

I bent over my special clover patch and right away spotted eight perfect four leafed clovers. I selected one.

After letting Pralph inside, I laid the clover down on the back of the couch and went to stand in front of the living room window and look out over the sloping hill that was my backyard. A 'ditch' of vines, weeds and sumac ran the line of houses on my side of the road which separated our dead end road from the street that ran adjacent to it. Through the brush, I could see the swimming pool in the neighbors' backyard.

Time to get down to business. We had an appointment to keep at the funeral parlor down the road.

How did I get to such a crazy place in my life?

Starr phoned as we were leaving and said she'd

meet us there. The funeral director was predictably somber, and thorough. He said he'd take Howie's fingerprint before he was sent for cremation and store it in a file.

And so after it was all over with, Starr had offered to get me the tooth and I'd declined. As it turned out the only people from my own family who turned up at Howie's funeral were my parents and the girl who seemed like family; Curly-headed Ginger with her husband Morton and their daughter.

The after-funeral get together was at Howie's sister's house.

Just over the hedge, was a big white house with a white garage beside it. It was good ol' Louis's childhood home. Louis couldn't make it to the funeral.

He had a more important thing to do, and that was to greet Howie "on the other side." I had read in the newspaper, just months before Howie's passing that Louis died suddenly in the basement of his mother's house.

Chapter Fifty: Whirlwind Summer

After a rain, the pavement smell was gorgeous. I know; I walked a lot. I had an easy relaxed stride. There was no quickened pace, no imminent dread of death.

It was just me, and Elliot the black cat who walked me home

from Kerry's bus stop every morning. He dashed out of the bushes to weave in and out of my legs as I passed. Sometimes I picked him up and he squirmed to get away. I set him down and patted him on his way. I went about my bus-iness as routinely as possible, trying to figure out what those new routines were.

I wanted to work; and had a feeling no one would give me the chance of knowing what it's like to see a paycheck before my eyes and have a pride for that.

Amy bought tickets to a huge outdoor concert in New York. In July, a month following the death, Jeff, Kerry, Amy and I ventured out for the trip. Once regular concert-goers, Howie and I had been to hundreds of them. This would be my first in years. The music was alternative, bordering on punk. It wasn't my favorite but it was my first trip in a long time and it would be worth it to see Kerry enjoying herself. Jeremy chose to stay home and mind the pets. He didn't want to miss out on seeing Heather, his girlfriend and preferred to be home so he could spend as much time with her as possible.

The hairstyles were like that ice cream store. There were snow cone heads and Neapolitans; every flavor. Mine was still shaved close to the head. A series of stages were spread across an expanse of field littered with rock stickers, flyers, and hordes of people drinking water. It was scorching hot. My short hair was tinted red and Kerry's was blue for the occasion. I still couldn't stop the compulsion to shave my head but it was growing. A little.

Pierced kids in tank-tops, falling-down shorts, and punk T-shirts were a menagerie of counter-culture; carrying overpriced water bottles and sporting everything from tall red mohawks to bleached spikes as they tread over the sunburned grass in every direction. Kerry wanted to be in the front row. I didn't figure it was such a good idea, since people were packed on the field like sardines in a tin, sweating on each other and fainting from heat exposure. Girls were carried away by concert personnel and ushered into a tent where they could re-hydrate.

Nonetheless I wanted her to have her way, and to my surprise she pushed through people and led us weaving in and out of the crowd toward the front. Jeff and Amy hesitantly followed the rude path we were cutting. Because she was a short insis-tent nine-year-old, they got out of her way.

We settled for a tight spot, ten or twelve rows back from the stage. Kerry was excited when the guitar players took the stage, their faces painted with dark crescents under the eyes. She realized she was too short to see and asked me to put her on my hip. I obliged, hot as I was and even though she was heavy I managed to hop up and down which seemed to be a required activity. I was "one of the herd."

A bald guy with headphones who apparently swallowed a watermelon whole, unashamedly sweated some stains into his Tshirt and stood in the corner of the stage studying the crowd and looking important. As the music first started in to scream-ing, I saw it was his job to keep the hopping hooting front row at bay. He gestured to uniformed security guards who alerted personnel to fainting girls and he made sure no one crossed the safety zone between row 1 and the stage. I didn't like the music but I could fake it. And I could appreciate the passion.

To Amy's horror, (I could see it on her face, Bless her!), some feet sailed our way over the crowd. My teeth grazed the crowd surfing boy's ankle as he passed over my left shoulder, above all our heads.

My left arm was weaker and since I was balancing Kerry on my right hip with that arm around her securely, it was tough helping the kid's body sail by me with my shoulder still sore from the time I fell behind Jill's shed. But I was oblivious to pain and I helped the body surfers, male and female alike, by ushering them along with my free arm until eventually the person fell onto the ground with a thud and got back up to do it again.

Sometimes a body would get close to Kerry's head and girls with their navels exposed rallied around us, pointing at the crowd to direct the teenager's body away from the little girl. Amy stood behind Kerry and I, and impressed me with her strength as she used her strong arms to keep body surfers away from Kerry and me by shooting them past me.

I ducked, bobbed, sweated and delighted in the frenzied ex-citement, waving my good arm and listening to Kerry sing along to songs I didn't know. Shoes passed within inches of my good ear; kids in black clothes with edgy hairstyles appeared beside my face and were staring up at the blazing sky, along the arms of bouncing kids. At last some *organized* chaos! LIFE was all around, oblivious, maybe foolhardy.

Chapter Fifty-One: August

Two months since his death. My exhaustion was shocking in its enormity. I felt I could sleep forever. When I was awake I did regular things like read the newspaper, feed the pets and walk downtown for leisurely excursions with Kerry at McDonalds.

I passed the puddle at the curve of the road which never seemed to dry up, where in the winter it froze over and kids from our street raced to it in the morning yelling, "I call dibs on cracking the puddle!"

I went to Vermont. It was nice to cuddle up at night in the big brass bed. My parents breathed easier when they slept in the recliners but I still felt that I was putting them out by taking their bed despite their assurances. At night, Kerry and I flipped through TV channels, staying up late into the morning and giggling at funny movies and SNL.

I walked down the hall every morning, secure in knowing that Jeremy, Jeff and Amy were back in Connecticut tending to the dishes, laundry and pets. I didn't have to say anything. My father greeted me at the table, no matter what time I dragged out of bed, with coffee and overdone toast, cut into threes.

My mother sat beside me doing a crossword and filling me in on gossip. She herself, had two years left to live but I couldn't have known that. None of us did. Life precariously, boldly sits upon an invisible precipice.

Kerry drew pictures and showed my father who remarked, "That's a humdinger-doozer boy!"

I was in Vermont for Ginger's sake too. She and husband Morton bought me a concert ticket to see Meatloaf. Ginger was no longer curly-headed; nor was she blond but I'd always think of her that way. Her hair was bobbed but resisted the style by stubbornly waving where she didn't want it to; and it was dyed purple.

Her friends, Andy and Don, came along with us to the concert. They chain-smoked, as did Ginger and Morton. Overall I was impressed with her family life. She had fine radiator heat in the apartment with a tea kettle on top of one of them. Her pets included trick love birds, a ferret, two dogs, a cat, and a parrot. I delighted in visiting with each and every one of them. She even had a teenage daughter who was diagnosed Asperger's like me. I gave purple Curly a copy of the anthology book *Women From Another Planet,* edited by Jean Kearnes Miller. It was a book I'd done with a group of other women that detailed the lives of women in the "universe of autism." She was entranced by my two stories, *Eraser Balls* and *'Cause Its Friday* and kept shushing me until she finished reading them.

I was surprised to see Andy and Don were coming along with us to New York for the concert. Andy was a big charismatic soft spoken guy, with a thick head of hair and glasses. His brother was a recovering stroke survivor and had little use of his arm. It was only apparent when he spoke that he had any difficulties.

I thoroughly enjoyed the concert which was orchestrated like a theatrical event and at times comical. At one point Purple Curly could not bear the itchy hives she had contracted from some sort of orangey cleanser that was on the tables where she worked; in a cafeteria. She reached up under her blouse, unhooked her bra and let loose her ample bosom from under her Meatloaf T-shirt. Ah, now she could breathe. She kept sneaking her hand up her shirt to scratch.

I whispered to her, "Fling your bra out over the crowd. Go on!"

But she replied, "You fling your own bra!" With that she tucked it into her pocketbook.

"I'm not the one with hives. Besides, I wear those camisole things," I said. "No fun you are."

In the van on the way home, I sat next to Don in the middle seat and Andy sat way in back with the cooler of food Ginger had prepared for us. I closed my eyes and could see the occasional wash of light from streetlights as, quite regularly, they cast over my eyelids. I wanted to fall asleep on Andy's great big arm. I surprised myself as it seemed I was starting to miss things like that. Even if he reeked of smoke.

Chapter Fifty-Two: His Birthday

Starr arrived on Howie's birthday and suggested we spread

some ashes. Now that's fun!

I kept baggies near the black plastic box of ashes. Earlier in the month Sue and Howie's sister Lorraine scooped some remains out for themselves.

Kerry and I went fishing together under the bridge down-town and scattered some ashes into the eddies. And now, Starr was here to drive us to a few of our fishing spots. We walked down a steep pine-needle covered path. I felt bad because the day was hot and Starr had trouble walking, but she joked the whole way and her daughter Kassi, who was a few years older than Kerry, helped her along.

I sat with my feet hanging over the edge of a cement platform. I told Starr that this was one of the last places we'd tried to fish.

Howie's hands were just starting to curl then and he was failing at all attempts to cast a line. In frustration he'd thrown down the pole. I'd scolded him that day, warning him that he was too close to the twenty foot drop and the waterfalls below.

It was like the time he had climbed the mountain and I had yelled at him "Are you trying to kill yourself?" He stood looking down from the cliff, a red blur on a rocky outcropping...

When he came back down he said, "It's the last one I'll ever climb." I had known but not fully grasped that there would be so many "lasts" for him. But now I understood. I was glad, in retrospect we'd known how to laugh at the absurd degradation death brings. I was glad we knew to be in every crazy moment.

I sat near a watershed booth which was made of concrete and had giant gears inside that you could see if you peeked in an open window. A green metal door was locked closed with a rusty hasp and padlock. I was worried, on this particular day, which would've been Howie's forty-third birthday, that Starr might get too close to the edge. But she didn't.

She stayed perched on a rock at the foot of the woods, weaving a wreath from vines and lacing yellow flowers through it. You could tell she was Native American. Kassi and Kerry threw stones into the open window of the little graffiti'ed building and into the water below us.

Kerry sat beside me and we let loose the contents of our

baggies. The Howie dust fell into the water below, churned in grey swirls and disappeared. Starr had given me three silk flowers: a black one, a light blue one, and a yellow.

I dropped the black one into the water stem first and watched the dark green and seemingly bottomless water as it ate up the flower. Bubbles rose from around the 'silk' petals as it sunk like a stone straight down and went out of sight. I was surprised because I'd expected it to float. He always told me, when he was a teenager he wasn't ready to die till the day

they made black roses. When I saw them on the internet I didn't have the heart to tell him.

I sat beside Starr on a nearby rock and watched as Kerry resumed throwing stones. Her laughter was always good for me, but I found myself completely speechless. Starr tried to say a few things to me, about the pretty flowers she'd found, about this and that, and I could only answer monosyllabically. She called to her daughter Kassi and asked her to put the wreath against the building so she could take a picture.

Starr took a picture of the wreath and we started to make a path through the woods, uphill, to the car. We would leave the wreath there and scatter the rest of the ashes and the two remaining silk flowers in Howie's favorite trout brook. That was the plan.

Starr would stack stones there in a pile to mark the spot, like Indians did. She had become very spiritual, was having prophetic dreams and believed in the power of crystals like me.

"Maybe we can come back and spray paint 'Kim and Howie' on the building sometime," she said boldly, surprising me with her brashness. We all turned back one last time to glance at the beautiful wreath laid against the building. And we all had a good laugh. Right above the wreath, spray painted above it on the concrete wall was somebody's crude drawing of a great big penis.

Chapter Fifty-Three: Surprise E-mail, Full Circle Life

I awoke at noon. It was Saturday. I read the newspaper, let the dog out and turned on CNN for background noise. Blurring out the violence on the TV, my mind floated back to the day Howie died; five months previous.

Father Jamison stood beside his hospital bed saying prayers and making the sign of the cross on Howie that day. Of course none of us knew he would be gone that night. As Father Jamison spoke I let my gaze wander out the picture window to the side of Howie's bed. There was a winding road with offshoots of quaint streets lined with gingerbread houses; with children's' bicycles and recycling bins in their yards. In the distance was a church steeple.
We were several floors up from the ground and had a view, fairly close to the hospital window, of the scant topmost branches of a spindly tree. The white-hot sun backlit the branches and I saw it! I pointed and asked Father if he saw what I did. Silhouetted against the sunlight was a perfect cross, illuminated by a gorgeous ethereal light.

Father Jamison said he saw it too, and I turned Howie's head gently for him to see. I had spent almost two weeks sleeping in this very room; why hadn't I noticed it before? In fact it was my habit to seek out crosses that appeared naturally in the environment or in nature. I had a collection of digital photos of that very subject matter. I carried my camera everywhere and if a window pane or cracks in the road formed a cross I took the picture. Howie's eyes matched the color of the sky. He had not wished to communicate with me all day but just then we looked out the window and he was smiling peacefully. The topmost tree arms formed a natural cross backlit by sun.

I shook the memory from my conscious, got some coffee and waited for the computer to boot up. I liked responding or at least reading the daily posts from peers on the spectrum. Conversing with peers was an intellectual stimulation that put fuel in my day. Yawning, reading, deleting; I almost overlooked the e-mail from Donna Williams. I'd received a couple mails from her over the course of the season, inviting me to join her Autism Spectrum site, a place where people on the spectrum could list their skills and perhaps find work. But as I read the e-mail I realized this one was different. She proposed to me the idea that I get a book ready for publication. She said she'd be my editor and gave me one year as a deadline. I told her I'd have it done a whole lot sooner.

Chapter Fifty-Four: Seeking Gainful Employment

The first time I called the transit company to arrange a bus ride to my neurologist's office, I had to redial three times. My lips were quivering and as a result my voice was shaking.

They would pick me up right at my door and deliver me to my appointment a half hour early. If this could work for appoint-ments then why couldn't I use the service to get me to and from a job? I never managed to get somewhere on my own unless I walked. I punched in the numbers for the transit company into my cell phone. All I had to do was call when I was ready to go home. What independence!

If I could use the bus, then why not taxis? I punched the number of the local cab company into my cell phone when I saw it cruising by me one day as I waited for the bus. The phone number was emblazoned conveniently across the side door.

At home I let the housework pile up a little. I didn't wash clothes until I really had a monumental pile and I let the dishes stack up until dirty ones slid off and crashed on the floor. I was writing the book and it was taking a lot of time. I got after everyone with my best 'grouchy bear' impression to start washing their own dishes. When they all complied, I noticed a big welcome decrease in my workload.

But I couldn't feel happy. I was dragging through my life as if I were treading through waist- high water upstream in winter clothing.

I decided to go to a counselor in New Haven. I was shocked when, after I made the phone call and arranged for my first of eight appointments, the bus company informed me that they didn't deliver anyone anywhere outside of the Valley. That's where I found a service that would provide free cab rides to me, provided it was for a medical appointment.

I began to scour the classified ads in the newspaper for work. I phoned the library where just the month before I'd had my paintings on display in the front lobby. They weren't hiring but I could put an application at the Town Hall.

I climbed the steps and went into the brick building. The carpeted hall at the top of yet more stairs was lined with open doors on both walls bearing placards like "Tax Assessor's Office." After wandering into a few

empty offices I found the room with the long desk where I remembered getting all my fishing licenses and marriage license with Howie in 1988. A woman there directed me to a room full of people in skirts and suits. One of the suited men was our town's First Selectman. I managed to ask a busy woman for an application and headed down the corridor in the wrong direction. I tucked my application into my bag and turned around.

I reached the glass double-doors at the end of the stairs. I could see the outdoors; the mailmen across the road getting into trucks, women parking their cars at the curb and briskly trouncing down the sidewalk to important places. I pushed and the door wouldn't budge. I pushed mightier. Nothing. I pushed on the door to the right. I could see the outside but I couldn't get to it. The door wouldn't open, so I pulled it instead. It seemed locked!

Had I broken a rule and become trapped by some hidden restraining system until I could be apprehended? Did I just look shifty?

A white-haired man with wire framed glasses perched low on his nose appeared beside me. He was half-smiling in a thoughtful manner and much shorter than me, adding to the sensation that I was a big waste of space. He wore a suit a size too small that was rumpled around the edges. Gently, in the manner of someone talking to a child he told me to try pulling the door on the left. I grabbed for the lever and the door came open. I couldn't get through it fast enough. I thanked him and shot him a side-glance, trying to smile.

"Sometimes," he said softly, "these things can be tricky."

I hurried to the drugstore nearby and darted through the aisles, making sharp angles around displays and not knowing why I'd gone in or what I wanted. I picked up bottled water and choc-olate covered peanuts. I hurried outside to the bench I'd seen on the sidewalk. The peanuts were daring. Foolish. They could set off a migraine but I thought maybe I needed the protein and figured it was worth the risk. There was no way I was attempting to go home in my 'condition.' I called for a taxi and waited. People came and went through the Laundromat door on my left, bearing baskets and staring at me. People entered the drugstore through the automatic doors on my right. Staring. Snickering. Was it because I wore light green? With brown dress pants and suede boots? Was it the newspaper I had already read but was pretending to read again? I couldn't say. I would never know.

I had Amy get me an application from the hospital where she worked. I would try to be 'cafeteria help' or maybe I could clean rooms. It would be hard passing doctors and maybe even Michelle in the halls. Harder still, going into people's private rooms. But I needed money.

I could practice saying, "No habla English," if someone tried to talk to me.

I would have to let the applications sit where they were and wait for a call-back. I had done what I could. I had at least twelve "out there in the world." It was time to get some serious writing done.

Chapter Fifty-Five: Crazy

I went to Social Security but they couldn't take my information because the computers were down. What a waste of bus fare! I stood to purchase a Lotto but the machine broke right before my turn! My home computer booted up as I sat down, right before I turned it on. It gets stranger. I couldn't sleep and...

I figured I'd just fall asleep in Howie's reclining chair. I got up to use the toilet, passing the only portrait I had hanging in the house. I didn't like eyes looking at me. It was a family picture, a twelve by eighteen inch portrait of the family, hanging on a nail in the hall. It had been there for years.

On my way back to the chair I checked the time. It was past midnight and I was the only one awake in the house. I was now a full fledged insomniac.

Sometimes even commercials made me cry so TV was sense-less. I couldn't watch shows with couples. *Like Everyone Loves Raymond* or *King Of Queens*. Yuk! Shows with couples. That was not doable. This surprised me as I had always enjoyed these shows in the past. Now they set my churning stomach atwirl with loss. That was too painful. One commercial haunted me. It seemed to have been playing incessantly for years.

Howie and I had been watching TV early on right after his diagnosis and a commercial for calcium tablets came on.

"Hmmm" I said to him. "I think I should get some with the next grocery order. What do you think, hon? I don't want to be one of those older ladies who gets fragile and breaks a hip later on, huh?"

"Do whatever the fuck you want," he'd snapped. I had been shocked. He went on. "You get to have a life, you *get* to grow old. Buy your goddamn tablets. Who the fuck cares."

I couldn't turn my mind off sometimes. I lay there in his chair, reclined to the fullest, wrapped in Howie's favorite red Aztec print fleece blanket. Even when I did fall asleep, my body was still in the trained habit of waking every few hours. It would be a restless night. I cried in the darkness, startling myself with the sounds of my own sobs. I hadn't cried this long and hard since the death.
I cried for not having a person to grow old with.
I cried, remembering the night of his diagnosis with the dis-ease. I cried remembering when I was in the cellar folding laundry on the long Formica table when he jumped from the shadows and came up behind me like a wolf on prey. I gasped then, surmising he had been standing behind the hot water tank and a pile of junk; waiting for me to come down the
stairs.
I cried remembering his hands that came round from behind me, clutching my breasts through my sweatshirt. I felt his breath on my face but I couldn't let go of the shirt I was folding. I was paralyzed with a strange fear.

"These are mine," he'd growled at me.
"You're hurting me," I'd whispered.
"Put my head on the wall," he'd said. I cried there in the recliner, remembering that. Put my head over your computer like a stuffed animal when I'm gone, because I'll be watching you from over there. And I'll know. So don't forget what I'm telling you." He'd said to me.

I wiped snot across my face with the blanket and looked up at the ceiling, thinking these thoughts. I could remember laying in bed with him after a particularly rough day for me. It was full of phone calls and drop-ins and I was not doing well. I had sulked and been trapped in my thoughts, upset over the color of the recliner which had been delivered light blue, a tranquil color but nonetheless a color afraid of itself. It was *supposed* to be a brave cranberry and wasn't. He had said something in the night to me then... when the colors weren't right.

He had said, "Know what? I hope you *do* find someone someday."

When I spent Thanksgiving at my parents' place the first winter after his death, after making a snowman with Kerry outside, my father had greeted me with coffee, cheese and crackers and said to me that he wanted to live long enough (he was in his seventies) to see me remarry. I told him he'd be living forever, and I laughed. It was these thoughts and more that I whorled in my aching head, blind with falling tears.

Then *thud*!

Light illuminated the room.

My body jumped as my eyes blinked to adjust to the sudden light.

I dug fists into my eyes to see more clearly.

It came from the hall. The hall light was on, but how?

As I studied the situation it didn't take long to figure out what happened. There was the family portrait on the floor, leaning upright against the wall. It had come straight down off the wall, slid down the expanse of wall and hit the floor with a thunk. It had flicked right over the light switch; turning it on in the process.

Sort of like what happened in the funeral parlor with the *Hus-band* wreath.

I slept with the light on.

And I wasn't

crying after that.

Electricians replaced the electric box in that wall twice because it stopped working after that. Then it stopped

working and never worked again for three years.

Chapter Fifty-Six: Reflections

She favored wearing color combinations like light pink and soft green. I arrived at my appointments with her once a week for eight weeks in a row. She was a therapist, by the name of Donna and I did not break down the therapist word and think of her as 'the rapist' (of thoughts, feelings, etc.).

She was matronly like my mother, and had a beautiful face. Her voice did not hum at that frequency I find so disturbing. In the waiting area, the overhead fluorescence would flicker and hum like bug-killer contraptions. My free taxi usually brought me there early so I sometimes had time to browse my newspaper. Other times I was so keyed up from a particularly intrusive chatty cab driver that I just sat and fidgeted and got up repeatedly to get my self cold water from the burping water cooler.

The therapy room itself had a table and two chairs with a window to back-light the therapist and for me to become distracted with. It was not a bad set-up, but it was artificially bright, the fluorescence gave a surreal feel to the objects in the room which were otherwise pleasing to keep company with. It was an old building with interesting niches and crevices and even had a radiator in the room with a tea kettle on top, like the one at Ginger's house. I told her we would have to conduct the sessions with the light off. That was okay with her. There was just the one time she left the light on.

I was learning not to have all-or-nothing thinking. A black and white thinking style was not conducive to healing. When I arrived, disheveled, eyes darting everywhere but on her face, I would answer her usual "how are you" question with my usual response: "Okay." But after minimal prodding I spilled how dissatisfied I was at myself and what a lousy unproductive week I'd had. She taught me to "turn my thinking around" and recognize the positive things I'd accomplished. I told her I feared Howie died angry with me and I touched on some of the arguments we had. She said that I must know, deep inside, that it was his disease "talking," and I must remember to keep that in perspective.

I told her about my mother's open-heart surgery when I was 12. It intensified my fear of the color green. When my father and I readied to visit my mother, we were made to scrub our hands and wrists in green disinfectant lotion. Then they gave us green masks, green paper gowns and even sterile green tissue-shoes to put over our own street-shoes. I remarked on how it was always that way for me.

I assigned something evil to the color and for a long time everything that was green was bad. I would not even wear it. She told me that not everything green could necessarily be bad. That was a "guilty by association" type thinking.

It was an interesting concept.

Chapter Fifty-Seven: Stars And Coffee Cans

"I want a new couch. And a refrigerator," I told Donna Williams in an e-mail, proud to even know my own wants, and "feeling" weird not to run decisions by someone else.

She said that sounded like a good plan. I told her maybe I'd have enough money to finance a trip to Europe and meet Colin at last. If I could do any of those things then I would have a keen sense of accomplishment. She wished me well.

After five hours of nonstop writing I was almost done with the book. My upper back was numb. Every time I mailed Donna Williams my work, she would almost immediately e-mail back words of encouragement like: "It's looking riveting, isn't it? Good job, mate!"

I needed air. There was about a page left to write.

The climate was a seasonable twenty-two degrees, and that's below freezing. There had been a sixty mile an hour wind storm. That's as fast as cars go. I needed to pick up the garbage pail lids which had tried to run away from home by blowing over the back hill. I also needed to bring out the trash and put some clothes in the dryer. But I collapsed on the front step instead, hugging myself and waiting for Pralphdog to do his duty.

The sky was twinkling with stars and hung with a crescent moon. I couldn't help but think of my mother, and the recent operation she had; to put four stents in one leg and one stent in the other. She was mostly blind in one eye from the diabetes. I tried to call her once a week. I sat on the step, patting Pralphdog's bottom and he arched. I did not feel the cold although I wore no coat and had sock-feet. I saw the musical *Tommy* on TV just the day before on cable TV. It had brought back to me a cascade of memories. How my friendship with Starr had remained intact I didn't know. But I counted myself lucky. I thought about all the years Howie was sick and I hadn't been with my father to watch my mother wake up from her heart procedures. She had almost died during surgery while Howie was in the hospital. They understood why I didn't ask Amy, Monty, or Howie's Aunt Sally to take me to Vermont. I forgave myself. Howie had to come first. Here I was on my own stoop, in the dark blanket of cool night. In the house, on my PC, were snippets of my life written out like so many loose beads on a string, a series of seemingly disconnected events in a nearly completed book.

I looked up over the trees at the topmost of the mountain across the street, and up into the star-filled sky, black as Elliot the cat. Years ago, my mother would say, "It's in the pretending" and we saw stars in the cans we'd poked holes in, as the flickering candle inside made the holes twinkle.

Once upon a time I looked at coffee cans and I saw stars. Now here I was looking at real stars in their constellations, and I was thinking about coffee cans.

Every thing between the pretending and the real is merged.

Everything treasured is about "looking for perfection in imperfect moments."

A life just now, unfurling, and on its own brave new journey.

I smiled to myself, under the banana moon.

AFTERTHOUGHTS

I have come to this conclusion. Asperger's, in my own experience, has been a lifelong misunderstanding of cues.

In an attempt to make sense of a frustrating and confusing world, I assigned meaning to colors. Surely if the color green popped up more than once in association with terrifying or sudden unexpected changes, then green must be bad in some way.

In my early 40's, I got some cognitive education and learned that I was assigning bad energy to color, when in fact my life events would've transpired anyway, regardless of the colors of my life. I FEEL colors, do you feel colors and patterns? Do certain colors vibrate?

Since I tend to *feel* so deeply, I rely heavily on impressions, intuition, and gut feeling, to be the steering wheels for my intention. Colors are soothing mechanisms.

I am the kind of person who is inclined to prefer optimism, pro-action, truth, and hope. But depression can hinder even the most compassionate human being. So can mutism.

I did get my chance to go to a John Edward show. I hoped against for a reading. When the renowned psychic started speaking about *my* life, with things only he could know, and even mentioned the exact charm I held in my hand, I did not stand up, did not get my reading. This is what Selective Mutism takes from you. Free will. No one in the packed arena did stand up, because the message had been for me. Howie was keeping his promise to speak through John but I was overwhelmed and rendered unable to hear it.

I believe this, that if I had not been raised by a father with such high serotonin levels, a happy-go-lucky caring and compassionate optimist, I would be a very low functioning and sad "Aspie" today. If my mother had not rocked me when I had meltdowns, if she had beat me or patronized me because I had extreme food and tactile sensitivities, pica and did not speak to people, I would not feel worthy of love, as I do today. I may never have sought it out because I may have thought that 'someone like me' is unlovable because of my differences.

I am glad she enrolled me in catechism. I've realized the importance of spirituality even though it may or may not be Catholicism.

I am glad she gave me opportunities to mix with peers, like 4-H and Girl Scout camp. Even though I was not able to inte-grate into the cliques in these groups, as she'd hoped, I still enjoyed the experiences in my own way through parallel play. I got to work on badges *alongside* peers, I fluffed out countless tissue paper roses alongside the other girls; late into the night and affixed them to our Girl Scout parade float, I got to wear a uniform, I got to at least tell myself I was "part of a group" in my own way. I was solitary in these groups, involved in activities alongside peers. Even Starr gravitated toward the other girls when we were at camp or having a 4-H meeting. But I felt a belonging, and the other children learned acceptance. Who can truly berate you anyway when your mother is leader, right? (wink) My peers were offered glimpses of me, in a setting other than school.

I am thankful my mother took me with her to cooking classes and that I attended square dances with my aunt, Annie, watching from the sidelines. I was a part of these activities; not socially, no, but I was exposed to them and that was so enriching. My parents seldom left me with a babysitter. I was stimulated by experiences that left impressions on me.

I loved learning, still do. My parents knew that and always encouraged it, even when that meant buying an entire set of encyclopedias they couldn't afford, (pre-internet days) or enrolling me in a "music from other lands" club which sent records, artifacts, and pamphlets from an exotic place in the world, monthly. Through this experience I was more than a speck of a kid standing on a boulder in the woods. I was part of a wider world I could imagine and dream about.

They were not perfect people, my parents. But who is? I don't know anyone who is. They were the right parents for me. Perhaps the thing I learned by living my life the way I have, is that I am normal after all.

Normal for someone born an Aspie, who happens to also have selective mutism.

If Asperger's can sometimes feel like a thorn in my shoe, like when I am listening to small talk that I see no point in, or when I mistakenly take someone literally (the examples are in the multitudes here), then surely selective mutism is a cactus in my underpants or uh more to the point: in my throat.

It is not unusual for an Asperger's individual to have any number of co-morbid conditions like Tourettes, ADD, bi-polar, dyslexia, clinical depression, or even selective mutism like me. The possible cocktails are immeasurable. I encourage you to read about people "like me" and the ways we express ourselves. My brain has more plumage every time *I* do!

I know now, of course, that some of my "neuro-deficits" are in part spatial and also that I have a Broca's weakness in the brain. When I'm fatigued, stressed, overwhelmed or ill, spoken language and deriving meaning from what others say- is a monumental challenge for me!

To not have words is more than just scary. It usually takes you by surprise. "Why me?" is pointless. So are tears, self-injury, alcohol or drug misuse, and mentally beating up on one's self. All of which I've tried mind you, so I know!

Often it is after *all of the above* that a person like me finally reaches a point of self-acceptance. This is the greatest gift we can give ourselves. That, and forgiveness for things left

undone,

unsaid,

unexpressed.

I have object recognition deficit too, how many times have I tried to get into the wrong car in a parking lot? You may say ME TOO. With me, this deficit caused me to fear school. If I could summon sound to ask to use the rest room then that was half the hurdle because I'd get lost finding my way back to the classroom. I still have recurring nightmares about being lost in buildings because it happens so often. I find it hard to give directions to places I've been to a hundred times before.

Being object blind with low spatial ability means I cannot visual my path. I can't construct routes in my head.

Add a nonverbal learning disability and weak visual perception, sensory hyper- and hypo- sensitivity and that's just a bit of my *fruit salad* which makes up me, as Donna Williams would say. I love her choice of words.

I've heard memoirists use this term before,

"I could not have written this if I had ever for a moment thought others might read it."

This is true for me. Filling seventeen some odd diaries as I did, with rich detail, tear stains, and honest self- dissection, was an attempt at sorting through the confusing bits, trying to learn what made me tick, trying to make sense of my various foibles and eventual labels. The diaries have been destroyed and this book is my voice. In ink instead of sound.

Writing this book started in earnest on an electric Royal typewriter. Fun stuff, that was back when you had to rely on Wite-Out to erase mistakes. Finally I got my first desktop PC in the early 90s and my book began again, based on passages I'd transcribed from diaries, to my electric typewriter, to my trusty MSWord program and stored on floppy disks and in desktop files.

There has always been an indefatigable attempt on my part, a curious niggle inside my brain; to truly understand my self and why/how I relate the way I do.

I was trusted with life and death situations. I learned that maybe just maybe my core self is not so weak and bruised as it would appear, but instead is rich with seeds. The eventual publishing of this book is the germination of those seeds.

Donna Williams read each early chapter and helped with putting them in order. For some reason I sucked at that. But she only changed one line and she was right. There was a line about the grapes in the orchard that really was a bit sappy. She suggested I omit it and I did. But she didn't change a bit of my writing. That's all me! That first version of this book was longer and included more chapters. It was called Communication Breakdown (CM) and is no longer available. It was self published.

In 2011, a fine thing happened. I got an agent who believed in me. My agent's assistant cut lots of text so the book is shorter than CM. I took the self published Communication Breakdown offline, and in 2012 Inkwell published Under The Banana Moon (UTBM) with an extra two chapters: *I Get A Kick Out Of Steak* and *Knucklehead Billy*. The book you are reading now is Under The Banana Moon with a redesigned cover and a few extra lines here and there that the original UTBM didn't have. I liked the old book cover, designed with reproductions of two of my paintings, but I like this one too. Change can be good.

My next book deals with PTSD, borderline personality, and Manic depression to name a few topics. I've admitted a loved one to a psychiatric hospital. Mental illness, love, and continual learning about unconditional loving despite
roadblocks has been a theme since the funeral.

After trauma and heartbreak sometimes you fall down before you can walk tall again. Writing about people is a sensitive issue. For this reason, my next book is a delicate one. It was not my intent to upset anyone with this book but I did. For that I am sorry. Every single person in UTBM has taught me what I need to learn.

This book I'm working on now is a continuation of Under The Banana Moon. I want it to be written honestly, with compassion and sensitivity to all involved. There is a tightrope, invisible but shimmying beneath my personhood as I try to select the right words; as I balance the circus under the surface.

I had 13,000 visitors to my blog in 2014.

I sell my artwork yearly at AANE and Good Purpose Gallery in the Berkshires (and elsewhere).

I have several inclusions in books about autism and selective mutism.

I tried on jobs to see what fits and as of this writing, I've done a little paralegal stuff (not for me!),
volunteering at a library

and hospital,
and even ghostwriting (I wrote *Reborn Through Fire* for Miracle
Man burn survivor Tony Yarijanian)
and caregiving for which I receive a modest income.

Thanks to Judy Rosenfield, (she knows her stuff!) for instilling in me
that I am capable of anything, for believing in me, for helping me to
silence my gremlin, and for being everything a friend is.
Thanks to Allison and William, for their patience with me during
editing. Kim (my agent), you gave me an olive branch and you didn't
have to do that. I felt worthy.

Thank you Al for calming the terrors, thank you for all the little
reasons and all the big ones.
My Connecticut raised cousins (ALL four), thanks for defining
family and being so rich a part of my early life.
In no particular order, Jeff and Kim C., Jeremy and Heather, Chloe,
Sheri, my other Allison, Kerry/Silis, Keith, Jaden, Carly, Alexia, all
my Donnas, Clay (you are a poem too), and Daddy, remember I love
you all.
Amy, I appreciated you more than I let on.
I've learned a lot about life through each of you.
I'm very lucky. I'll shut up now. I've got some writin' to do. Why not
like Under The Banana Moon's Facebook author page and check out
my blog at: Ravenambition.wordpress.com

IN MEMORY OF
H, C, P and M

Made in the USA
Columbia, SC
21 June 2020